The Courts and the Doctor

D. J. Gee

CBE MB FRCPath DMJ

Emeritus Professor of Forensic Medicine
University of Leeds

and

J. K. Mason

CBE MD LLD FRCPath DMJ

Regius Professor (Emeritus) of Forensic Medicine
University of Edinburgh

OXFORD   NEW YORK   TOKYO
OXFORD UNIVERSITY PRESS
1990

Oxford University Press, Walton Street, Oxford OX2 6DP

Oxford   New York   Toronto
Delhi   Bombay   Calcutta   Madras   Karachi
Petaling Jaya   Singapore   Hong Kong   Tokyo
Nairobi   Dar es Salaam   Cape Town
Melbourne   Auckland

and associated companies in
Berlin Ibadan

Oxford is a trade mark of Oxford University Press

Published in the United States
by Oxford University Press, New York

British Library Cataloguing in Publication Data
Gee, D. J. (David John)
The courts and the doctor.
1. Forensic medicine
I. Title II. Mason, J. K. (John Kenyon) 1919–
614.1
ISBN 0–19–261967–5
ISBN 0–19–261786–9 (pbk)

Library of Congress Cataloging in Publication Data
Gee, D. J. (David John)
The courts and the doctor / D. J. Gee and J. K. Mason.
p.   cm. — (Oxford medical publications)
Includes bibliographical references.
1. Evidence, Expert—Great Britain.   2. Medical jurisprudence—
Great Britain.   3. Medical laws and legislation—Great Britain.
I. Mason, J. K. (John Kenyon)   II. Title.   III. Series.
{DNLM: 1. Expert Testimony. 2. Forensic Medicine. W 725 G297c}
KD7523.G44   1990   347.41'67—dc20   {344.10767}   90–6708
ISBN 0–19–261967–5
ISBN 0–19–261786–9 (pbk.)

Typeset by
Footnote Graphics
Warminster, Wiltshire
Printed in Great Britain by
Courier International Ltd., Tiptree, Essex

To Eileen
and all those like her

Preface

A main function of a Department of Forensic Medicine is to educate medical students as to the interplay between medicine and the law. It is said, perhaps with justification, that very few doctors are likely to be involved as principals in forensic pathology and one suspects that it is largely for this reason that forensic medicine has been virtually phased out of the curriculum in most British medical schools. But there are times when the doctor cannot avoid the law— he cannot avoid treating victims of violence in the casualty department or examining a suspected case of sexual abuse in his surgery and, as a consequence, he cannot avoid the courts. We are then faced with the difficulty that instruction in these inevitable contacts disappears along with the conventional teaching in forensic pathology.

This small book is an attempt to fill part of that gap. It has proved more difficult to write than we had anticipated—and, this, for two main reasons. First, its scope could extend from a short commentary on the model of 'Stand up, speak up, and shut up' to a major treatise on legal procedure and the law of evidence. We have attempted a middle road in the belief that, while the former approach *may* be applicable to doctors, the great majority of professionals would express some interest in the historical, theoretical, and ethical aspects of the doctor's role as a witness. Secondly, it is difficult to write for the whole spectrum of medical practitioners from the houseman in the coroner's court to the consultant neurosurgeon in the Courts of Justice. On the whole, we have the former in the front of our minds—and have paid particular attention to his needs in Chapters 4, 6, 7, and 8. We hope, however, that we have included some material which will be of help and interest to the latter. This may be particularly apposite at the present time since increasing concern over the methods and reliability of medical evidence has been expressed over the past few years.

We have each been fortunate in that our medical schools have been among those which have retained an element of medico-legal teaching for undergraduates so that we have been forced to take a broad look at the subject; nevertheless, we are very conscious that we have no formal training in philosophy or the law and we can only hope that this is not too apparent. In this respect, we acknowledge most gratefully the advice and help that has been given by many friends, among whom we would particularly mention Professors Brian Hogan and Neil MacCormick, Drs John Cairns, Derek Chiswick, and Nick Reid, Mr J. A. Turnbull and Mrs Yvonne Aitken. Any errors remaining are, of course, entirely our own responsibility.

Finally, we offer sincere thanks to our publishers who have been more than usually tolerant of their authors' failings.

September 1989   D.J.G.
                                                                 J.K.M.

Authors' note

In general, this book follows the Interpretation Act 1978, s.6 in that, unless the contrary intention appears, words importing the masculine gender include the feminine and words importing the feminine gender include the masculine.

Contents

Table of Statutes

List of Cases

1

The development of the law in the United Kingdom

Some subjects pervade the whole fabric of a society—every member is directly affected by them and is frequently made aware of them. This is probably more true of law than of any other discipline; indeed, many would say that without law there can be no society:

Law is both a product of civilisation, in that whatever groups of individuals have attained that stage of organisation and of control over their environment which we call civilisation, some kind of legal ordering of society is found, and it is also an essential of the continuance and development of civilisation, in that without a legal order to regulate conflicting claims and to resolve differences, civilisation would slip back into anarchy. [1]

Others have, however, been more sceptical:

Society is not based on the law, that is a legal fiction, rather law must be based on society; it must be the expression of society's common interests and needs, as they arise from the various material methods of production, against the arbitrariness of the single individual. [2]

Shakespeare's rebels are even more forthright:

DICK. The first thing we do, let's kill all the lawyers.
CADE. Nay, 'that I mean to do. Is not this a lamentable thing, that the skin of an innocent lamb should be made parchment? that parchment, being scribbled o'er, should undo a man? [3]

Destruction of the current legal system has been, and will continue to be, an early aim of many revolutions. This may result from no more than the fact that practitioners of the law tend to be identified with the ruling classes—for professionalism of any sort goes in hand with paternalism. This would not, however, explain the number of lawyers who become dedicated revolutionaries. Rather, it is a natural representation of the conflict between the two views already expressed—if society is based on the law, then the existing law must be destroyed if society is found wanting. For, if society is unjust, it follows that the law represents injustice. Indeed, Marxist theory, in some interpretations, envisions a society in which there is no need for law.

Law, justice, and morality

For many people, the distinctions between law, justice, and, even, morals are ambiguous—it is unclear whether there are valid distinctions or whether the three concepts are equivalent. Thus, one can speak of 'Courts of Law', or of 'Courts of Justice'; magistrates are synonymously 'Justices of the Peace', and so on.

Such distinctions are of particular relevance to a bit-part actor, such as an expert witness, who is not a lawyer but who, nevertheless, has a role in expediting the judicial process. At the conclusion of a case, such a person may be more inclined to look at the outcome in terms of the apparent justice or injustice of the result rather than of the correctness of the legal procedures that have been followed.

The definitions of the three subjects show that they are distinct semantic entities. Thus, the *Shorter Oxford English Dictionary* has it:

Justice Exercise of authority or power in the maintenance of right; vindication of right by assignment of reward or punishment.
Law The body of rules whether formally enacted or customary, which a state or community recognizes as binding on its subjects.
Moral Of or pertaining to the distinction between right and wrong, or good and evil, in relations to actions, volitions, or character.

Other conceptual distinctions include:

Law is a collection of rules of human conduct, prescribed by human beings for the obedience of human beings. The difference from moral precepts is that laws are enforced by the State, morals are not.[4]

For morality prescribes a course of conduct, both positive and negative; it bids men not merely to eschew evil, but actively to do good. But the precepts of law are mainly, though by no means entirely, negative.[5]

Justice concerns authority and its impartial application. Thus, justice is less concerned with the content of the law than that it should be impartial; there should not, for instance, be one law for the rich and another for the poor. This has not always been seen to be the case. Justice as defined by Greek philosophers such as Plato was not so much concerned with equality as to see that each man was dealt with according to his position in society. Closer to home, we have the cynical judge who is widely quoted as saying: 'The law, like the Ritz hotel, is open to rich and poor alike'[6] and this holds good today when the cost of litigation and the operation of the system of legal aid combine to make it almost impossible for those of moderate financial means to seek justice through the courts.

Nevertheless, this quality of justice as our society understands it—that is, of ensuring equal opportunity for redress to all men—is sufficiently fundamental to be one of the clauses in Magna Charta: 'To none will we sell, to none will we deny or delay right or justice'.

In summary then, morals are those views of an individual or of society which express the totality of what is considered to be good or bad. Laws are the rules laid down by society for its control, so as to endeavour to maintain at least the social conditions of social justice. Legal justice is concerned to see that all men have equal access to, and responsibility under, the law. The relationship was summed up admirably by Lord Chief Justice Coleridge in 1893:

It would not be correct to say that every moral obligation involves a legal duty; but every legal duty is founded on a moral obligation.[7]

Even so, there are alternative interpretations of this relationship between morality and law—a subject, let it be said, which fills shelves in the average law library. Effectively, this resolves itself into deciding whether the law should enforce only basic moral principles, whether it should follow public opinion and insist on implementation of the morality so indicated, or whether it should be disinterested in morality save when immorality leads to positive social harm—matters which form the basis of what has become known as the Devlin/Hart debate. The former, in summary, believed that immoral activity *per se* should, in extreme cases, be criminalized whereas the latter held that an act should not be punishable simply because it offends other people's moral sensibilities—but only when it causes actual harm or offends by impinging directly upon the others' senses. Devlin's view embodies the concept that the integrity of society depends upon its 'moral cohesion' and it is, accordingly, the function of the law to protect the state through the imposition of contemporary morality.[8] Hart denies that such moral cohesion, beyond a general condemnation of harmful behaviour, is either necessary or possible in a pluralistic society.

Although it can only be a blatant simplification, the resolution of that argument can be seen, at the conceptual level, as being represented by the major legal systems, civil or codified law on the one hand and the common law on the other.

Common law and codified law

Probably the most extreme example of code law is to be found in the traditional Islamic law or Shari'a:

Floating above Muslim society as a disembodied soul, freed from the currents and vicissitudes of time, it [the Shari'a] represented the eternally valid ideal towards which society must aspire.

Law, in classical Islamic theory, is the revealed will of God, a divinely ordained system preceding and not preceded by the Muslim state, controlling and not controlled by Muslim society.[9]

As far as we are concerned, the code law with which we are familiar is that which has been a particular historical feature of continental European law—as, for example, laid down in the codes of Charlemagne, Pope Gregory IX, and later, the Caroline and Napoleonic codes. These legal systems owed their origin to the highly developed and sophisticated Roman law which still survives as a distinct legal discipline. Its influence has persisted—whether or not in a continuous form is still debated—in the legal systems of countries and communities which came under the control of the Roman Empire. Britain, however, remained an exception. There, the normal civilized process of learning and government virtually broke down following the retreat of the legions and simultaneously, all trace of the form and structure of Roman law vanished along with the material evidence of its civilization; a remarkably complete destruction when one considers that Roman government of much of the British Isles lasted for some four hundred years, roughly the same time as separates the present day from the Tudor period.

All the evidence which persists of a form of legal structure in the following barbarian period is contained in such basic codes as those of Ine, King of Wessex (AD 690). These were based on the customary tribal laws of the successive Anglo-Saxon and Danish communities—in short, the form of law became the law of custom or the common law. The Norman conquerors brought their own law which could be blended successfully with many such existing Anglo-Saxon concepts of legal theory; thus, there was no impulse to revert to Roman law when it was widely revived in the twelfth century.

Anglo-Saxon society was essentially tribal and decentralized. The major Norman contribution to the evolution of English law was to establish the feudal system under which society was arranged with the people owing allegiance to a superior lord and the King being established as the ultimate pinnacle of the system. Although some major feudal magnates had the right of dispensing justice in their own courts, the King and his Council, rather than the local gatherings of members of the community became the source of the administration of the law. This became increasingly concentrated in the King's Courts, the *Curia Regis*, which were, at first, situated where the King was physically situated, for example at the Palace of Westminster. Later, these were carried to the people in the community by itinerant judges travelling on well defined routes through the country, forming the primitive Assize circuits.

Law derived from common custom is admirable so far as it goes but it must be added to in order to accommodate the complexities of an evolving society. Thus, the Normans introduced ecclesiastical courts which dealt with matters of religion and of the family under the canon law. Henry II introduced many new developments by way of enactments of the Royal Council, such as the creation, already mentioned above, of judicial circuits and the development of the jury system of trial as an alternative to the earlier forms of trial by battle or ordeal. Initially the jury, composed of local men, decided matters on the basis of their own local knowledge. It was not for about another 200 years that witnesses other than jury men began to appear at and give evidence in trials (see also Chapter 2 for more detail).

Laws that were introduced to supplement the common law during this early medieval period were made by the King in council; the people had no say in the matter. However, the rule of the King was not always acceptable, as, for example, in the case of King John (1199–1216), whose misrule resulted in Magna Charta in 1215. The first sign of a Parliament in which people other than the great feudal lords were represented appeared in 1265 when Simon de Montfort summoned a parliament which included representatives from cities and boroughs as well as barons, knights, and clergy. The climax of absolutist monarchy was reached in the period of the Tudor and Stuart kings and queens, and the increasing determination of Parliament to participate in law-making and government culminated in the Civil War, or English revolution. Cromwell's commonwealth introduced many legal reforms which even included an early concept of legal aid. Englishmen were increasingly discontented with the Restoration form of absolute monarchy, and the reign of William and Mary signalled the establishment of parliamentary democracy as we know it in which it was the ordinary people who, through their representatives in Parliament, formulated new statute laws that were to be added to the existing body of law. Such statute law represented the will of the people, and although it was administered and interpreted in the courts by the judges, the power to alter such law remained vested in Parliament alone.

Statute law, however, is essentially specific in its application; if there is conflict as to the generality, the common law will usually take precedence[10]—and this despite the overall doctrine of the sovereignty of Parliament. A classic example is the common law rule which imposes liability on the state to pay compensation in respect of property destroyed in time of war; this rule still subsists irrespective of the specific exception provided by the War Damages Act 1965.[11] A main qualification of the general rule of precedence applies where the major part of the law is a creature of statute—as is the case in industrial relations law. However, it is a feature of a system of law which evolves from custom that it must, itself, change as the customs of the community change. As recently as 1985, the House of Lords, which is the ultimate legal forum in the United Kingdom, confirmed the view that the law cannot remain static but must be sensitive to human development and social change; it must be flexible in the absence of Parliamentary direction.[12]

Thus, much of the law as it affects the ordinary citizen is defined by what is sometimes referred to as judge-made law. This is, in fact, a misnomer; the judiciary cannot *make* law—that is the prerogative of Parliament.[13] What the judges can do, and do frequently, is to interpret the law as it stands at the moment and, thereby, to establish a legal precedent which can only be overturned by a court of equal or higher standing in the hierarchy of the Supreme Court (see Chapter 3). Therein lies the importance of an independent judiciary—for the basis of the greater part of the common law lies outwith the party political arena. English judges were regarded as servants of the Crown for some considerable time after their establishment. It was not until the Act of Settlement 1701, that their salaries became safeguarded and that their removal from office could only be effected through action of both Houses of Parliament. [14]

Civil and criminal law

The principal division of law which concerns witnesses today, and in which procedures of evidence are somewhat different, is the division into criminal and civil law. The distinction was certainly not clear in Anglo-Saxon England where wrongs committed by one person against another might well result in a blood-feud between families. To avoid such vengeance, a system was established for the payment of financial compensation in the form of *wergild*, or 'blood-money'. Even at this time, there was some concept of national concern, in that offences might be considered to infringe the King's Peace. The distinction between offences which affected the community rather than the individual became clearer after the Norman conquest. The former were distinguished as crimes, which required prosecution and punishment by the State on behalf of the community. The latter, offences only affecting an individual, were called torts, which were dealt with by way of financial compensation; tort law represents one beginning of civil law. Originally, civil matters were mainly dealt with centrally, at first by the King in council and then by the courts which derived their authority from the centre; these included the Court of Common Pleas, which stayed and worked in London, even when the King and the court were travelling elsewhere. The travelling Assize courts dealt primarily with criminal matters. Later, however, they took on civil matters as well under the statute of *Nisi Prius* 1285, the object being to save litigants from the time and trouble involved in travelling to London. *Nisi prius* means 'unless before', the idea being that the matter would be dealt with at Westminster unless it could be dealt with previously at Assize; it was common to see some of the main Assize courtrooms entitled *Nisi Prius* on the door before their replacement by Crown Courts in 1971.

The other fundamental development in the provision of law was the creation of the 'custodians of the peace' who originated in the early fourteenth century as a device to relieve the Assize judges of some of the increasing burden of work. They soon became known as Justices of the Peace and their role grew steadily. By the middle of the sixteenth century they were empowered to make preliminary enquiries into crimes which would pass subsequently to the Assizes for trial by indictment, that is, before a jury. Before he could be appointed a justice, a person had to satisfy certain property requirements and this arrangement lasted until early in the present century. The justices were entitled to try minor offences without a jury, that is by summary trial, from their inception. The importance of their work has remained so that the bulk of criminal work, involving the less serious offences, is still dealt with by Justices of the Peace sitting in the magistrate's courts.

The coroners' system

The role of the coroner developed on a completely different judicial line. It is a part of the legal system which is so fundamental to the medical profession that it merits separate and relatively lengthy consideration.

The office of coroner is of ancient origin. It is suggested that coroners existed in Saxon times, although not under that name, and that their powers were reinforced soon after the Norman conquest as being the officials whose function was to enquire into sudden unexpected deaths; in that capacity, their primary duty was to determine whether the deceased was English or Norman and, if the community could not prove the former, to impose the fine known as the '*murdrum*', a primitive form of counter-resistance movement.[15] It is certain that an act of Richard I in 1194 established officials known as '*custodes placitorum coronae*', or keepers of the pleas of the crown. These pleas of the crown involved certain criminal prosecutions in which the public good was affected; among other duties, the 'coroners' kept lists of and presented suspects to the justices at the Assizes, thus acting as a form of public prosecutor, not unlike the present Procurator-Fiscal in Scotland (see Chapter 3). In due course these duties were removed but the status of the coroner has survived a long and eventful history—including the near extinction of the post in the seventeenth and eighteenth centuries—and the office has regained a position of importance in the English legal system in the last 100 years as the principal route for the investigation of sudden death.[16]

The Scottish legal system[17]

In Scotland, customary law was found in the Gaelic areas while Scandinavian law applied to the Isles of Orkney and Shetland for many centuries. From AD 1100 onwards, lowland Scotland came under the influence of Norman England, especially during the reign of David I. A feudal system was developed and itinerant justices perigrinated dispensing royal justice. The baronial courts of great feudal chiefs often rivalled the royal courts in importance. The office of sheriff was probably instituted during David I's reign, being held by a local baron who was the royal judicial and administrative officer for that region. The sheriff court was originally sited at the office holder's castle. Ecclesiastical courts also developed during this period and introduced canon law into Scotland; burgh courts grew in importance along with the status of the developing townships.

The first Parliament met at Cambuskenneth in 1326 and, in the frequent absence or minority of Scottish monarchs, Parliament assumed an increasingly significant role. Various committees with legal functions were developed from it and some of these were later converted into the Court of Session. The alliance of Scotland with France against England resulted in forms of French practice being incorporated in the Scottish legal system. The College of Justice was established, with papal support, by James V. The ecclesiastical courts were secularized as commissary courts at the time of the Reformation, and their jurisdiction was taken over eventually by the Court of Session; however, canon law remained as an integral part of the system. The High Court of Justiciary, consisting of the Lord Justice-General, the Lord Justice-Clerk and Lord Commissioners of Justiciary, was created in the seventeenth century.

The maintenance of separate legal systems was an integral part of the Act of Union between England and Scotland in 1707. The 'compromise' reached (in Article XVIII) was that laws relating to public government were to be drawn up on a United Kingdom basis but, otherwise, the courts and laws were only to be altered when it was to the evident utility of the Scots. While much of this agreement was left in a relatively nebulous state, the practical result was that the civil and criminal courts of Scotland—the Court of Session, the High Court of Justiciary, and the Sheriff Courts—were to remain independent of the English judicial system.

The essential differences between English and Scots law lie in concepts of jurisprudence. As an extreme simplification, it can be said that, for the reasons given above, supported by the fact that the majority of law students received their further education in France or in the Low Countries, Scots law is heavily influenced by Roman law and is, thus, based on principles laid down by great legal thinkers— the institutional writers; it is, therefore, dominated by an appeal to reason. A reviewer of one of our books expressed surprise at 'the inexorable logic of Scots law'—but that is precisely what it is about. English law, on the other hand, prefers to look at the circumstances surrounding the case and to apply the decisions reached in previous similar conditions to the case in question; the system is, in effect, evolutionary by way of analogy. As an example, you cannot rape a sleeping woman in Scotland because, in reason, a sleeping woman has no will to overcome; this does not follow in England because, as a matter of simple fact, the woman has not consented to sexual intercourse. However, Scots law can get round such problems in so far as, although it is scarcely necessary nowadays, the courts can formulate new law by way of declaration when reason demands it. Thus, while you may not be able to rape a sleeping woman in Scotland, you can inflict clandestine injury upon her and be punished equally severely.

The rights of nobles to hold courts was removed, together with the principle of hereditary sheriffdoms, after 1745. Sheriffs were appointed for each county, the official who we would now designate the Sheriff Principal, but who was originally called the Sheriff Depute, being drawn from the ranks of the advocates; he generally employed a substitute who, until the nineteenth century, was seldom an advocate. Nowadays, an increasing number of appointments to Sheriff are being filled by those who have been solicitors. There is no coroner in Scotland, comparable responsibilities being undertaken by the Procurator-Fiscal whose office dates from the sixteenth century[18] (see Chapter 3).

A further result of the different origins of English and Scots law is that statute law is found to be less necessary in the latter. Thus, for example, there is no statute in Scotland comparable to the Offences Against the Person Act 1861 because the various classes of assault are not seen as requiring specific delineation, the principles being adequately laid down in the institutional writings. However, public law must be uniform throughout the United Kingdom and the statutes of the Parliament at Westminster covering this field will generally run to Scotland. This is to be seen, for example, in the Road Traffic Act 1988 and its companion Road Traffic Offenders Act 1988. There being no separate Scottish Parliament, Scottish statutory private law must also be enacted at Westminster. There, the special position of the Scottish legal system is recognized by the establishment of a Scottish Grand Committee which consists of the Scottish members of Parliament supplemented by a number of other members so as to maintain the political balance of the House of Commons as a whole—a practice which causes some difficulty in the face of the increasingly polarized political ideologies of the two countries. The Grand Committee is supported by two Scottish standing committees whose function is to consider Bills which will apply only to Scotland. The practical result is that there are a number of statutes which are qualified by the word (Scotland) and which have a counterpart in English legislation. These need not necessarily reach the identical end-point—there are, for example, fairly marked administrative differences between the Mental Health Act 1983 and the Mental Health (Scotland) Act 1984 while the definition of incest in the Sexual Offences Act 1956 differs from that now given in the Sexual Offences (Scotland) Act 1976.

European Community law

The latest historical influence on the law of the United Kingdom stems from our membership of the European Community.

The European Communities Act 1972 allows for the United Kingdom to comply with the obligations and to exercise the rights flowing from membership of the three major European Communities of which the Economic Community is, perhaps, the most important. Thus, the Act gives the force of law in the United Kingdom to any community law which can be applied directly to individual member states. Of rather greater importance in the present context, the Act also allows citizens of the United Kingdom to appeal to the European Court of Human Rights or to the European Court and the judgments, subject to appeal, will take precedence over our own law. The Mental Health Acts have already required amendment in the light of such action.[19] Other litigation has involved the husband's rights in relation to the abortion of his child[20], the rights of an operatively converted transsexual to marry,[21] and the legality of corporal punishment in state-controlled schools.[22]

In general, Community law prevails over national law and, while the extent of this still seems to be a matter for argument and interpretation, United Kingdom statutes now have effect 'subject to Community law'. From the point of view of the medical profession, it is to be noted that the Medical Act 1983 allows for the automatic registration in this country of doctors who have qualified in any of the states in the Community and this type of professional exchange is bound to exert its effect on the various memberships.

Whether this supranational activity will be for better or for worse—or, indeed, whether it will be encouraged or stifled—remains to be seen. Certainly, one can expect the volume of code or statute law to increase and it is unlikely that either the English or the Scottish common law doctrines, which have, for so long, been the pride of administrators over a large part of the world, will remain inviolate. The likely difficulty may well be to maintain an evolutionary progression in the face of increasing imperative pressure.

References

1. Walker, D. M. *The Scottish Legal System* (5th edn, 1981) Edinburgh: W. Green & Son, p. 6.
2. Marx, K. 'Speech in his defence' quoted by McLellan, D. in *Karl Marx, His Life and Thought* (1976) St Albans: Paladin, p. 215.
3. Shakespeare, W. *King Henry 6th* IV.ii.86.
4. James, P. S. *Introduction to English Law* (7th edn, 1969) London: Butterworths, p. 4.
5. Hanbury, H. G. and Yardley, D. C. M. *English Courts of Law* (5th edn, 1979) Oxford: University Press, p. 1.
6. Lloyd, D. *The Idea of Law* (1964) Harmondsworth: Penguin Books, p. 121.
7. *R* v. *Instan* [1893] 1 QB at 453.

8. Harris, J. W. *Legal Philosophies* (1980) London: Butterworths.
9. Coulson, N. J. *A History of Islamic Law* (1978) Edinburgh: University Press, pp. 1–2.
10. Bell, J. and Engle, G. (ed.) *Cross' Statutory Interpretation* (2nd edn, 1987) London: Sweet and Maxwell, pp. 41–4.
11. *Burmah Oil Co (Burma Trading) Ltd* v. *Lord Advocate* 1964 SLT 218. Also, the English case *Shiloh Spinners Ltd* v. *Harding* [1973] AC 691 per Lord Wilberforce.
12. *Gillick* v. *West Norfolk and Wisbech Area Health Authority* [1985] 2 All ER 402 at 421 per Lord Scarman.
13. *In re F (Mental Patient: Sterilisation)* [1989] 2 WLR 1025 at 1035 per Lord Donaldson.
14. Curzon, L. B. *English Legal History* (1968) London: Macdonald & Evans, pp. 3–23.
15. Havard, J. D. J. *The Detection of Secret Homicide* (1960) London: Macmillan, pp. 1–28.
16. Havard, ref. 15 above at p. 11.
17. In general, see Walker, ref. 1 above.
18. Normand, W. G. 'The public prosecutor in Scotland' (1938) 215 LQR 345.
19. *X* v. *United Kingdom* (1982) 4 EHRR 18.
20. *Paton* v. *United Kingdom* (1981) 3 EHRR 408.
21. *Rees* v. *United Kingdom* (1987) 9 EHRR 56.
22. *Campbell and Cosans* v. *United Kingdom* (1982) 4 EHRR 293.

2

The history of the medical witness

Contrary to what might be expected, the acceptance of the medical witness as a recognized cog in the machinery of justice is a comparatively recent phenomenon. This is all the more surprising in view of the fact that medicine and law, being the original courses offered at most of the medieval European universities, are very old academic subjects.[1] While the law has had a fundamental effect on the nature of society from its outset and has dealt with a wide range of problems that affect the personal lives of ordinary men and women, the contribution of medicine to the solution of legal problems has been slight until comparatively recently. This is, at least, true as regards Britain, where medical evidence in court was almost unknown before the seventeenth century. However, it must be accepted that doctors in Continental Europe had achieved a role as medico-legal experts much earlier.[2]

Early times and the influence of Roman law

There is comparatively little information to go on in respect of very early times. Every medical student knows of the origins of medical ethics in the Code of Hammurabi, with its descriptions of penalties imposed on physicians found to be guilty of what appear to be early examples of medical negligence. Even so, there do not seem to be any remaining records of physicians giving evidence to the courts on such matters.

The arising Greek civilization gave birth to the great, if shadowy, figures of Hippocrates and his successors among the physicians and to the more tangible forms of the philosophers—Socrates, Plato, Aristotle, and many others. Simultaneously, a more defined form of legal consciousness arose in association with the first flourishes of a political system. However, many historians deny that medical evidence was used in any form of legal process. The prosecution of a case was essentially a private matter; an action, even in instances such as homicide, was brought by an individual assisted by orators to speak on the salient points. There was little public law, in the sense that we now understand it, under which crimes are matters for prosecution by the state. Yet, despite the dearth of documentation of actual medical evidence, passages in some of the orators' speeches dealing with individuals' wrongs have been described as indicating the acknowledgement of a role for such evidence—certainly in the form of supplying depositions.[3]

Law became a much better established discipline during the period when much of the civilized world was under the control of the Roman Empire. At the same time, very substantial medical figures such as Galen were appearing but, despite the survival of a comprehensive body of writings in the individual schools of law and medicine, there was still little evidence of a clear role for the physician in the courts. Undoubtedly, there were a number of conditions mentioned in legal rules which were of a medical nature, such as the state of health of slaves or the existence of a chronic illness which could exempt the sufferer from some legal obligation. Under both the legal arrangements of the earlier formulary system, where a magistrate made preliminary enquiries and a judge heard the case, and the latter *cognitio* procedure under which a judge dealt with both stages, there were few rules of evidence and the judge applied the principle of free weighing of evidence according to his own lights. The only experts whose evidence was considered mandatory in certain circumstances were land surveyors and midwives— the latter to certify the existence of pregnancy. Although there are some isolated instances, such as the record of a physician having examined Julius Caesar's wounds so as to compare their severity, there is, in general, no reliable indication of physicians having actually *given* expert evidence.[4]

This may, of course, be due to no more than a lack of surviving court records rather than represent a proof that medical evidence was unused in Roman legal processes. Thus, in one area of the Roman Empire—Egypt—records have survived in fragmentary form which describe the use of medical evidence either by way of requests for medical examination of persons or as actual reports of those examinations.[5] One wonders whether such a system was peculiar to Egypt or whether it is simply that conditions in that country facilitated the survival of records which have disappeared elsewhere.

None the less, the breakdown of civilization which followed the

Roman withdrawal from Britain had less catastrophic consequences on the continent of Europe where the structure and methods of Roman law were taken over and absorbed by many of the barbarian groups which conquered Italy and its adjacent areas.[6] As a result, a balanced system, which included a pattern for the examination of witnesses, remained in force continuously[7] or, at least, was easily retrievable.

At the same time, a new civilizing force arose adjacent to, and invaded, parts of Europe with the emergence of Islam as a power. Schools of law, such as those of Hanbali and Maliki, were created at a relatively early stage in the development of the structure of Islamic society. These defined specific roles for expert evidence within their procedures.[8] Great centres of learning developed in cities such as those of southern Spain and Italy; their disciplines included law and medicine in which scholars from Islamic, Jewish, and Christian backgrounds worked together. These centres ensured the survival of the learning of the Greek and Roman civilizations. To visit them now, when only the architecture remains, still conveys a sense of their vitality and importance at that time.

Medieval evidence

With the end of the dark ages and the emergence of the medieval period, universities began to appear in various cities, such as those at Salerno and Bologna, followed, for example, by Paris, Montpelier, and Palanca. These included law, theology, and medicine as their earliest faculties. There are indications from as early as the beginning of the thirteenth century of the existence of a medical man with legal responsibilities in Bologna.[9] Not long afterwards, there is some evidence, albeit scanty, of medical testimony being provided on the Continent.[10] Rashdall reports a case of 1332 in which students of law were making a disturbance in the streets of Toulouse. An official and the watch tried to arrest one of the demonstrators; the mob attacked the official. One of the students struck him in the face with a poignard, cutting off his nose and part of his lips and chin and either knocking out or breaking eleven teeth. The surgeons *deposed* that, if he recovered—which he did eventually—he would never again be able to speak intelligibly. Another of the watch was killed. The student was sentenced to death.[11] At the comparable time in China, an official text for coroners, the *Hsi Yuan Lu*, contained detailed descriptions of medico-legal matter such as wounds, hanging, and the like.[12]

In England, on the other hand, there was no provision for medical officers having legal responsibilities, and no indication of medical evidence being given in court, until much later. The form of legal procedure in Britain was substantially different from that on the Continent. One is tempted to speculate whether the comparatively belated acceptance of the role of medical evidence in court, and, indeed, of forensic medicine as a discipline, in England may have been due, as already mentioned in Chapter 1, to the very complete destruction of the Roman legal system in this island while it developed elsewhere in Europe. Moreover, although Oxford and Cambridge share equal antiquity with the continental universities, they did not set out to be centres for the study of medicine and the development of other universities in Britain was delayed until considerably later. It is, perhaps, significant that the universities established next after Oxford and Cambridge were in Scotland. After the wars against the English, the Scots forged close links with the Continent in learning as in much else and it may well be more than coincidence that the first chair of forensic medicine in Britain was established in Edinburgh in 1807.

But, to return to early medieval England: at the time of the Norman conquest, justice tended to be very much a local matter to be decided from within the community in which the case had occurred. Even after the advent of the King's Justices in Eyre, who travelled the countryside to administer royal justice from the time of Henry I, decisions were based on the opinion and views of local people who knew the parties to the law suit. In the early days, the local township was called to describe the events and to give their opinions on the contestants in the case, while the role of jurors was to act as witnesses as well as to decide upon guilt. The functions of jurors and witnesses became distinct only much later and jurymen could still act both as witnesses and jurors even into the seventeenth century.[13] In effect, therefore, the expert witness in medieval times, rather than being an independent person called in from outside, was the neighbour or fellow-citizen who knew all about the event.

Some very interesting examples can be found among Stenton's translations of medieval court records for the early thirteenth century which show that patterns then were much the same as they are today even if the methods used for solving them were different:

Aldusa de Elton appealed Simon son of Alan that in the peace of the lord king he took from her her virginity and this she offers to prove against him. Simon comes and denies the breaking of the peace of the lord king and that he took from her her virginity, as the court shall adjudge, but he wishes to tell the truth. He had her for almost a year with her good will, and when it did not please him to keep her any longer, she brought this appeal against him for hatred because he put her away.

The jurors bear witness that it is true that he had her with her good will for a year and that he took another to wife and for this reason she has appealed him. Therefore it is adjudged that the appeal is null. Therefore Simon is quit therein and she is in mercy. She is pardoned because she is poor.[14]

Evidently Aldusa had reason for jealousy and spite, having been superseded as mistress, and brought a false accusation of rape—but the neighbours knew all about it and, also, everyone pitied her.

Where an opinion on a wound, or on a person's medical condition, was required, it was provided by a layman of some official standing.

Thomas de Hoton appeals Peter of Wadworth that in the peace of the lord king John he wickedly and in felony wounded him in the head with a hatchet where he was in his wood of Wadworth.

Peter comes and denies the [breaking of] the peace of the lord king, and the felony and the whole word for word as the court shall adjudge. But it is true, he says, that he found him cutting in his wood and sought his pledge, whence he says that he appeals him for hatred and malice and he seeks that the wound may be viewed. The sergeant of Tickhill comes and bears witness that he certainly came to him and showed him recent blood and one flow but no wound. The coroners bear witness that he showed them dry blood and not the wound, and shire court says the same. Therefore it is adjudged that Thomas is in mercy and Peter is quit therein.[15]

The amount of detail of a medical nature entered in the records increased in the succeeding centuries but this was still without any sign of the involvement of a doctor in the provision of the evidence.

Inquest was taken before the . . . coroner . . . [in 1366] on view of the body of a certain John Clark, tiler, on the oath [of twelve men]. They say on their oath that . . . Adam Case, an inhabitant of London, came to the vill of Stepney, namely to a certain field below that vill, and there insulted the said John Clark, tiler, with opprobrious words, and forthwith drew a certain knife thirteen inches long, with which he feloniously struck John Clark, making severe wound on his left shoulder one inch long and thirteen inches deep and this wound at once caused his death. Being asked whether [Adam] did this by the abetment or procurement of any person, they say, No. Being asked whether the felon has gone, they say that he was arrested forthwith and taken to Newgate gaol. [16]

By the fifteenth century, some records exist of doctors themselves being involved in the legal process as defendants where their medical skill was called into question. In one well known case, in 1424, which is referred to by both Forbes and Havard, a man suffered an injury to his thumb, and was treated by barber surgeons. The result was not very satisfactory, but a panel of physicians called to arbitrate considered that a substantial responsibility for this lay with the astrological constellations at the time of the incident. [17, 18]

Emergence of organized medicine

The medical profession began to develop as a recognizable body in the sixteenth century. The first Medical Act, of 1511, attempted to control those who could practise, and the Royal College of Physicians was granted its charter in 1518. Yet, as evidenced in several famous cases in which legal inquiry was made into the deaths, the profession was still not playing a significant role in the courts. Thus, after Amy Robsart was found dead at the foot of the stairs in the home of her husband, the Earl of Leicester, in 1560, rumour was rife that she had been murdered by her husband because of his infatuation with Queen Elizabeth, who was said to be aware of the circumstances. Even so, such a politically precarious situation as this did not apparently merit the services of a physician to give evidence to the coroner's inquest into her death. [19]

A fascinating case is described by Forbes involving the death in 1514 of Richard Hunne, who was apparently murdered by the gaolers of the Bishop of London, by having a wire pushed up his nose into his brain; the body was then hung up in order to simulate the appearances of suicide. The case was fully and most astutely investigated by the coroner and his jurors, again without any trace of medical assistance. [20] It is remarkable that in France, where medico-legal practice was, by this time, well established, Ambroise Paré

published his book *Reports in court* in 1575.[21] There are several
examples of medico-legal reports prepared by him in his *Apologie and
treatise* of 1585.[22]

In the famous murder of Darnley, husband of Mary, Queen of
Scots, following an explosion at Kirk-o-Field, Edinburgh in 1567,
his body and that of his servant were found in the garden of the
house undamaged by gunpowder but apparently strangled. Darnley's
body was apparently subject to some medical inspection[23]; again, it
is interesting to note a contrast between the English and Scottish
approaches to forensic medicine.

However, the medical witness at last made a recognizable appearance on the English legal stage in the seventeenth century. For
example, doctors testified as to the duration of pregnancy in the case
of *Alsop* v. *Bowtrell* (1620).[24] Medical evidence was given in the trial
following the murder of the Revd John Talbot in 1669.[25] An oft-
quoted example is the evidence, although hardly laudable, of Sir
Thomas Browne at the Suffolk witch trials in 1665, who informed
the court that, in his opinion, the children in the case had undoubtedly been bewitched.[26]

Evidence which sounds more acceptable was given by medical
witnesses at the trial of the Earl of Pembroke, in 1678, for the
murder of one Nathaniel Cory. Pembroke, a man of notoriously
violent temper, got into a brawl with Cory in a tavern in the
Haymarket and, according to the indictment

... with his right fist did strike the said Cory on the left part of his head,
and knocked him down, and being so down, did strike, bruise, beat and
kick the said Cory upon the head, neck, breast, belly, sides and back, of
which the said Cory did languish from the said fourth of February until the
tenth of the same month, and then died.

During the giving of evidence, it transpired that Cory had been
subject to fits or fainting spells in the past. A Dr Hemes testified to
having treated Cory for his injuries, and said that an autopsy was
carried out after the death and 'a large quantity of congealed blood
was seen in the abdomen'. Evidence on behalf of Pembroke was
given by a Dr Conquest, who stated that he had treated Cory in
the past for fainting fits; he thought it possible that Cory, while
drunk, had fallen from a chair in the tavern. The court, in this case
being the House of Lords, found Pembroke guilty of manslaughter.[27] The case is of particular interest as being one of the first

recorded examples of medical evidence being called in an adversarial context.

Recently, Stephen Knight has linked the same Earl of Pembroke with one of the most famous unsolved murders of the seventeenth century, that of Sir Edmund Berry Godfrey, a London magistrate who was found dead on Primrose Hill with extensive bruising of the neck and chest and transfixed by his own sword. Knight suggests that Pembroke was Godfrey's murderer. Be that as it may, quite extensive medical evidence was certainly given at the coroner's inquest which was held a week after Godfrey's body had been found.

Evidence was given of an autopsy examination of the body, performed at the inn to which the body had been taken. This was to the effect that the sword wound had been inflicted after death, that death itself was due to strangulation, and that he had been dead for four or five days before his body was found.[28] Here, we have the makings of real forensic medical evidence including estimation of the time of death and the distinction between ante- and post-mortem injury. Three men were convicted of the murder but some of the gloss is taken off by the fact that they were almost certainly innocent scapegoats.

Examples of medical evidence become more frequent and there are many such during the eighteenth century, most of them being very well known. Not all were in London. For example, at the trial in 1705 at Dorchester of Mary Channing for the murder of her husband by means of mercury poisoning, a doctor who had treated the deceased gave evidence of his symptoms during his illness, and of the results of an autopsy: '. . . the bottom of the stomach, lungs and part of the liver black and several black spots in the guts'. Mary was convicted and sentenced to death. She 'pleaded her belly', was examined by a jury of matrons and was found to be pregnant; execution was therefore delayed. She was eventually strangled at the stake and then burned eight months later[29]—a horror story which serves to emphasize that English justice at the time was deficient in more qualities than that of its expert evidence.

Another notable poisoning case was tried at Oxford in 1752. Mary Blandy was accused and convicted of poisoning her father with white arsenic. The poison was given to the victim both in tea and in gruel. Servants noted a white powder in the gruel and became suspicious, especially when one also became sick after eating it. A doctor, Dr Addington, was called to treat Mr Blandy. He told the court how he became suspicious that his patient was being poisoned because of his symptoms. After death he performed an autopsy and found extreme inflammation of the stomach:

> ... The internal coat of the stomach and duodenum, especially about the orifices of the former, was prodigiously inflamed and excoriated. The redness of the white of the eye in a violent inflammation of that part, or rather the white of the eye just brushed and bleeding with the beards of barley, may serve to give some idea how this coat had been wounded.

He did not carry out any tests for poison on the body itself but investigated the powder which had been saved from the gruel. He used such techniques as throwing the powder on a hot iron and treating a solution with syrup of violets. These tests were certainly crude, but he also performed control studies using a known sample of white arsenic and obtained identical results.[30] Dr Addington was, thus, one of the first to attempt to sustain his medical opinion by way of scientific proof.

In 1720, Lord Ferrers was tried for murder, and evidence was given of his state of mind. This is, perhaps, the earliest example of psychiatric evidence being offered in an English criminal trial.[31]

Evidence of identification of human remains was given in another famous trial, that of Eugene Aram, in 1759 at York. Aram, a schoolmaster, was accused of the murder of a shoemaker, Clarke, whose body had been buried in a cave and was only discovered thirteen years later by reason of the confession of an accomplice. A complete skeleton was unearthed from the cave floor. Two local surgeons pronounced it as being human, of a young man, of the same age as the deceased and buried for a corresponding period to that which had elapsed since the deceased was last seen. In addition, the skull bore a depressed fracture, consistent with having been caused by a particular hammer, a mason's pick, which the accused was known to have possessed. The fact that the surgeons had given very similar identification evidence about another skeleton, found in the vicinity just before the accomplice confessed, was not alluded to in the court. Even at that time, persons accused of a felony could not have the services of counsel to cross-examine witnesses.[32]

Towards the end of the eighteenth century, Donellan was tried for the murder of his brother-in-law, Sir Theodosius Boughton, by cyanide; the case is often quoted as an example of a great doctor failing to be an adequate expert witness. At the trial, in 1781, in which Donellan was accused of having prepared and administered some cherry laurel water to Sir Theodosius, the famous John Hunter was called to give evidence for the defence. He had not been present at the autopsy which had been carried out on a decomposing corpse and which had been less than complete. He was therefore obliged to express an opinion on the evidence given by other doctors who had made the examination and who had given evidence for the prosecution. He confessed himself unable to form an opinion, and said that he wished the head had been opened, as he felt that death could have been due either to apoplexy or to poisoning, and such an examination would have resolved the doubt. Later, the judge was dismissive of Hunter as a witness:

For the prisoner you have had one gentleman called, and a very able man. I can hardly say what his opinion is, for he does not seem to have formed any opinion at all of the matter. He, at first, said he could not form an opinion whether the death was, or was not, occasioned by the poison, because he could conceive that it might be ascribed to other cause. I wished very much to have got a direct answer from Mr Hunter if I could, what, upon the whole, was now the result of his attention and application to the subject; and what was his present opinion; but he says he can say nothing decisive.[33]

Hunter obviously made a very poor and indecisive showing against the definite opinions of the four experts called by the prosecution. He certainly did no good for Donellan, who was hanged soon after. And yet his evidence, in fact, indicates very well the difficulties experienced by a really expert witness in conveying the uncertainties of a case to a legal audience. His approach seems to have been grounded on good ethical principles and his criticism was valid. At all events, it can be seen that the evidence, the problems and the procedures are beginning, by this time to have quite a modern ring. Expert witnesses can now be said to have at last fully emerged into the legal forum in a role which is important to the dispensing of justice.

Modern developments

The functions of the witness as a component in the adversarial system became much clearer from the beginning of the nineteenth century. Hand in hand with this came improvements of knowledge and techniques in the relevant scientific disciplines, notably in that of toxicology. Marsh's development of his test for arsenic was a major step in providing the courts with more accurate opinions, as were the work and writings of such authorities as Christison, whose comprehensive textbook on poisons first appeared in 1829.

Academic posts in the discipline of forensic medicine began to be established at the same time. First was the approval of a Chair, at Edinburgh, in 1807. In 1831, Alfred Swaine Taylor became lecturer in medical jurisprudence at Guy's Hospital and in 1838 Sir James Risdon Bennett was appointed at Charing Cross Hospital, London. Chairs of medical jurisprudence appeared in Glasgow in 1839 and in Aberdeen in 1875. Textbooks on the subject were published from 1816 onwards, Taylor's first book being published in 1836. Thus, the atmosphere was changing dramatically from that which had existed in Britain in earlier years. It is significant for our present purpose to note that a book entitled *An analysis of medical evidence* by J. G. Smith, appeared in 1825.[34]

The nineteenth century contains many examples of famous cases of homicide where medical evidence played an extensive and import-ant part. Obvious instances are the trials of Burke and Hare (1828), Palmer (1855), Smethurst (1859), Pritchard (1865), Staunton (1877), and Bartlett (1886). Concern for the accuracy of medical evidence had reached such levels that there might be an occasional review of the evidence after conviction, as in the cases of Smethurst and the Stauntons, and for it to provoke a lively correspondence in the medical press.

The role of medical evidence in psychiatric cases also became prominent around this time, especially in the two famous cases of M'Naghten in 1843 and of Hadfield in 1880. These two cases resulted in substantial legislation on the subject of mental respon-sibility and the defence of insanity, notably the formulation of the M'Naghten rules and the passing of the Criminal Lunatics Act 1880.[35]

After centuries of neglect, the provision of medical evidence at inquests was at last encouraged by statutory provision for the pay-ment of medical witnesses[36] and by the passing of the Births and Deaths Registration Act 1836; the former was not really effective until the passing of the Coroners Act 1887 and nearly another fifty years passed before medical witnesses became a regular feature of inquests. [37]

The role of the expert medical witness could at last be considered to be fully established by the end of the nineteenth century. In the early years of the twentieth century, a tendency to a cult of the omniscient expert emerged, most noticeably in the figure of Sir Bernard Spilsbury who dominated criminal trials until the end of the Second World War—the cases of Crippen (1910), Voisin (1917), Armstrong (1922), Thorne (1825), and Rouse (1931) spring easily to mind. There appears to have then been a reaction against such an authoritative stance, and this coincided with the passing of the great histrionic barristers such as Sir Edward Marshall Hall. There has been a strong swing of the pendulum and the increasing tendency now is to express concern about the methods and standards of medical evidence, a movement which is, perhaps, given impetus by such notable instances as the Australian case of *Chamberlain*. [38] We return to this case later; for the present, it is salutary to repeat the words of Mr Justice Morling in his report of the Royal Commission of Inquiry into the Chamberlain Convictions, 1987:

In criminal cases, where the standard of proof is proof beyond reasonable doubt, it is highly desirable that complex scientific evidence called by the prosecution should be so carefully prepared and expressed that the necessity for the defence to challenge it is reduced as much as possible ... It will often be the case that experts will disagree on matters concerning which there is little prior experience. However, in the present case a number of opinions given in evidence at the trial have been shown to be plainly erroneous ... It is appropriate to discuss some of them in the hope that lessons may be learned which may prevent similar errors being made in the future. [39]

We have come a long way from those first fumbling attempts at expert evidence in the seventeenth century. But with greater experience and scientific knowledge now available, the direction of the legal process is to require increasing expertise of its professional witnesses.

The types of medical witness

Concurrently with such requirements, the specification of professional persons in the role of witness has become more precise. It is, perhaps, premature to discuss any differences as to provision of evidence before addressing the law of evidence (Chapter 5); some understanding of the subject is, however, essential to much of what follows.

A professional person may attend court as a witness in one of three capacities. He or she may be an ordinary witness, a professional witness, or an expert witness. The distinction reflects the type of examination which will be undergone in court.

As an ordinary witness, the doctor, or other professional, may be called upon to give evidence as to what was seen as an ordinary member of the public. Thus, a doctor might see someone robbing a bank and be called to court subsequently to give evidence of identification.

A professional witness is defined as a witness practising as a member of the legal or medical professions, or as a dentist, veterinary surgeon, or accountant, who attends to give professional evidence as to matters of fact.[40] Thus, a casualty officer may have admitted to hospital a man suffering from a stab wound. As a professional witness, he will be asked details as to the identity of the victim, how he got to hospital, what injuries were present, what was the man's condition, and where was he sent from the casualty department.

There is no comparable definition in the secondary legislation of an expert witness but the British Medical Association describes him or her as someone specifically called in by one side or the other to interpret the facts using his or her expertise. This is slightly limited as a witness may become an expert witness although called for another purpose. The casualty officer may, for example, be the only person in a position to give an opinion as to how and by what means the injuries were sustained. In the event that the victim died, however, the pathologist will be employed specifically to determine and provide evidence and opinion as to the type of knife that was used, from which direction the blow was struck, whether it could have been self-inflicted, and the like. Even so, the definition makes it clear that the expert witness need not have direct experience of the facts themselves. Thus, it may be alleged that our victim died not from the stab wound but as a result of a negligently performed operation. In such an event, an independent surgeon might well be called to give his opinion which would be based almost entirely on what he had gleaned from the clinical notes. This indicates an important distinction—that, in general, the expert witness is a volunteer; no one can be summoned to give an independent opinion but, once the appointment is accepted, the responsibility must be carried through to the end.

The role of the witness may, of course, become mixed. A good example is that of a doctor witnessing a vehicular accident. In such circumstances, he could be a witness as to fact, a professional witness as to the extent of the injuries received, and an expert in using these as a way of assaying the speed of the vehicle. This example is used again in relation to the law of evidence (Chapter 5).

In civil cases, it is always the judge who determines whether the witness' expertise is sufficient for the court to accept his evidence and also whether expert evidence, and its quantity, is required on the point at issue. The decision in a criminal case as to whether the witness is 'ordinary' or 'expert' lies with the legal authorities and is demonstrated in practice by the fees the court is willing to pay (see Appendix B). In general, these are related to the expertise necessary in a particular case, not that which the individual is qualified to provide; this condition exists throughout the United Kingdom. We consider such matters as the proof of expertise in Chapter 8.

References

1. Rashdall, H. in Powicke, F. M. and Emden, A. B. *The Universities of Europe in the Middle Ages* (1936) Oxford: University Press.
2. Havard, J. D. J. *The Detection of Secret Homicide* (1960) London: Macmillan, pp. 1–10.
3. Amundsen, D. W. and Ferngren, G. B. 'The physician as an expert witness in Athenian law' (1977) 51 *Bull. Hist. Med.* 202.
4. Amundsen, D. W. and Ferngren, G. B. 'The forensic role of physicians in Roman law' (1979) 53 *Bull. Hist. Med.* 53.
5. Amundsen, D. W. and Ferngren, G. B. 'The forensic role of physicians in Ptolemaic and Roman Egypt' (1978) 52 *Bull. Hist. Med.* 336.
6. Rashdall, ref. 1 above.
7. Ackerknecht, E. H. in Ciba Symposium, 11 *Early History of Legal Medicine* (1950) No. 7, p. 1286.
8. Farag, M. Personal communication.
9. Rashdall, ref. 1 above.
10. Ackerknecht, ref. 7 above at p. 1313.
11. Rashdall, ref. 1 above at p. 433.
12. Ackernecht, ref. 7 above at p. 1286.

13. Devlin, P. *The Judge* (1981) Oxford: University Press, p. 117.
14. Stenton, D. M. (ed.) *Rolls of the Justices in Eyre for Yorkshire, 1218–1219* (1937) Selden Society, Vol. 56, p. 251.
15. Stenton, ref. 14 above at p. 197.
16. Gross, C. *Select Cases from the Coroners' Rolls, 1265–1413* (1895) Selden Society, Vol. 9, p. 55.
17. Forbes, T. R. *Surgeons at the Bailey* (1985) New Haven & London: Yale University Press, p. 43.
18. Havard, ref. 2 above at p. 4.
19. Havard, ref. 2 above at p. 2.
20. Forbes, ref. 17 above at p. 75.
21. Ackerknecht, ref. 7 above at p. 1290.
22. Keynes, G. (ed.) *The Apologie and Treatise of Ambroise Paré* (1951) London: Falcon Educational Books, pp. 217–20.
23. Frazer, A. *Mary Queen of Scots* (1969) London: World Books/Weidenfeld & Nicolson, p. 339.
24. Hand, L. 'Historical and practical considerations regarding expert testimony' (1902) 15 *Harvard Law Rev.* 40.
25. Birkenhead, Earl of *More Famous Trials* (1938) London: Hutchinson, p. 114.
26. Havard, ref. 2 above at p. 5.
27. Birkenhead, ref. 25 above at p. 181.
28. Knight, S. *The Killing of Justice Godfrey* (1984) London: Grafton Books, p. 127.
29. Gutteridge, R. *Dorset Murders* (1986) Wimborne: Roy Gasson Assoc's, p. 9.
30. Roughead, W. (ed.) *Trial of Mary Blandy* (1914) London: Hodge & Co, Notable Trials Series, p. 84.
31. Hand, ref. 24 above at p. 47.
32. Watson, E. R. (ed.) *Eugene Adam. His Life and Trial* (1913) London: Hodge & Co, Notable Trials Series.
33. Forbes, ref. 17 above at p. 157.
34. Forbes, ref. 17 above at p. 30.
35. Forbes, ref. 17 above at pp. 177–89.
36. 6 & 7 William 4, Ch. 89.
37. Havard, ref. 2 above at pp. 44–65.
38. *Chamberlain* v. *The Queen* (1983) 46 ALR 493 (FC); [No 2] (1983) 153 CLR 521 (HC).
39. Morling, Mr Justice T. R. (Commissioner) *Report of the Royal Commission of Inquiry into the Chamberlian Convictions* (1987) Darwin: Government Printer of the Northern Territories, pp. 311–13.
40. Costs in Criminal Cases (General) Regulations 1986 (SI 1986/1335), r. 15.

3

The form of legal process

We are concerned in this chapter to consider actual court practice
and its effect on the medical witness. It has been noted in Chapter 1
that there are two major legal systems which operate within our
immediate spheres of interest: the English speaking world and the
European Community. The law in the latter, based as it is on civil or
Roman-Germanic law, is codified and it is the code, not the decisions of the courts, which provides the authoritative and exclusive
source of the law. The common law, on the other hand, was
developed by the judges whose decisions, within a system of precedent by which lower courts are bound by decisions of higher
courts, established the law with very little legislative interference
until the nineteenth century. Progressively, the legislature has taken
over the law-making role and most of English law is now to be found
in statutes. In addition, the Law Commission was established in
1965 to review *all* the law 'with a view to its systematic development and reform including, in particular, the codification of the
law'; and significant aspects of the common law have been codified
since 1965. The idea behind the Law Commission—and the move
towards codification—was not to bring the common law into line
with the civil law. There are still differences, an important one
being that English judges will, within the framework of the code,
continue to apply the law within the doctrine of precedent with its
emphasis on case law and its respect for the decisions of superior
courts. In civil systems, at least in theory, much less importance is
attached to judicial decisions and the code remains the exclusive
source of law.

By and large, there are, correspondingly, two major forms of legal
process: the inquisitorial, which generally finds favour in those
countries governed by the civil law, and the accusatorial or adversarial,
which is very much a product of the English system. The essential
differences have been summed up as being that, whereas the inquisitorial system is concerned to discover the truth without restriction as
to a specific matter having been raised, the adversarial approach

is designed to adjudicate on the strength of the rival contentions that the opposing parties have presented;[1] there is little wonder that the medical scientific witness, other than one who normally works within the immediate medico-legal circle, finds himself more at home in the former environment.

The inquisitorial system

In its pure form, it is the accused who is on trial rather than an objective assessment being made as to whether or not the prosecution has proved its case against him. To this end, great importance is attached to pre-trial inquiries which are conducted by an independent legal officer.[2] At the trial, the duty of eliciting the evidence is given to the 'inquisitor', or judge, who conducts the examination of the case himself and who is given wide powers to investigate all aspects of the case. The functions of such advocates as appear are to draw the judge's attention to any points he may have missed, to suggest questions that the President, or chief judge, might put,[3] and to represent their clients by way of summaries or closing speeches. Since the presiding judge is concerned to find the answer to a specific problem he will address the matter directly and will have no interest in 'scoring a point'. As a consequence, the expert witness may be given considerable latitude, particularly as to the exposition of the facts; the examining judge may, for example, give the witness an opportunity to verify a fact or opinion. The need for potentially dangerous snap decisions is, thus, eliminated and a single confession of ignorance—'I don't know'— is unlikely to prejudice the strength of the rest of the evidence.

Of greatest significance in the present context, the inquisitorial system is intended to apply in the English coroner's court and in the public inquiry. It is appropriate, here, to discuss the coroner's inquiry as a distinct entity.

The coroner's inquiry

The development of the English coroner's system, which has been adopted in Wales and Northern Ireland, has been discussed in Chapter 1.[4] The modern coroner may be either a lawyer—that is, a barrister or a solicitor—or a doctor of not less than five years' standing; both professions are subject to this condition. Some coroners are in full-time posts while others combine part-time involvement with other professional activities.[5] In practice, most coroners are qualified as solicitors although a few are doubly qualified in both law and medicine; in view of the fact that the main function of the coroner nowadays is to decide on the cause of death, there is reason to question whether this is, in fact, the ideal distribution.[6] The coroner is appointed by the local authority;[7] each has his own geographical area of jurisdiction and each must have a deputy coroner to act in his or her absence. Full time coroners are usually established in large cities where they have courtrooms and offices, sometimes as part of a major court complex. So far as we are aware, only Sheffield has developed the concept of the medico-legal centre thus far.[8] Other coroners may play a more peripatetic role, performing their function in more thinly populated regions and being accustomed to hold inquests in appropriate rooms anywhere within their area (see also Chapter 4). Within his jurisdiction, the coroner has a duty to investigate any death that is reported to him (see Appendix A); very infrequently, he undertakes other duties such as the investigation of treasure trove and acting as sheriff.

The person with whom a doctor is most likely to have immediate contact when one of his patients dies is the coroner's officer. This official may be either a serving police officer or a civilian—often one who has seen previous police service. He is responsible, under the coroner's supervision, for initiating police inquiries into the death and for organizing an inquest when appropriate.

The coroner must hold an inquest if the cause of death proves to be unnatural or in other circumstances as described below. Since the implementation of the Coroner's Rules 1984,[9] it has been possible for the inquest to be completed using mainly documentary evidence. Thus, a doctor may be asked to provide a report and will then play no further part in the proceedings. However, he may be asked to attend the inquest and give oral evidence especially when questions arise as to the cause of death or the medical treatment of the deceased. In practice, this may be mainly for the benefit of relatives and other 'properly interested persons' who are present[10] though it must be understood that the investigation is for the state and not for the individual. The occasions on which a coroner *must* sit with a jury are now infrequent[11] and can be summarized as being when it is suspected that death:

(a) occurred in prison or in such circumstances as to require an inquest under any Act other than the Coroners Act 1988;
(b) occurred while the deceased was in police custody or resulted from an injury caused by a police officer in the purported execution of his duty;
(c) was due to an accident, poisoning, or disease that must be notified to any government department, or an officer of a government department or an inspector appointed under the Health and Safety at Work etc., Act 1974, s. 19;
(d) occurred in circumstances, the continuance of or possible recurrence of which is likely to be prejudicial to the public;[12]
(e) in any other case where the coroner deems a jury appropriate.

A number of persons may, then, have a serious interest in the outcome and may be represented. In such circumstances, adversarial attitudes may become grafted onto an inquisitorial process—conditions which may be less than ideal. We have noted elsewhere (p. 144) the importance of the medical witness maintaining his balance under examination. It is worth observing that this may be, paradoxically, far less easy in the coroner's court where an examination of the witness may not be directed to the identifiable single question of innocence or guilt or to the probability of a given proposition being correct. The almost inevitable jockeying for position by the parties represented in an important case can become frustrating in practice; the witness must, therefore, be particularly careful not to lose objectivity. Occasionally, the medical witness himself may be the object of an accusation as to negligence or improper conduct. If such is believed to be the case, he can, and should, be legally represented himself; he is entitled to refuse to answer questions which may be incriminating—and very often, it is only another lawyer who will see the potential danger in a line of inquiry. It is, however, to be noted that 'incriminating' is interpreted in this context as meaning in a criminal, and not in a civil, sense.

The doctor called to the coroner's court is obliged to attend just as is the case with any other court. It is important to remember that, even though the court may sit in informal locations and although few of the legal figures are ever robed or bewigged, the evidence which the doctor gives is given on oath and the rules relating to perjury and contempt of court apply just as much as they do in more august surroundings. The coroner's court is an inferior court of record and, as a result, any evidence which appears in the coroner's depositions or which has been taken on oath can be used in, say, relevant civil proceedings; the subsequent litigation may be both protracted and expensive. [13]

The adversarial system

The inquisitorial system may have advantages in the pursuit of justice and be attractive to the expert for that reason. Ludovic Kennedy has said: 'over the years I have become more and more concerned at the weaknesses of the system of justice ... which is called the adversary system'; while not advocating a complete change to the French system, he has asked: 'ought we not be thinking of moving in that direction?' [14] Nevertheless, English— and, indeed, Scottish—legal practice will, when possible, revert to an adversarial system whenever matters are in dispute. Quite why this should be so is, at times, difficult to understand.

The law of evidence, which has been subject to much modification by way of statute is, effectively, a system of *ex*clusionary rules based on the general principle that the only evidence which should be given is that which can be tested in court by counsel. Whether this resulted from or led to the adversarial system as we know it is difficult to say. Whatever the true answer, the system fits well with the sporting instincts of the British. This national characteristic takes shape in the idea of 'sides' within the courtroom and the legal vernacular is full of phrases such as 'giving the man a run for his money'; the mere suggestion of winning or losing a case introduces an element of sporting rivalry and Professor Usher, for example, when referring to an awkward moment in the witness box, put it well when he said: '... [in being concerned slightly with the law] I account it a singular advantage to have been a sportsman ... in my youth'. [15]

Given that the advocate is there to make the best case he can for his client, the doctor in the witness box must expect, and accept, questioning on a partisan basis. In the majority of cases, a doctor's main evidence will be as to fact: what did he see? What did he do? In answering these questions he is doing no more than setting

the scene in which the adversarial contest is to be played out. If the
sporting analogy is to be continued, he is the groundsman whose
function it is to prepare a fair pitch. As such, he is relatively
unaffected by the system; his answers are factual, and in the event
that an opinion is sought, it can be given unreservedly. Neither side
can seriously challenge this though they may, later, dispute its
significance: it is the 'expert' who knowingly enters the adversarial
arena. We discuss later (Chapter 10) the question of partisanship on
the part of the expert witness. Here, it is sufficient to emphasize that
the witness' function is to propound his professional belief. He
would not be there unless invited by the legal advisers of one side or
the other and he would not be invited were it not apparent that his
views were, in general, favourable to that side. Inevitably, therefore,
he is part of the adversarial system but his participation is, so to
speak, second-hand; he is representing neither the accused nor the
crown, neither the plaintiff nor the defendant, but his opinion. One
opinion may be 'worth more' in evidence than that of another in
terms of the experience and prestige of its presenter but, no matter
what his eminence in the profession, he must expect his views to be
challenged by the other party. It follows that no one should offer
himself as an expert witness unless he at least feels confident that his
opinion will withstand the efforts which will be made to undermine it.

The lawyers

Although his initial dealings may well have been with the police or
coroners' officers, the doctor will soon come into contact with
lawyers whatever may be the variety of proceedings in which he first
became involved as a witness.

In practical terms, lawyers can be classified as solicitors, barristers, or judges. Loosely speaking, solicitors represent the legal
general practitioners. They deal with much legal material which
never goes to court, such as preparing wills, conveyancing, and
acting in the commercial world. They may take the role of advocates, pleading their clients' cases in the lower courts; currently,
they may not do so in the High Court but recent suggestions for the
reform of the legal system indicate that they may well be able to do
so in the future. Most solicitors have law degrees but the essential
qualifying exams are governed by the Law Society. They work from
legal firms with offices in all parts of the community.

Barristers can be looked on as the consultants of the legal world. Some work in branches of the law where they never go to court but the majority have advocacy in court as their principal role—indeed, in Scotland, they are known as advocates. While they may act in any court, they are usually to be found in the Crown Court, the High Court, and the Courts of Appeal where they are always dressed in wig and gown. They also may have law degrees but they become members of one of the Inns of Court while training and their qualifying exams are the Bar Finals.

Any case going to the High Court or the Crown Court requires a solicitor to prepare the case who will then brief a barrister who, in turn, will plead the case in court. In major cases, there will be two barristers, one being a junior and the other a leader who is usually a QC or 'silk'. The latter term derives from the material of the barrister's gown and denotes a senior member of the profession, appointed to the rank by the Queen on the recommendation of the Lord Chancellor.

Circuit judges, styled as His Honour Judge X, and High Court Judges, who are knighted on appointment and styled the Honourable Mr Justice X, are appointed by the Queen on the recommendation of the Lord Chancellor normally from barristers of ten years' standing. Circuit judges will normally have prefaced their appointment as full-time judges by serving as recorders, the title of recorder now being reserved for a part-time judgeship. The qualification for appointment as a recorder is ten years' standing as a barrister or as a solicitor. Furthermore, the qualification for a circuit judge is either ten years' standing as a barrister *or* five years' standing as a recorder. A solicitor may, thus, aspire to a full-time judicial appointment as a circuit judge. Judges of the Appeal Court are styled Lord Justice X but a 'Law Lord' is one who sits in the House of Lords and is, therefore, a peer. There is no reason why anyone in the legal profession should not be appointed a life or hereditary peer in his or her own right; such a peer would not, of course, be a member of the Appellate Committee.

The English legal structure

The constitution of the English legal system is detailed, firstly, in the Supreme Court Act 1981. The Supreme Court consists of the

Court of Appeal, the High Court, and the Crown Court. The last
has replaced the old Courts of Assize. It is to be noted that the title
'Supreme Court' is something of a misnomer perpetuated by historical
accident; the highest court of appeal is the House of Lords which
hears both civil and criminal appeals of major importance arising in
England and Wales and also civil cases deriving from the Scottish
jurisdiction.

The Court of Appeal is divided into criminal and civil divisions.
The Lord Chief Justice presides over the former and the Master of
the Rolls over the latter.

The High Court consists of three divisions: Chancery with the
Lord Chancellor presiding and with the Vice-Chancellor as the
administrative head; the Queen's Bench Division presided over by
the Lord Chief Justice; and the Family Division the head of which is
known as the President. The principal site of the Court is in the
Courts of Justice in the Strand, London although a hearing may take
place at any 'first tier' Crown Court centre in England and Wales. In
practice, much Queen's Bench and Family Division work is done
outside London but this is rarely the case for Chancery work. It is in
these courts that civil litigation is fought out and the medical profession is likely to be heavily involved in providing expert opinion.
Clearly, the most obvious instances will be in the adjudication of
personal injury cases of all sorts and particularly in those which
involve medical negligence, in which case the doctor may be involved both as a principal and as a witness. Many apposite cases will
also be heard in the Family Division, especially those related to the
control of reproduction by those who are incapable of giving a
consent which is valid in law. Many such cases will arise as a result
of a further function of the High Court, Family Division, which is
to order, or discharge an order, that a minor be made a ward of
court—evidence of abuse or as to qualities of treatment offered or
refused will be very much a matter for testimony. The High Court is
also responsible for appeals from the Crown Court, except when the
judgment of the Crown Court relates to trial on indictment, and
from inferior courts, of which the Coroner's Court is the most
significant example in the present context. If the Divisional Court
quashes a coroner's inquisition, the court may order the same or
another coroner to hold a fresh inquest with another jury; evidence
once given may, therefore, have to be repeated and the ambience
may have changed dramatically. The High Court's further function

of judicial review is essentially a matter of administrative law and will rarely affect the doctor.

The Crown Court[16] is effectively the superior court of record for criminal offences and hears all cases that proceed on indictment. It is here that the medical witness, both in a professional and an expert capacity, is likely to come up against the full panoply of the law. The Crown Court for the City of London is called the Central Criminal Court, or, more popularly, the Old Bailey.

Despite the 'glamour' and the notoriety attached to the Crown court, the doctor who is not a forensic expert is as likely to appear in courts of inferior record as in the Supreme Court and it is well to remember that the consequences to the principals involved may be just as serious in their effect as are those following a trial in the High Court. There are, for example, many whose lives and livelihood will be destroyed should they lose their driving licence for a year; their cases merit as much attention to detail as do those involving a potential prison sentence.

The county court[17] is an inferior court of record—inferior in so far as a superior court can prohibit such courts from exceeding their jurisdiction. The jurisdiction of the county court in civil litigation is very wide but is simultaneously circumscribed, in the main, by the extent of the damages that can be awarded. From the doctor's point of view, the most important cases to be dealt with at this level include actions of tort—which may involve personal injury; however, such actions cannot currently include those in which the demand for damages exceeds £5000. A county court exists in most large towns and boroughs; it is presided over by a circuit judge who deals with several courts in a county court district.

The Justices of the Peace

Magistrates' courts represent the work-horses of the legal system; they are to be found in all reasonably sizeable towns and have jurisdiction over defined geographical areas which used to be known as petty sessional areas.[18]

There are some 26 000 lay magistrates (Justices of the Peace) in England and Wales. The only statutory requirement for the office is that a magistrate must live within fifteen miles of the commission area to which he is appointed. In practice the aim is to ensure that persons of standing and discretion are appointed and that the magistracy is fairly representative of the community as a whole. Legal qualifications are not a prerequisite and the vast majority of magistrates have none. All magistrates are required to receive training in which the emphasis is on their judicial role and on sentencing. The court magistrates may be advised on points of substantive law, evidence, and procedure by the justices' clerk.

In addition to the lay magistracy, there are stipendiary magistrates who are legally qualified and who are salaried. This office originated in London in the late eighteenth century owing to dissatisfaction with the quality of the lay magistrates. The number that may be appointed is limited and, nowadays, additional stipendiaries are likely to be appointed only where there is a shortage of lay magistrates. The stipendiary magistrate sits alone and has all the powers of his or her lay counterpart.

While magistrates' courts deal qualitatively with minor matters, they are very important quantitatively. On the criminal side, nearly all cases begin in the magistrates' courts and over 90 per cent end there. Apart from the trial of cases, magistrates are involved in committal proceedings, bail applications, and the issue of warrants of arrest and search. Their civil jurisdiction is less extensive but is, none the less, important—especially in relation to minor domestic proceedings. In addition, magistrates staff the juvenile courts (see Juvenile justice below).

For jurisdictional purposes, crimes are classified as:

(a) those triable only on indictment;
(b) those triable only summarily; and
(c) those triable either way.

It will be appreciated that some crimes are, by their nature, so grave that they can be tried only on indictment in the Crown Court where trial is by jury; obvious examples include murder and rape. Where the charge is of an offence that is indictable only, the function of the magistrates is simply to determine whether there is a *prima facie* case against the accused such as to justify his or her committal for trial. At one time this was an elaborate procedure requiring the prosecution to outline its case in open court. This process is still possible if the accused insists upon it but a new style of committal proceedings was introduced in 1967 whereby the magistrates may commit the accused for trial without considering the prosecution's evidence provided that the accused is legally represented and consents. This is the style that is usually adopted; English legal process has, thus, taken on a major feature of Scots practice. It follows that an expert witness would be involved in committal proceedings only rarely and there are severe restrictions on the reporting of proceedings unless the accused chooses to lift them.

At the other extreme, some offences are so obviously minor that they are triable only summarily before a magistrate's court—the majority of road traffic offences fall into this category. Three magistrates usually sit although the required quorum is two. Although there is no jury, the form of the trial is virtually the same as that in a trial on indictment (see p. 106). Counsel will rarely be engaged and, if the accused is represented at all, it will be through the medium of a solicitor. None the less, an expert who is engaged in a summary trial—as he may well be, say, in driving offences involving alcohol or drugs—should not make the mistake of thinking that his examination is likely to be less searching than in a trial on indictment.

In between these two extremes, there are offences in which the gravity of the offence depends on the circumstances; theft is an obvious example of such offences that are triable either way. Charged with such an offence, the accused may always insist on trial by indictment; but, in a suitable case, the magistrates may try the case summarily if the accused consents. It follows that for an apparently trivial theft the accused may insist on trial by indictment (perhaps because he feels his chances of an acquittal are better before a jury) and many have suggested that thefts below a certain amount should be triable only summarily. Such a suggestion was rejected by Parliament in 1977 though a similar suggestion was accepted in relation to offences of criminal damage which are now triable only summarily where the damage is below a specified amount (presently £2 000).

Convicted following summary trial, the accused may appeal against sentence or (if he pleaded not guilty) against conviction to the Crown Court. Where he appeals against conviction the appeal is in effect a re-trial of the whole case so that an expert who gave evidence at the trial may have to rehearse that evidence at the appeal. There is also an appeal by way of case stated to a Divisional Court of the Queen's Bench Division which may be used only where an issue of law is involved and the expert witness will not be involved.

Convicted on indictment, the accused may appeal against sentence or (if he pleaded not guilty) to the Criminal Division of the Court of Appeal. Only exceptionally will the Court of Appeal admit new evidence but there have been appeals which have turned on newly admitted expert evidence and, when such evidence is given, the expert is examined and cross-examined in the ordinary way (for which, see Chapter 8).

A final appeal lies from the Divisional Court or the Court of Appeal to the House of Lords but only where a point of law of public importance is involved.

The Scottish legal process

The judicial apparatus of Scotland is, as in England, based on a division between civil and criminal law—the main practical difference being that the judges in Scottish courts are not specialized. In fact, those sitting in the High Court, which is the highest criminal court, are the same as those in the civil Court of Session; the same senior judge is known as the Lord Justice-General in the former and as the Lord President in the latter. The Court of Session is made up, firstly, of an Outer House, consisting of twelve judges who sit singly as courts of first instance; appeal, or, indeed, recourse by the judges themselves, is to the Inner House which, in turn, is divided into two divisions, each of four judges. The First and Second Divisions, as they are known, are of equal standing; there is no footballing analogy.

The High Court has fewer categories but functions as a court of trial, when one judge sits, and as a court of Criminal Appeal when at least three judges hear the case. By contrast with the Court of Session, whose decisions can be appealed to the House of Lords in London, the High Court has supreme jurisdiction.

The bulk of both run-of-the-mill civil and criminal work is undertaken in the Sheriff Court which corresponds most closely with the English county court—though the similarity is very tenuous. A great many cases which would be dealt with by the English magistrates' courts are heard by the Sheriff who may also sit with or without a jury. The sentencing powers of the Sheriff are limited—two years' imprisonment is the maximum permissible on indictment—but, in the event that the Sheriff considers this to be inadequate, he can refer the case to the High Court for sentencing.

The District Courts, presided over by laymen, lie below the Sheriff Courts and deal with really minor offences for which the maximum penalty is two months' imprisonment or a fine of £100.

Doctors will certainly appear in the Court of Session as both professional and expert witnesses in cases concerned with personal injury and, here, the conditions are no different from those obtaining in the English civil courts. In the event of an appearance in the High Court, conditions will be found to be similar to those in England with one major exception—that is, that all evidence in criminal cases in Scotland must be corroborated. Thus, for example, two doctors must perform a post-mortem examination and two doctors must examine a case of rape or incest. Corroboration is of fact, not necessarily of opinion but, perhaps surprisingly, the two doctors cannot normally appear on opposing sides—the defence must produce their own experts. Even so, the fact that two doctors, who may not listen to each other's evidence, can be examined and cross-examined does a great deal to modify the concept of the 'expert witness' as opposed to that of the expert who gives evidence—a matter which we address in Chapter 10. There is now no *need* to call both witnesses to trial[19] but it is often to the accused's advantage to do so. A double cross-examination is that much more likely to expose any weaknesses in the prosecution's case.

Most often the non-specialist doctor will appear in the Sheriff Court and it is here that he will meet the Procurator Fiscal. The Fiscal is often equated with the English coroner but this is to over-simplify the facts. It is true that he, or increasingly she, is responsible for the investigation of sudden and unexpected death but the Fiscal is always a lawyer who is employed full-time by the Crown Office. The Fiscal system represents the prototype of the English Crown Prosecution Service. Thus, the major function of the office is to prosecute in the Sheriff Court and to prepare the case for the advocate in the High Court; the Fiscal also prepares and presents the evidence-in-chief in a Fatal Accident Inquiry.[20] The procedure in the Sheriff Court is similar to that in any court of criminal justice but, even when the Sheriff sits with a jury, conditions are less redolent of tradition than is the case in the High Court. Despite the relative lack of formality, the Sheriff is addressed as 'My Lord' or 'My Lady' in the same way as is the judge in the High Court or the Court of Session.

Juvenile justice

Very different systems of justice have evolved in nearly all countries in respect of juveniles, whether this affects the young person as a criminal or as a victim of criminality. The general premises are that a child should not be subjected to some of the more formal aspects of legal procedure and that a child's best interests are more appropriately served in an investigative rather than an adversarial setting.

By the time this book comes to publication, the law relating to child care will have altered markedly.[21] In due course, the juvenile court will be abolished in favour of courts at several levels sitting as family proceedings courts. A person under the age of 17 may be brought before the court if he or she is, or is likely to be, suffering significant harm as a result of a breakdown in child/parental relationships.[22] The power of the court to make a care order in respect of a child who has committed an offence only will be done away with. Comparable Scottish legislation is contained in the Social Work (Scotland) Act 1968. The conditions under which a charge against a child may be heard are detailed in the Children and Young Persons Act 1933, Part III. The doctor may be called upon for evidence in such situations—although an alternative and equally likely association with child care will be through the prosecution of adults either under the common law or under the 1933 Act, ss. 1 and 11 or the Children and Young Persons (Scotland) Act 1937.

At present, a person under the age of seventeen who is to be prosecuted for an offence in England and Wales will be brought before a juvenile court.[23] The juvenile court is, to an extent, one of last resort in so far as recourse represents something of a failure of the social services system or of community policing. A child below the age of ten years cannot be guilty of an offence but, beyond that age, it is possible for the prosecution to prove that a child is capable of forming a criminal intent. However, the test as to how the presumption of an inability to do so may be rebutted is strict—not only must the child be aware that his or her action was beyond childish mischievousness but he or she must know that what was done was seriously wrong.[24] Such considerations are less material in the context of care proceedings which may be initiated either to protect the child or if he or she is beyond parental control.

There are a number of rules which define the role of, and representation of, the child, its parents, and the extended family in relation to care proceedings. In particular, in the event of a conflict between the parents and the child, the court must appoint a guardian *ad litem* who must protect the child's best interests; moreover, the parents are not entitled to be full parties to the proceedings unless the child is subject to a separate representation order—a comparatively new acknowledgement of their special status.[25] These niceties will scarcely concern the doctor although it is as well to appreciate the loyalties of those who examine his evidence. Despite the existence of representatives and respondents, care proceedings are, strictly speaking, non-adversarial[26] and, indeed, both in England and Scotland, the rules of evidence may be 'bent' to accommodate the model of the child's best interests.[27]

The juvenile court as presently constituted is, in essence, the magistrates' court in another format. It is rigidly protected from association with adult practice and, although a large number of persons may be present by right, the hearings are private; at least one of the justices sitting must be a woman. Examination of the witness may, therefore, be conducted in relatively informal surroundings but will be no less searching than in an adult court.

There is no juvenile court as such in Scotland where the function is taken over by the Children's Hearing.[28] This is essentially an informal discussion conducted by a Children's Panel; this consists of three members who are drawn from, so far as is possible, all walks of life and whose qualification need only be an understanding of children. Before a case is taken to the Panel, it is screened by the Reporters to the Panel who also present the case. It is important to remember that the hearing is not a court in so far as it can only hear cases which are agreed, and understood, by the child and the parents—each of whom must attend the hearing and may be represented, albeit without the benefit of legal aid. In the event of any dispute, the case must be remitted to the Sheriff for a finding; the Panel is, in any case, responsible for the disposal of the case which may be by way of discharge or by the imposition of a supervision order of graded severity. The medical evidence to the Panel may, therefore, be presented either to the Panel or the Sheriff. In the former case, it will normally be in the form of a report although the Panel may, rarely, ask the doctor to amplify his report in person and psychiatric assessment of both the child and the parents may assist in disposal of the case. In front of the Sheriff, the reporter will lead the evidence but will act essentially as a fact finder rather than a prosecutor—both parents and child may, however, be represented and may obtain legal aid for the purpose.

Public inquiries

Public inquiries provide a way by which Parliament or Ministers may obtain an independent investigation into matters of public concern. The final results and recommendations are passed to the responsible Minister who may or may not take action as a result. Some public inquiries, for example those dealing with the site of an airfield or a motorway, are obligatory; others, although authorized by statute, are discretionary. These very commonly relate to dangerous or disturbing aspects of public health—inquiries into major disasters such as the loss of an oil rig or concerning widespread child abuse[29] are examples and, therefore, doctors and health carers may be intimately involved.

The atmosphere of a public inquiry may be daunting even to the experienced witness. The arrangements as to evidence, which is taken on oath, and the like are derived from the Tribunals of Inquiry (Evidence) Act 1921 and thus the atmosphere is that of a Court of Law. Theoretically, the proceedings are inquisitorial in nature but the sheer importance of the issue ensures that many parties are involved and will be represented by high quality legal expertise. The result is that, the medical evidence having been led by Counsel for the Inquiry, the doctor is effectively cross-examined by numerous lawyers each of whom is anxious to make a specific point for his or her specific client. The Chairman is always conscious of the duty to make findings of fact and recommendations and will generally intervene should the atmosphere become too adversarial; perhaps more importantly, he is likely to request a considered reappraisal of the evidence should this have become confused in the course of cross-examination—a revision process which may be helpful to the expert witness.

Arbitration

The medical witness may, very occasionally, be involved in an arbitration—a reference of a dispute to a private tribunal for hearing in a judicial manner, the dispute being related to an issue which is triable in the civil courts.[30] Thus, expert evidence may be required, for example, as to how certain injuries were caused when this is related to the question of liability.

The parties to the dispute choose their own arbitrator (or arbitrators) and can set their own rules of procedure subject to these being of a sort which would be acceptable to the High Court on appeal. Thus, it is not possible to state the way in which a witness will be examined. He will normally be on oath (1950 Act, s. 12(2)) but this is not necessarily so. Similarly, the process will usually be by way of examination, cross examination, and re-examination by counsel but different tactics could be agreed; the arbitrator himself is likely to take an active part in the presentation of the evidence. The expert witness may well be asked to assist his side in the interrogation of his opposite number.

By the nature of an arbitration agreement, proceedings are likely to be amicable and relatively informal. Despite this, the knowledge that the finding of the arbitrator is final—subject only to appeal to the High Court on a point of law—should be sufficient to impose a heavy sense of responsibility on the witness both as to preparation and presentation of his case.

References

1. Caplan, L. 'The expert witness' (1979) 47 *Med-Leg J.* 124.
2. Sheehan, A. V. *Criminal Procedure in Scotland and France* (1975) Edinburgh: HMSO. The close association between the Scottish and French legal systems is shown by the important role of precognition (see p. 85) in the Scottish criminal law.
3. In France, three judges sit in serious cases and they join the jury's deliberations, and cast their vote, when a jury is called.
4. See also Hunnisett, R. F. *The Medieval Coroner* (1961) Cambridge: University Press.
5. The function of the coroner was fully explored in Brodrick, N. J. L. (Chairman) Report of the Committee on *Death Certification and Coroners* (1971) (Cmnd. 4810) London: HMSO.
6. Mason, J. K. 'Coroners from across the border' (1983) 23 *Med. Sci. Law* 271.
7. Local Government Act 1972.

8. Usher, A. 'The Sheffield Medico-legal Centre' (1978) **18** *Med. Sci. Law* 96.

9. SI 1984/552, r.37. The primary legislation is now to be found in the Coroners Act 1988.

10. Chambers, D. R. 'Medical evidence in the Coroner's Court' (1985) **25** *Med. Sci. Law* 103.

11. Coroners Act 1988, s.8(3).

12. But only if someone is capable of taking appropriate action. See *R* v. *HM Coroner for Inner Hammersmith, ex parte B Peach* (No 1) [1960] 2 WLR 496.

13. For more recent texts as to the coroners' system, see Burton, J. D. K., Chambers, D. R., and Gill, P. S. *Coroners' Inquiries: A Guide to Law and Practice* (1985) Brentford: Kluwer Law; Knapman, P. A. and Powers, M. J. *The Law and Practice on Coroners* (1985) Chichester: Barry Rose Ltd; Matthews, P. and Forman, J. C. (ed.) *Jervis on the Office and Duties of Coroners* (10th edn, 1986) London: Sweet and Maxwell.

14. Kennedy, L. 'The rectification of miscarriages of justice' (1984) **29** *J. Law Soc. Scot.* 351.

15. Usher, A. 'The expert witness' (1985) **25** *Med. Sci. Law* 111.

16. Established under the Courts Act 1971. When acting as a court of appeal from the magistrates' court, the Crown Court may consider matters other than criminal; certain appeals from decisions of local authorities may also be heard.

17. County Courts Act 1984.

18. Magistrates Courts Act 1980.

19. Criminal Justice (Scotland) Act 1980, s.26(7).

20. Fatal Accidents and Sudden Deaths Inquiry (Scotland) Act 1976.

21. Children Act 1989—not applicable to Scotland. The statute is imprecise as to implementation.

22. This wide remit replaces the specific conditions detailed in the Children and Young Persons Act 1969, s.1—now due for repeal.

23. Prosecutions for homicide must be heard in the Crown Court and there are other conditions, including the severity of the offence and the shared responsibility with adults, that may shift the venue of trial. For easy access to the details, see Hoggett, B. M. *Parents and Children: the Law of Parental Responsibility* (3rd edn, 1987) London: Sweet and Maxwell, Chapter 4.

24. *McC* v. *Runeckles* [1984] Crim LR 499; sub nom *J. M.* v. *Runeckles* (1984) 79 Cr App R 255.

25. Children and Young Persons (Amendment) Act 1986, s.3. In view of the new legislation, this right may never be brought into force under the 1986 legislation which is repeated in the 1989 Act.

26. *Humberside County Council* v. *R* [1977] 1 WLR 1251; *R* v. *Birmingham Juvenile Court, ex parte G and R* [1988] 1 WLR 950.
27. *W* v. *Kennedy* 1988 SLT (Reps) 583.
28. For full exposition, see Kearney, B. *Children's Hearings and the Sheriff Court* (1987) London/Edinburgh: Butterworths.
29. Of which, the most recent is to be found in Butler-Sloss L. J. (Chairman) *Report of the Inquiry into Child Abuse in Cleveland 1987* (1988) (Cm 412 and 413). London: HMSO.
30. Arbitration Act 1950.

4

The environment of the legal process

In earliest times, a court would have been likely to be held in the open air. In the Saxon and early medieval eras, the provincial courts, the Shire and Hundred courts, were *al fresco* meetings, the site being designated by custom and often cleared and dug to an appropriate form. Some of these open air court sites are still visible.[1] The one described by Stenton near the Fosse Way lies today as a great rectangular depression in a ploughed field, close to the roadside on the brow of a hill. This natural format is often commemorated at the present time—the basic parliament of Switzerland, the *Landesgesmeinde*, still meets in the open air once each year.

However, here and in other northern countries, the vagaries of the weather dictated an early move to an enclosed building. Once inside, other aspects of the environment could be controlled. Acoustics could be designed so as to make witnesses and lawyers more easily audible and a suitable layout could provide a forum in which the judge was made to appear of enhanced importance and awe-inspiring significance; the witness, for his or her part, could be so placed as to attract the maximum psychological disadvantage, thus enhancing the chances of persuading him to tell the truth.

One of the oldest buildings set aside in this country for the purpose of acting as a court of law is the Westminster Hall, built by William Rufus; this is now rarely open to the public and is mainly used, it seems, for the lying in state of deceased notables. In 1270, however, it accommodated three courts—those of Common Pleas, Chancery, and King's Bench; all sat in the same hall, at different corners and they were still in site when preparations were being made for the trial of Charles I in 1649, as were shops selling ink, paper, spectacles, and the like.[2]

The development of the feudal system after the Norman conquest led to local magnates having their own rights of justice in addition to those of the Crown. Thus, the local seat of the administration of justice was usually the castle which might have been, either, a royal possession or one held by a principal baron. Baronial rights were gradually eroded but the royal castles remained important centres; even to this day some Crown Courts are still held where they succeeded Assize Courts in the remains of large castles—as at Chester, York, Lincoln, and Lancaster. Siting courts in such imposing buildings results in court rooms full of character and architectural style. The ancillary areas for the attending witnesses tend, however, to be cramped and lacking in comfort; stone flagged corridors in winter are apt to sap the strength of the nervous witness who may be held in attendance for several hours.

Less important courts would be held in less imposing places. The village inn, or ale house, acted in that capacity quite often. There are examples throughout the country, one being the Bingley Arms, at Bardsey near Leeds, the site of the local court from AD 1000 until the last century. Until comparatively recently, coroner's courts were often held in public houses. In fact, the inn has been a medico-legal focal point for centuries, it being a convenient place to lodge unidentified bodies for the purpose of identification; the outbuildings of a public house could, thus, become a makeshift mortuary— one of the authors has, in the relatively recent past, performed an autopsy in such circumstances and for the same reason.

Local and mercantile courts increased in importance in later medieval and early Tudor times. As the volume of work increased, small courtrooms began to appear in areas quite remote from the castles. Some of these early courtrooms still survive and may be centres of civic pride and ceremonial. The court in the Guildhall at Sandwich, Kent is one example. Another, in a remarkable state of preservation, is the courthouse of the Honour of Knaresborough, situated in a seventeenth century building within the castle grounds. The records show the existence of a court as far back as the fourteenth century. In the rectangular room, the judge's bench is literally that—a great block of tree-trunk raised above the level of the court at one end of it. Benches for jurors and other participants enclose a central space with a trapdoor leading to a prison cell beneath the courtroom. And that, in essence, is the basic design of a courtroom which has persisted until the present day.

In some of the older Crown courtrooms the design is elaborated so as to accentuate the roles of the different participants in the drama. Often, the judge's bench is elevated to such a height above the well of the court that the Judge, enthroned on high, in red robes and full-bottomed wig, develops an awe-inspiring majesty when seen from the floor of the court itself and it may, indeed, be difficult for him to sublimate a sense of omnipotence. The other person commonly raised by the architecture of such courts is the witness who is, then, exposed to full public view for everyone to decide whether or not he is telling the truth. The witness box is usually sited alongside the judge's bench, or the jury box but, on occasion, it is completely separate, standing in splendid isolation in the well of the court. In either case, the witness is thrust into prominence so that, not only can his every word be heard, but also his demeanour and play of expression can be seen and remarked upon; even his body movements, how he stands and what he does with his hands attract attention. Thus, a witness who is being less than truthful, or who is not really sure of himself, is likely to betray the fact and one objective of a skilled barrister will be to ensure that the Judge, or the jury, are aware of it. For some witnesses, this tension may prevent the adequate presentation of evidence and, thus, be counter-productive. This may be especially so in the case of children giving evidence of sexual assaults; provision is now being made for the use of video cameras, the child being in an adjacent room, away from the court, although visible to the judge and to the barrister on TV monitors. Whether such arrangements are strictly fair to the accused is a matter of debate;[3] nevertheless, the use of live television links is now approved by statute.[4] In these days of violence, it is becoming increasingly common for witnesses to be shielded from public view; fortunately the time when professional and expert witnesses will require such protection has not yet arrived.

The modern courtroom

Viewed from the entrance, a modern custom-built court appears as a much more normal, level room. But, even here, the bench for judge, magistrate, or coroner is prominent and is clearly singled out for precedence, not least by the Royal coat of arms on the wall behind it. The witness box, also still manages to occupy a fairly prominent position. Unless contra-indicated on medical grounds, evidence is given standing. This is something of a double-edged weapon. The inexperienced witness may feel that he is the focus of all eyes and be, to an extent, cowed by the impression; on the other hand, to be at least on the same physical level as one's interrogator can give an encouraging sensation of equality. We revert to the psychology of the witness box in Chapter 8.

However, there are many people in a courtroom apart from the judge and the witness. A witness entering an average Crown courtroom, dealing with criminal cases, will first see the bench raised above the rest of the court. In front of the bench, and below it, facing the court, is a table at which the Clerk of the Court sits; this official is responsible for the administration of the court and the trial. In front of that, facing the bench is a long table and seat; here, the leading counsel in the case sit: prosecutor and defender side by side. Behind is a second row of seats, occupied by instructing solicitors and other participants in the prosecution or defence; advisers, police officers, and the like, who need to be easily accessible to leading counsel, are also accommodated here.

Behind them, and generally in the centre of the courtroom, is the dock, enclosed and usually accessible by stairs from beneath the court, although this feature is replaced by a more conventional entrance in very modern courts.

The jury are seated in two or more rows of seats on one side of the court, near to the bench. They face across the court and towards the witness box. The court stenographer sits nearby, making a typed transcript, on silent typewriter or in shorthand, of the evidence. Usually there are further rows of seats near the witness box for members of the Press.

Finally, there has to be adequate provision for the accommodation of members of the public wishing to attend the trial; there are rows of seats for this purpose situated either to one side or at the back of the court. In older courtrooms, this accommodation often takes the form of a gallery, rather like the balcony of a theatre. The not infrequent movement of members of the public and court officials can be distracting for the witness, a distraction which is often compounded by the verbal disapproval of the bench, but it has to be taken in one's stride.

In the future, computer terminals and video monitors are likely to appear increasingly often in courtrooms. A recent report of the Court Procedure Working Party of the Society for Computers and

Law has recommended much greater use of these machines in the Official Receivers' courts. Such facilities are bound to be made more widely available in other courts in due course.

Most modern magistrates' courts, situated in the newly constructed court complexes which are beginning to spring up around the country, are of much the same pattern as the Crown Court; indeed, magistrates' courts and lower tier Crown Courts are likely to be held in the same room on different days.

Other particular courts may take on a rather different form. Thus, civil courts usually do not use a jury and the benches for them may be used for other purposes or even be absent. Juvenile courts avoid all the more dramatic trappings, looking much like a normal room, with tables and chairs strategically placed; the Scottish Children's Hearing commonly takes place around a table. Most coroners' courts in large urban jurisdictions are purpose built and conform to the general pattern just described, but in rural areas the coroner uses whatever room may be available. His only restriction is stated in the Licensing Act, 1964, s.190 under which he must now avoid using licensed premises unless there is nowhere else available. As a result a witness may find himself attending loci ranging from police station games rooms to church Sunday school rooms. Some places can be positively disconcerting. On one occasion one of the authors was summoned to attend an inquest in the Council offices of a small Pennine industrial town. Expecting a dingy yellow-brown municipal spare room, he was amazed to find a sumptuous oak-pannelled room, with a long dark table covered in a rich burgundy-coloured baize cloth, lit by sunlight shining through stained glass in stone-mullioned windows; unfortunately, such delights are rare.

The public inquiry is, perhaps, one of the most complex venues to which the doctor may be called. Sites may vary from town halls to five-star hotels and even the most hardened witness may be surprised at what he finds. An essential difference from any other judicial or quasi-judicial court is that very many parties may be legitimately interested and represented. The Commissioner and his assessors will be clearly demarcated but the remainder of the hall is generally occupied by a number of tables each accommodating a legal team and their advisers. The use of microphones is essential and the sense of direct contact with one's questioner is lost. Again, we will return to this psychological aspect in Chapter 8.

The geography of Scottish courts is very similar to that described above and witnesses giving evidence on their less familiar side of the border have no need to fear the unexpected. The judge in the High Court is certainly more impressively gowned than his counterpart in the Crown Court but that is unlikely to affect the professional witness. Counsel in the High Court tend to be rather more mobile than in England but the almost invariable effect of this is to distance himself from the witness; the result is helpful for all concerned for it ensures that the exchange of question and answer is conducted in a tone which can be heard by the whole courtroom.

The Sheriff Court in Scotland is less flamboyant than is the High Court but is, nevertheless, thoroughly formal. The Sheriff may sit with or without a jury; in the latter case, the atmosphere approximates to that of a more formal version of the English magistrates' court. The layout of the court is similar to any other although, as described above, the actual room will vary from the very old, and atmospheric—but, often, uncomfortable—courtroom to one which is brand new and of modern design; a visit to the new Sheriff Court complex in Glasgow compares with one to another world for those who do not usually practice in the metropolis. The most likely reason for the non-forensic doctor to give evidence in the Sheriff Court is in connection with a fatal accident inquiry.[5] Here, the Sheriff sits without a jury but the nature of the case often attracts a number of legal representatives and considerable press coverage; the ambience of the fatal accident inquiry is, in many ways, unique.

We will return to the witness' general preparation for giving evidence later. Here we are concerned, in the main, with geography and we would specifically advise the inexperienced witness to discover, in advance of his attendance, the precise whereabouts of the courtroom and, most particularly, the parking facilities or how far the building is from a public transport route. There may be more than one court building in a town and, although the modern building tendency is to include all varieties of court under the same roof, it is not unusual for the civil or magistrates' courts to be quite remote from the criminal courts. Frantic searches for a building in an unknown situation lead to arrival in court harassed, dishevelled and breathless—and/or with a parking ticket, an item which sits uneasily in an expense account. Save in relatively uncommon situations, there is enough anxiety in the air without adding to it unnecessarily.

References

1. Stenton, D. M. *English Society in the Early Middle Ages (1066–1307)* (1959) *Pelican History of England*, vol. 3, p. 133.
2. Wedgewood, C. V. *The Trial of Charles I* (1964) London: Collins World Books, p. 108.
3. See Williams, G. 'Videotaping children's evidence' (1987) 137 *N.L.J.* 108; 'More about videotaping children' (1987) 137 *N.L.J.* 351, 369; Morton, J. 'Videotaping children's evidence—a reply' (1987) 137 *N.L.J.* 216.
4. Criminal Justice Act 1988, s.32. See Children Act 1989, s.96(5).
5. Fatal Accidents and Sudden Deaths Inquiry (Scotland) Act 1976.

5

The law of evidence

No medical witness needs to have a detailed knowledge of this complicated subject—indeed, he would be hard-pressed to do so. There are several books devoted wholly to the subject; the most widely quoted, *Cross on evidence*,[1] comprises 641 pages. It would be foolish for any doctor to attempt to master the subject, and yet some knowledge is useful even at the risk of its being a dangerous thing. It serves to give those doctors who are likely to be called to court some understanding of the procedures under which the lawyers work and of the rules which control them when dealing with evidence, whether it be medical or otherwise.

The section in Walker[2] on the law of evidence is very clear and this chapter relies heavily on the scheme laid out in that book. The interested reader must consult the original for more detail. The scheme starts with the premise that in order for a court of law to deal with a case it must prove certain facts and then apply legal rules to them. It is necessary to establish what facts may be proved—in legal parlance, a matter of relevance and admissibility. Then it must be decided on whom the burden of proving these facts rests and what standard of proof is required—the onus of proof. There is also the question of what the means of proof are—witnesses, documents, and real evidence—and which means may not be used or what evidence is inadmissible. Obviously the rules apply to evidence of any sort but we will see that medical evidence can have certain aspects which are peculiar to it.

In its widest sense, evidence includes both the facts in issue in a case and, also, the means of proving those facts. Legally speaking, there are varieties of facts. The most important are facts in issue, which are the main facts that have to be proved to establish a case. Thus, in a case of alleged murder, the facts in issue that the prosecution have to prove are that A killed B and that A did so with malice aforethought. The facts in issue may be proved of themselves, as when someone saw A kill B, or by means of other facts, which are not themselves facts in issue, as when someone saw A go off with B shortly before B was found dead.

One classic definition of evidence is that it is:

First, the means, apart from argument and inference, whereby the court is informed as to the issues of fact as ascertained by the pleadings; secondly, the subject matter of such means.[3]

An alternative explanation of this is:

The evidence of a fact is that which tends to prove it—something which may satisfy an inquirer of the fact's existence. Courts of law usually have to find that certain facts exist before pronouncing the rights, duties and liabilities of the parties, and such evidence as they will receive in further-ance of this task is described as 'judicial evidence'.[4]

Classifications of evidence

Judicial evidence can be classified into certain types, and this classi-fication affects the way that the evidence is used. Thus, we can have *direct* evidence, which means evidence of the fact itself, for example an eyewitness may have seen one man strike another. Alternatively, the evidence my be *circumstantial*, which means that there is evidence of a fact which itself might lead one to suppose a fact in issue. Thus, it may be that no one saw a blow struck, but someone may have seen the two men quarrelling, have seen them go into an empty house and have seen one come out with a wound. The inference is that the other man struck him but other explanations are, of course, possible, for example that the victim received his injury in an accidental fall.

Another classification is between original evidence and hearsay evidence. *Original* evidence has been called 'firsthand evidence',[5] when it may be the oral evidence of a person who actually saw a fact, or an original document, or a real object such as a weapon. On the other hand, *hearsay* evidence is 'secondhand evidence', as in it the witness relates what someone else said or did, or what they wrote.

Hearsay evidence is itself divisible into first- and secondhand hearsay. Firsthand hearsay refers to evidence of what another person said when that other person knows about the facts to which the witness is speaking; alternatively, it may be in the form of a report and there is increasing statute law which allows for hearsay of this type. Reports without oral support are, for example, admissible evidence under the Road Traffic Offenders Act 1988, s. 15 or under the Misuse of Drugs Act 1971; expert evidence allowed in this way may be both as to the fact and to opinion (Civil Evidence Act 1972, s. 2; Criminal Justice Act 1988, s. 3). Nevertheless, some distinction is to be made between civil and criminal litigation. The objections to hearsay evidence in the former are now virtually abolished,[6] the objective of the court being to reach a just solution by the best possible means. Hearsay rules are, however, more strict in the criminal courts, the reason being that:

The truthfulness and accuracy of the person whose words are spoken by another witness cannot be tested by cross examination and the light which his demeanour would throw on his testimony is lost.[7]

Exceptions are rare and, even then, will only be admitted at the discretion of the court when the evidence is of direct and immediate relevance to an issue at the trial;[8] exceptions to the hearsay rule can only be made through legislation. The majority of these points are of little import to the expert witness save in one aspect—that is that a statement made previously by the witness which is inconsistent with what he gives in evidence can be produced as admissible evidence;[9] this would also apply to the expert's previous writing in articles or books. The witness must, therefore, be prepared to justify any change and it may sometimes be a source of relief to find that Counsel is reading from a superseded edition. By the same token, of course, the other side may use articles written by others in an attempt to refute any expert evidence.

The law also distinguishes between *best* and *secondary* evidence. This means that if both an original and a copy of a report exist that can be produced in evidence, the original is the 'best' evidence while the copy is inferior or 'secondary' evidence. This rule does not now have much importance but would apply to medical evidence where a doctor has his original notes of an examination. These would constitute best evidence.

The production of evidence

Evidence can be produced in different forms. It may be *oral*, that is given by a witness in the witness box; it may be *documentary*, as when a statement is read out, or a report submitted as evidence, or a letter which has been written from one party to another; and it may be *real*, which relates to exhibits, or actual objects such as weapons, clothing, blood samples, etc. An occasional variation of real evidence which may occur for instance in murder trials, is known as a view, when judge and jury leave the court and go to visit the scene of the events. This is uncommon, but one of the authors was involved in a trial for murder in which one of the points against the accused was that features of the body at the scene were described as allegedly seen from the doorway. The evidence of other witnesses was that this was impossible due to the shape of the room and position of its contents; this implied that the accused must have been much closer to the body than was admitted. So judge, jury, and counsel adjourned to the scene to see for themselves the layout of the room. In this sense, the scene, as an actual object, constituted real evidence.

It has to be remembered that rules of evidence do not apply equally to all courts or tribunals. Thus a coroner's court is much more likely to accept evidence which could be described as hearsay than is a Crown Court. Certain professional tribunals, such as the General Medical Council in its disciplinary role, tend to look and sound very like a court of law, but may modify their procedures so as to achieve their specific purposes. [10]

Having considered the nature of and the basic classification of evidence, it is necessary to understand which facts need to be proved, and which are to be excluded—in other words the relevance or admissibility of facts.

Relevant evidence

To be relevant a fact must either be a fact in issue, for example whether A killed B, or a fact from which a fact in issue can be inferred—that is, something to indicate that A killed B, for instance that A was the only person with B at the appropriate time, even if no one saw the event; this is circumstantial evidence. Facts that are neither direct nor circumstantial evidence of the matter before the courts are irrelevant. However, even if a fact, which is not a fact in issue, *is* relevant, there may be a reason for its being inadmissible; such a reason generally derives from one of the other rules of evidence, such as the hearsay rule which we have discussed above. Thus, if a witness heard a victim protesting and shouting out the accused person's name, that would constitute admissible evidence towards the fact that the victim did not consent to the act, but it would not be proof of the identity of the assailant as, for this purpose, it would constitute hearsay evidence.[11] In civil actions, strict rules of evidence apply in some cases, such as in the matrimonial jurisdiction but not in others, for example wardship cases.[12] The decision of what is relevant or admissible in criminal cases rests with the judge and this accounts for an appreciable number of appeals to the Court of Criminal Appeal. In one of our cases, evidence was given that the sound of blows and of the accused's voice shouting the dead child's name were heard coming from a flat in a council block. This was admitted but was destroyed by the defence on the grounds that there were several other children in the area with the same name and that the witness could not be sure that the name being called out referred to the dead child.

The fact that an accused person's previous, similar actions or convictions for other crimes, will be held to be irrelevant often appears illogical to medical eyes. Much scientific research is based on the study of phenomena which can be shown to be specific to a certain event in that they recur in similar circumstances. Thus, if a person suffers from hay fever, a severe attack of rhinitis after driving through the countryside in June will be ascribed to the same cause and an attack of rhinitis after exposure to another dusty atmosphere, even if it does not contain pollen, is likely to be ascribed to an allergic reaction because of the patient's known tendency. Legally, however, 'similar fact evidence' is held to be irrelevant. An authoritative statement of the rule, quoted by Walker, was given by Lord Herschell LC in 1894:

It is undoubtedly not competent for the prosecution to adduce evidence tending to show that the accused has been guilty of criminal acts other than those covered by the indictment, for the purpose of leading to the conclusion that the accused is a person likely from his criminal conduct or character to have committed the offence for which he is being tried. On the other hand, the mere fact that the evidence adduced tends to show the commission of other crimes does not render it inadmissible if it be relevant to an issue before the jury, and it may be so relevant if it bears upon the question whether the acts alleged to constitute the crime charged in the indictment were designed or accidental, or to rebut a defence which would otherwise be open to the accused.[13]

Thus, if a man were accused of murdering a child, evidence that he had been convicted in the past of murdering other children would not be relevant. However, if on this occasion the child had died by drowning and the defence was that it had died accidentally due to submersion during a fit, it would probably be relevant to show that he had given the same explanation for the deaths of other children in which he had been involved. An actual example of such a situation can be found in the 'Brides in the bath' case of 1915.[14]

It may also be possible to use similar fact evidence to establish the identity of an accused as having committed a particular crime. Thus, if a particular murder has special features, such as an unusual mutilation of the body, the fact that the accused is known to have carried out other murders in the past in which the victims were similarly mutilated may be used in evidence to indicate his responsibility for the one now under investigation. Such was the situation in the 1952 trial of Straffen[15] who was accused of killing a small girl; evidence was allowed to the effect that he had killed other small girls in the past: all by strangulation, without sexual interference and without concealment of the bodies.

The general rule accepted by lawyers in the vast majority of cases is that proof that a person has acted in a certain way on previous occasions is no proof that he has acted in same way on the occasion in question; in this way, evidence of an accused person's character or of any previous convictions is normally considered irrelevant and, thus, inadmissible. Such evidence would obviously have an effect on the minds of the jury and so could prejudice a fair trial. Inevitably, there are exceptions to this rule—for instance, in cases of alleged defamation of character—but it is the general attitude adopted by the law; it may be puzzling to the scientist but he must be very wary of letting slip any such inadmissible material in his enthusiasm for giving 'complete' evidence.

Even if some evidence is both relevant and admissible, a trial judge may refuse to admit it, on the grounds that it would be prejudicial to a fair trial. In *Scott and Another* v. *The Queen*,[16] the defendants, who had been convicted of the murder of a special constable in Jamaica, appealed on the grounds that the only evidence of their identification was the statement of a man who had died before the trial; it was averred that the judge should have refused to admit that evidence. The Court of Appeal had rejected this submission as did the Privy Council who held that the trial judge, in exercise of his discretion to ensure a fair trial, had power at common law to refuse to admit a deposition but that that power should be exercised only in rare circumstances. This discretionary power is now statutory; under the Police and Criminal Evidence Act 1984, s.78 the judge can refuse to admit evidence if it appears from all the circumstances that its admission would affect the fairness of the proceedings adversely. Relevant evidence can also be excluded if this is felt to be in the public interest as for instance in matters of national security.

This is not to say that the courts are at pains to exclude evidence which is of probative value. The basic rule here is that, while the decision must rest with the judge, the way in which the evidence is obtained is, in general, irrelevant as to the reaching of that decision. [17] The main exception is that evidence that is obtained by coercion or oppression would not be admissible and this applies particularly to confessions by the accused[18]—but such problems are unlikely to affect the expert witness.

One rule which may come to the notice of, and confuse, expert witnesses is that which precludes the witness from giving evidence on the actual question at issue before the court—a rule which expresses the fear that expert evidence might take over the role of the court itself. Such a rule could have particular influence on the evidence of psychiatrists who, undoubtedly, have a very special place in the criminal legal system. However, the rule has been steadily eroded and, provided his opinion is based on personal observation of the fact, it is now permissible for the expert to answer such questions in both civil and criminal cases. [19] The question of whether the court *must* accept the unopposed evidence of an expert is, in our view, still open, particularly in criminal matters. In some cases, it has been held that such evidence should not be discarded;[20] in others, the supremacy of the court has been emphasized. [21] It is best for the expert witness to realize that he is not an oracle but that he is, at all times, only an expert whose expertise is open to evaluation by the court.

The onus of proof

Next, we come to the onus of proof—or who is obliged to prove certain facts. In the first place, there are certain facts which do not need to be proved and prominent among these are 'notorious facts' or facts which are within the knowledge of the judge or jury. You would not have to prove, for example, that a large number of cars use the M25 or that Edinburgh is more crowded in festival time than in February; such are matters within 'judicial knowledge'. The expert witness must, however, be careful to appreciate that what is routine to him may not be so to the court. An apparently simple manoeuvre such as taking the blood pressure may well not be clear to the layman; on the other hand, taking an oral temperature would probably be within judicial knowledge—the decision is, again, one for the judge.

By contrast, there are some things which cannot be *dis*proved and these are known as irrebuttable presumptions. Probably the best known of these, by virtue of its manifest absurdity, is that a boy aged less than fourteen years is incapable of sexual intercourse;[22] another, almost equally improbable, is that a child less than ten years old is incapable of forming a criminal intent. However, some presumptions *can* be disproved—these are known legally as rebuttable presumptions. The most obvious and general of these is that a man is innocent of a criminal charge; this is manifestly rebuttable on the evidence. A more specific example is that a woman's husband is the father of her child—something which holds in law until paternity is disproved by better evidence.

However, where facts cannot be presumed, it becomes a matter of deciding who has to prove them or on whom the burden of proof rests. Strictly speaking, the burden of proof is divisible into the persuasive burden, which is that of establishing one's case, and the evidential burden, which is that of establishing the facts on which the persuasive burden depends. In so far as a party to an action would fail if it produced no evidence, the evidential burden applies to both sides. In a civil action the persuasive burden lies on the plaintiff, the person bringing the action. In criminal matters it lies with the prosecution, on the principle, as mentioned above, that an accused person is presumed innocent until he is proved guilty. There may be uncommon variations in both civil and criminal cases. Thus as to the former, and of particular significance in the present context, it is well known that, in a case of medical negligence, the burden of proof lies on the patient to prove that the doctor was negligent. However, if the plaintiff has suffered an injury in circumstances which are explicable only as being attributable to negligence on the part of the defendant, the maxim of *res ipsa loquitur* meaning 'the thing speaks for itself' may be applied. The plaintiff is then entitled to succeed unless the defendant can bring evidence to rebut the possibility of negligence.[23] Such conditions would include, say, the leaving of a swab or forceps within the abdominal cavity, or undertaking a course of treatment which was universally condemned.[24] It is then up to the defendant to produce an explanation of the accident which is as consistent with the absence of negligence as with its presence; if he succeeds, the plaintiff then has to prove negligence in the normal way. It has to be said that the courts are very reluctant to apply this principle in medical cases.

Similarly, in criminal cases it is for the prosecution to prove that a person has been, say, guilty of murder—that is, that he has killed another person and that at the time he either intended to cause his death or was reckless as to the outcome. However, even if there is no doubt that he killed his victim, the defence may still seek to show that at the time he could not be held responsible for his actions because of insanity; in that case, since everyone is presumed to be sane until proved otherwise, the burden of proof of insanity lies on the defence. The law on insanity in relation to criminality is extremely complex and beyond the scope of this chapter but, again, the doctor may wonder why such a defence is not led more often. In practice, the plea was only of 'value' to the accused at the time of capital punishment; nowadays a term of imprisonment is probably preferable to an indefinite sojourn in a top security special hospital. The defence is far more likely to plead—and, at the same time, have to prove—diminished responsibility but this is only available in a charge of murder.[25] We take this humane approach to a presumption of innocence until proved otherwise very much for granted these days. Yet it is worth remembering that a person accused of murder was not allowed to call any witnesses for his defence until 1703 and he was not permitted to be represented by counsel until 1836.[26]

Having decided who has the responsibility for proving the facts in any particular case, we should, next, consider what standard of proof is required. The fact that the test has to be a subjective one, decided in the minds of the judge and the jury, may again appear unusual to scientific eyes. Nevertheless, it is rarely possible to have an objective decision, of mathematical precision, in the circumstances in which the courts work. The medical expert witness who is asked how sure he is of the opinion he is expressing may well find it difficult to match his level of certainty to the standard in the minds of the lawyers.

It is well known that the level of proof required varies between a civil and criminal action, though it has been suggested that nowadays there is little to choose between them, a court needing only to feel that it is sure of its facts.[27] A witness involved in several cases of either type will detect differences in the standards exerted. In essence, the standard of proof required in a civil case is of a balance of probabilities. This balance is a fine one and normally needs to be no more than 51 per cent against 49 per cent in order to succeed; any more severe test may be regarded as being unacceptable.[28] However, there are some indications that this will not always hold. Lawton LJ has, for example, indicated that a greater degree of probability is to be desired when a professional reputation is at stake[29] and this may also be necessary in civil proceedings which carry an element of criminality such as in care proceedings.[30]

In a criminal trial, the facts need to be proved beyond reasonable doubt. Lord Denning has said that:

Proof beyond a reasonable doubt does not mean proof beyond the shadow of a doubt . . . If the evidence is so strong against a man as to leave only a remote possibility in his favour, which can be dismissed with the sentence 'of course it is possible but not in the least probable' the case is proved beyond reasonable doubt but nothing short of that will suffice.[31]

It is to be noted that although the prosecution has to achieve this high standard of proof, the standard falls to the lower level of a balance of probabilities where the burden is on the defendant, for example, in order to prove diminished responsibility.[32]

Evidence will be accepted in English courts without corroboration on most occasions. Sometimes, however, corroboration is required, as in certain offences under the Sexual Offences Act 1956; the need for corroboration of unsworn children's evidence has been removed by the Criminal Justice Act 1988. While this will not normally affect the medical witness, it may, on occasion, have tangential importance. One of the authors had to give evidence to corroborate a child's testimony under the old rules. The case concerned a person who had died of stab-wounds. The eyewitness to the attack was the deceased's child, aged about nine years, who said that the accused had struck the victim in the face before inflicting the stabs. There was a small laceration of one eyebrow but the accused said that this was an older one resulting from an accident a day or so previously. Pathological evidence regarding the age of what had appeared a comparatively trivial wound at the autopsy, became of considerable importance in corroborating the child's evidence, the inference being that, if it was correct in this, the rest of the evidence was also likely to be correct. This book is not primarily concerned with autopsy technique but the case demonstrates the maxim that the obvious is often of relative unimportance in forensic pathology; it may well be that the ancillary findings are the most significant in indicating how the obvious came about.

Evidence in practice

Finally, we come to the means whereby facts may be proved—the evidence itself. As mentioned earlier in this chapter, such evidence may be oral, documentary, or real. Much of what concerns evidence in this sense forms the subject matter of other parts of this book; however there are some aspects of the rules governing this aspect of evidence which we should consider here. Witnesses giving oral evidence are not the property of either side; a witness who has provided a report or made an examination for one side can still be called to give evidence by the other side.[33] In criminal cases, prosecuting counsel will himself pass any evidence which comes to light which might favour the other side to his colleague acting for the defence. In any event, a witness who is summoned to court must attend, no matter who calls him. Obviously, as a matter of courtesy, he should tell the side that originally approached him if the summons is from the other party. Although it is a very rare occurrence, he could be ordered to attend a criminal court by the court itself.[34] One notable example of the type of situation which can arise was in the case of *R* v. *Arthur*;[35] the circumstances are described in Chapter 10.

Although there are many exceptions, some of which we will consider shortly, the basic rules as to witnesses themselves are that they should attend personally to give oral evidence and should only talk about things that they have seen personally. The normal rules are that the side calling the witness can only allow him to present his evidence in response to questions which must not be leading—that is, they must not be questions that would, by themselves, tend to lead to a preconceived response; counsel should not cross-examine his own witness. There is no reason—particularly in Scotland—why the question should not be widely embracing. The invitation: 'Would you describe to the court what you found in your examination' saves a great deal of time and allows the witness, who can refer to his notes, to express himself in his own words. Rarely, if the witness alters his testimony in the box to a substantial degree, counsel may obtain permission to treat this witness as 'hostile'—as though he had been called by the other side—and may then submit him to rigorous cross-examination. This could occur to a medical witness who appears to have changed his mind about facts or opinions he had expressed prior to going to court; such a situation must be rare and is then most likely to be due fundamentally to misunderstanding aggravated by inadequate pre-trial discussion (see Chapter 6).

Medical professional privilege

Before leaving oral evidence, note should be taken of its relationship to medical confidentiality. Contrary to the situation obtaining in many countries of the European Community and in some Common-wealth jurisdictions, the doctor's evidence in relation to his patient is compellable in both civil and criminal courts of law and this is fully acceptable to the General Medical Council as to the criminal law;[36] permissible disclosure extends to information given to a coroner's officer or the Scottish Procurator Fiscal's precognition.

Once in the witness box, the extent of the doctor's duty of professional confidentiality is dictated by the judge. Given a question that invokes a technical breach, the doctor may answer and, in so doing, cannot be exposed to any action on the part of an aggrieved patient—the immunity of the witness in court 'is settled in law and cannot be doubted';[37] to that extent, the doctor's *position* is privileged within the legal process. Alternatively, he may seek the court's permission to decline to answer, in which case, he will probably be asked to give his reasons. At this point, the judge may well ask to see a potential answer, for example a specific diagnosis, in writing. The judge may then accept the doctor's reasons for refusal or may order him to answer the line of questioning. The essential judicial test will be whether or not it is proper and necess-ary in the ends of justice that the question be put.[38] In Scotland, the matter would be decided on its relevance.[39] The doctor who refuses the order of the court may then be convicted for contempt of court; the fact that this so rarely, if ever, happens may be due to judicial wisdom or to common-sense medical pragmatism generally overriding rigid principle. Nevertheless, it will be seen that there is no medical professional privilege as to *evidence* in the British courts—privilege being here defined as 'the right of a person to insist upon there being withheld from a judicial tribunal information which might assist it to ascertain facts relevant to an issue on which it is adjudicating'.[40] There are arguments to be adduced on both sides as to whether this should or should not be so but this is scarcely the place to discuss them in detail; the interested reader is referred to the very critical view of a Secretary of the British Medical Association.[41]

Documentary evidence

The rules of documentary evidence can be dismissed fairly briefly. On the basis of the best evidence rule, the notes that the doctor uses in the witness box to refresh his memory should be the original notes which were made contemporaneously with the examination or other event, or as soon as practicable afterwards. Counsel for the other party may demand to see the notes and challenge them if this does not appear to be the case. In Scotland, the definitive report derived from the notes would be regarded as best evidence in criminal cases save in very exceptional circumstances.

The hospital case-notes may have a significant bearing on the case in so far as, rather than representing no more than an *aide-memoire* for the doctor, they may form an article of evidence on their own. The compulsory production of relevant documents is discussed in Chapter 6. Once civil litigation in respect of personal injuries has begun, the court may order production of relevant documents which are held by persons who are not concerned in the action and this may be at the behest of either the plaintiff or the defendant;[42] hospital case notes may, therefore, be called for even though the matter does not affect the hospital directly.

Real evidence

Real evidence in the form of exhibits or productions is generally outwith the control of the expert witness. However, he may be asked to identify, for example, a specimen of blood which he had

supplied. The importance of maintaining continuity of evidence
cannot be over-emphasized. Thus, the identifying label on any
specimen must be clearly receipted by anyone who has had possession of
it. A typical sequence in respect of an autopsy specimen would be

pathologist→police officer→laboratory→police officer→court official.

It is only in this way that the originator can state on oath that he
recognizes the specimen. To the non lawyer, such pedantry can seem
superfluous—it is little less than absurd to infer that a now putrified
globule in a test tube bears any practical relationship to the specimen originally tested. The point may, however, be important legally.
In one unfortunate case in our experience, the first name of a widely
used forensic scientist was the same as the surname of the deceased
and the wrong specimen was produced in evidence; the case almost
disintegrated on a technicality.

Inadmissible evidence

Finally, we draw attention to two areas where evidence as a means of
proving facts is not allowed. One is by the expression of opinions in
the capacity of an ordinary, as opposed to expert, witness. The other
relates to hearsay evidence.

The rule that an ordinary witness may not express an opinion is
based on the view that it is for evidence to establish facts for the
court's use and for the court itself to form opinions which are based
on those facts. The ordinary witness is supposed to relate what he
has personal knowledge of, not what conclusions he has drawn from
his observations. Thus, a doctor may witness a road traffic accident
and later, become involved in the treatment or post-mortem examination of a victim. Then, as regards the accident, he is an ordinary
witness. He can say that he saw the car skid and he might, as a
driver of many years' standing, be permitted to estimate the car's
speed as 50 mph. But he cannot, as a doctor, opine that the skid was
due to an inadequate tread on the tyres. By contrast, he could,
having examined the injuries, estimate the speed and direction from
which they were caused. The distinction is that the expert is entitled
to express opinions based not only on impression but also by
inference—always provided that the latter derives from his particular
expertise. [43]

The admissibility of hearsay evidence has been addressed above. This is another area which often appears rather absurd to a doctor who is accustomed to questioning patients and taking histories. In essence, hearsay includes any evidence which a witness may have given of what another person said, or did, or of any opinions expressed by them. If applied rigidly, the exclusion of such evidence would render the work of the court very difficult and, over the years, many exceptions to the rule have grown up. This is well typified in the medical context. For instance, a person who has described his own sensations, such as having had a pain in the chest, knows that the doctor is likely to include this in his store of factual knowledge and, as such, it will not be considered hearsay. However, any opinion which the patient expressed to the doctor as to why he got the pain would be a secondhand opinion and would not be admissible in the doctor's evidence. Such factors may well have to colour what a medical witness reports concerning things said to him by a patient.

As we intimated at the beginning of this chapter, the law on evidence is a highly technical area and one where the interested witness would be well advised to seek his information in legal textbooks. The application of the rules is the responsibility of the lawyers conducting the case, not of the individual witness, but a superficial knowledge of their effects may help to make some of the more puzzling aspects of court practice comprehensible to the doctor.

References

1. *Cross on Evidence* (6th edn, 1985) London: Butterworths.
2. Walker, R. J. *Walker and Walker 'The English Legal System'* (6th edn, 1985) London: Butterworths, pp. 559 *et seq*.
3. Bizzard, J. H., May, R., and Howard, M. N. *Phipson on Evidence* (13th edn, 1982) London: Sweet and Maxwell, p. 2.
4. Cross, ref. 1 above, p. 1.
5. Walker, ref. 2 above, p. 563.
6. Civil Evidence Act 1972, s.1; Civil Evidence (Scotland) Act 1988, s.2. And see now Children Act 1989, s.96(3).
7. *Teper* v. *The Queen* [1953] AC 480 per Lord Normand at 486.
8. *R* v. *Blastland* [1985] 2 All ER 1095.
9. Criminal Procedure Act 1865, s.3; Civil Evidence Act 1968, s.3. See also Civil Evidence (Scotland) Act 1988, s.3.
10. Cross, ref. 1 above, p. 15; Polson, C. J., Gee, D. J., and Knight, B.

The Essentials of Forensic Medicine (4th edn, 1985) Oxford: Pergamon Press, p. 611.

11. Walker, ref. 2 above, p. 569.
12. _In re H (a Minor); K_ v. _K_ (1989) Times, 9 June.
13. _Makin_ v. _A-G for New South Wales_ [1894] AC 57 at 65.
14. _R_ v. _Smith_ (1915) 11 Crim. App. R. 229.
15. _R_ v. _Straffen_ [1952] 2 QB 911.
16. (1989) Times, 20 March.
17. _R_ v. _Sang_ [1979] 2 All ER 1222; _Fox_ v. _Gwent Chief Constable_ [1985] 1 WLR 1126.
18. See Police and Criminal Evidence Act 1984, s.76.
19. Brownlie, A. R. 'Expert evidence in the light of _Preece_ v. _H M Adv_' (1982) 22 _Med. Sci. Law_ 237 quoting _Ireland_ v. _Taylor_ [1949] 1 KB 300; _R_ v. _Holmes_ [1953] 1 WLR 686.
20. _R_ v _Matheson_ [1959] 1 WLR 474; _R_ v. _Lanfear_ [1965] 1 All ER 683.
21. _R_ v. _Turner_ [1975] 1 All ER 70; _R_ v. _Bailey_ (1977) 66 Crim. App. R. 31.
22. But this may only apply in the criminal context: _L_ v. _K_ [1985] 1 All ER 961.
23. See Atiyah, P. S. '_Res ipsa loquitur_ in England and Australia' (1972) 35 MLR 337.
24. _Clark_ v. _MacLennan and another_ [1983] 1 All ER 416.
25. Homicide Act 1957, s.2.
26. Curzon, L. B. _English Legal History_ (1968) London: Macdonald & Evans, p. 233.
27. Walker, ref. 2 above, p. 17.
28. _R_ v. _Swaysland_ (1987) Times, 15 April.
29. _Whitehouse_ v. _Jordan_ [1980] 1 All ER 650 at 659.
30. _In re G (a Minor) (Child Abuse: Standard of Proof)_ [1987] 1 WLR 1461.
31. _Miller_ v. _Minister of Pensions_ [1947] 2 All ER 372.
32. Walker, ref. 2 above, p. 619.
33. _Harmony Shipping Co. SA_ v. _Davis and others_ [1979] 3 All ER 177.
34. Criminal Justice Act 1967, s.9.
35. (1981) _The Times_, 6 November, pp. 1, 12.
36. General Medical Council _Professional Conduct and Discipline: Fitness to Practise_ (1987), para 81(f).
37. _Watson_ v. _M'Ewan_ [1905] AC 480 per Earl of Halsbury LC at 486.
38. _Attorney General_ v. _Mulholland; A G_ v. _Foster_ [1963] 2 QB 477.
39. _H M Adv_ v. _Airs_ 1975 SLT 177.
40. Law Reform Commission _Privilege in Civil Proceedings_ (1967) (Cmnd 3472) London: H M S O.
41. Havard, J. D. J. 'A question of privilege' (1985) 25 _Med. Sci. Law_ 242.
42. Administration of Justice Act 1970, s.32.
43. Walker, ref. 2 above, p. 655.

6

Pre-trial evidence

There are, in essence, three types of report which the doctor may be called upon to prepare in a medico-legal context. The first can be regarded as purely factual and describes what has happened in the course of a professional relationship—given that a patient presented in the casualty department or in the surgery, what were the findings, what treatment was given, and what was the manner of disposal?

The potential difficulties here lie not so much in the writing of the report—save to remember that, when it is in the form of an affidavit the writer is under oath to tell the truth—but rather, in the conditions which lead to the report. It scarcely needs to be emphasized that one cannot write a retrospective report in the absence of good contemporary notes. Preparation of this type of report often falls upon relatively junior doctors who have been working under considerable pressure in the accident and emergency department. Many will, therefore, feel that, while it may seem easy to pontificate from the lofty heights of academia, it is often too much to transfer the theoretical ideals to the practical working world. None the less, good notes made at the time can save the doctor embarrassment later; more importantly, poor notes can, and often do, result in miscarriages of justice.

The doctor's notes

Although the notes themselves do not constitute a 'report', it will be seen later that they become important evidence in their own right. There are a number of apposite features which have proved to be significant in our experience and which are worth recapitulating.

1. All notes should be written in the expectation that they may be scrutinized by other doctors and by lawyers in an unemotional atmosphere. Subjective observations should be avoided unless they

are very pertinent. It may well be that a patient's conduct tries one's patience to the limit but that is no reason to refer to 'this dreadful person' in the treatment notes! Similarly, pleasantries should be of a formal nature only. One of us remembers, as a very inexperienced practitioner, referring an apparent psychiatric case to hospital with the words: 'Sorry to inflict this snag case on you'; it sounded very different some weeks later when it was read out in the coroner's court, the patient having died while under treatment for congenital syphilis.

2. Ideally, the notes should not be changed. Should this be necessary, the alterations must be signed, dated, and the doctor responsible ready to justify the action. We have come across instances where the times of incidents have clearly been altered in the notes following an allegation of negligence in attendance; unacknowledged factual changes of this type, even though they may be true, can have an adverse effect on the court's appreciation of the professional evidence.

3. It is well to include copies of all observations made by way of line drawings or photography in the patient's notes. For example, one can envisage colour transparencies of injuries being made for teaching purposes only. Such productions would be the property of the hospital were they prepared using hospital equipment and materials; even in the event of their being a purely private venture, it is likely that the court could order their publication if it was thought to be in the interests of justice. [1] In normal circumstances this would be of little import and indeed, such 'private' notes would constitute a valuable *aide-memoire*; however, this might not always be the case and it is a matter which must always be borne in mind, particularly when undertaking investigations or research which are not strictly germane to patient care.

There is little particular advice which can be given as to the preparation of a report based on one's notes. For the benefit of the doctor facing this task for the first time, we suggest that it is helpful to follow a fairly standard pattern. There is less chance of forgetting anything of importance and the procedure of giving oral evidence is already being anticipated. The report can be thought of as being divided into three parts.

First comes the identifying section. This contains the doctor's name, qualifications, and professional position or appointment. It also records details of the patient or person examined and the date or dates of the examination together with the names of any other persons present at the time. The next section contains the facts discovered by the examination: the nature and size of any wounds together with the general condition of the examinee. The final section is composed of any conclusions or opinions that the doctor has been able to reach, such as what agent caused the injuries. By preparing a report in this way, the doctor is clarifying in his own mind what is factual, what is opinion and therefore what is likely to be subject to dispute.

Accuracy of terminology

We would draw particular attention to the need for accurate terminology; all too often terms such as 'bruises', 'abrasions', and 'lacerations' are used without precision when, in fact, specificity may be all-important in assessing causation. A bruise results from vascular —commonly capillary—disruption and extravasation of blood in the tissues. By and large, this requires pressure and as a consequence, the same amount of force will provide a different degree of bruising when applied, say, to the lax abdomen or to the bony chest wall; moreover, the extravasation of blood will be contained in dense tissue whereas it will diffuse in lax tissues. The extent of a bruise may, therefore, be a poor reflection of the force applied. It is also well known that bruises change colour with time; the precise age of a bruise cannot be assessed but it is generally easy to distinguish a 'fresh' bruise from an 'old' one and this is of greatest importance in a *comparative* situation—a matter which is discussed in greater detail under non-accidental injury in children. We believe that bruises often give as much or more information in the analysis of cases of assault than do the much more obvious lacerations and incisions. Although they may very well be insignificant in a clinical context, they should never be ignored in any notes which may become the subject of legal scrutiny. In this context, it is worth mentioning that bruises often become more obvious with the passage of time; a re-examination of the victim of an alleged assault twenty-four hours later is often well repaid.

Abrasions result from damage to the dermis without involvement of the subcutaneous tissues—subsequent 'scabbing' is often due to extravasation of tissue juices or cellular breakdown products. The

essential element in their production is differential movement between the skin and an external surface—the direction of the movement often being apparent in 'piling up' of the abraded epidermis.
Abrasions may also be produced by direct force, but in these circumstances, the differential movement is between the skin and the
side of the abrading object as the tissues directly beneath it are
depressed; thus, an excellent reproduction may be produced, say, of
the heel of a shoe. It should, however, be noted that a narrow object,
such as a cane, will produce parallel lesions of the skin; intervening
bruising due to direct pressure on the underlying tissues is often
present in addition or as an alternative. A slap from the hand will
produce similar 'tram-line' marks in which the abrasions or bruises
are, in fact, related to the interdigital spaces. A point of major
forensic interest in abrasions is that the lesion is very strictly confined by the epidermal structure—abrasions, therefore, tend to
mirror the object which has caused them. It is to be noted that well
marked abrasions, which appear to be typically parchmented or
scabbed, can be produced in the cadaver and may be a source of
confusion to the uninitiated.

A laceration can be of any depth and may go so far as to expose the
underlying bone. It results either from tearing of the skin due to
distension forces or, more characteristically, from pressure between
an applied force and bone—the boxer's so-called 'cut eye' is, in fact,
a laceration induced by direct pressure over the supra-orbital ridge.
This example draws attention to the importance of distinguishing
lacerations from incised wounds which are due to cutting instru-
ments. The incised wound is characterized by free bleeding, its
edges are unbruised and all structures within its depth are severed;
by contrast, the laceration is irregular and bruised and the tougher
fibres within it will remain intact—the resulting appearance is
known as 'bridging'. It is to be noted that the shape of a pressure
laceration is dictated by the shape of the underlying bone; the lesion
will not necessarily reflect the shape or size of the causative object.

Special reports

The second type of report which is commonly called for relates to an
examination or investigation undertaken with a specific purpose in
mind. It may be instigated by the subject himself as, for instance,

when a doctor seeks an expert opinion on his own behalf when appearing before the Health Committee of the General Medical Council. The investigations may also be requested by the subject's legal representatives. Such reports are not necessarily destined for adversarial scrutiny; more often they will be designed to indicate whether a cause of action exists, to indicate a line of defence or simply, how to present the client's case as, for example, before the Mental Health Tribunal. In such circumstances, the solicitor has chosen his expert because he knows him and respects his opinion. It is, therefore, unnecessary to 'prove' ones expertise in the body of the report. The requirements in this respect are relatively simple and may be limited to a statement of degrees and qualifications obtained together with the position held which is appropriate to the examination. The authority for and the reason for the examination should be clearly stated as these will dictate the extent of the conclusions. Since the report may, at the discretion of the client or subject, be used as evidence in a court or tribunal, it should contain the minimum of hearsay—only that without which it would not be possible to come to a conclusion (Fig. 1).

By the same token, the reporter should weigh carefully the likely effect of altering the report at the request of the solicitors. Very often such requests will have no purpose other than to clarify a point; occasionally, however, lawyers may wish to delete something which they see as being unfavourable to the client.[2] In such circumstances, the reporter must search his conscience closely; a significant deletion from an independent report may represent an important departure from professional ethics—the instructing solicitors can always seek a further opinion should they so wish.

The expert's report

The reporter's ethical position is most difficult in the third example—that is, the report which is called for when litigation, either civil or criminal, is already in train and an expert opinion is sought not only to support one side of the case but also, positively to refute the opinion on the other. Thus, since experts' reports must be exchanged when ordered by the court in both criminal and civil actions,[3] at least part of an expert's role will consist of destructive criticism of the opposition. It will be clear from Chapter 10 that we

I, John Brown, MD, FRCP, am currently Director of the Institute of Comparative Psychology in Memobridge. I have been asked by Messrs Green and Black, of Legalville, to examine James White and to prepare a report. The purpose of the report is to indicate Mr White's suitability to apply for restoration to the register of Chartered Animal Keepers from which he is currently excluded on health grounds.

The examination took place on ... beginning at ... and ending at.... There were no witnesses to the examination.

I took a clinical history from Mr White and elicted the following...

I made a physical examination, the results of which are as follows...

I arranged for a specimen of ... to be examined for the presence of.... The results of the examination are attached.

As a result of my examination I conclude that Mr White is fully recovered and that an appeal to the Registrar is likely to be successful.

> John Brown
> MD, FRCP
> Dated...

Fig. 1. Outline of a report in a 'tribunal' case

do not regard the adversarial arena as the ideal place in which to decide complicated questions involving medical causation, prognosis, and the like. Nevertheless, many of the unsatisfactory aspects of the system can be obviated by the preparation of reports of high quality, as a result of which the experts from each side can narrow their differences. Before considering the form of the report, we must consider the rules which govern its disclosure. This requires a short digression into the concept of legal professional privilege.

Legal professional privilege

Privilege was defined in Chapter 5 as 'the right of a person to insist upon there being withheld from a judicial tribunal information which might assist it to ascertain facts relevant to an issue on which it is adjudicating'.[4] Legal professional privilege is therefore a misnomer as the privilege belongs to the client, not to the professional adviser.[5] This is less important than is the way in which it is circumscribed. It applies only to communications between a legal adviser and his client which are prepared for the purpose of obtaining legal advice, including advice in non-litigious business[6]—verbal answers to questions addressed to the legal adviser are similarly protected. However, it does not include every communication within the ordinary business of the solicitor and, of greater importance to the health professional, it does not extend to confidential reports which are no more than indirectly related to litigation;[7] for example, the malign influence on preventive medicine of accident reports not being guaranteed confidentiality is, in our opinion, very disturbing. Moreover, the consequent reluctance of the doctor to expose himself to criticism in an accident investigation may result in unjustified adverse publicity for the medical profession.

It will be seen that there is no certainty of 'privilege' being extended to medical reports prepared for legal advisers. Havard[8] has pointed out that, following a medical examination related to litigation, what was said to the doctor would have received absolute privilege had it been said to the lawyer. At that time, it seemed at least possible that such doctor/patient communication would also attract privilege but recent developments indicate that this would not be so. The case of *W* v. *Egdell*[9] concerned the allegedly non-consensual release of an independent medical report. In the present context, the words of Scott J in the court of first instance are significant:

There was a clear and important distinction between, on the one hand, instructions given to an expert and, on the other, the expert's opinion given pursuant to those instructions, the former being covered by legal professional privilege while the latter was not.

In reaching his conclusion, the judge is reported to have relied very much on two cases involving hand-writing experts.[10] Whether the examination of documents is comparable to history-taking and examination in a medical setting is debatable. We also find it difficult to see how the confidentiality of a question can be dissociated from that of its answer. Nevertheless, the significance of the judgment to doctors who would not expect or wish their findings to be broadcast is obvious.

Disclosure of documents

Medical documents, other than advice which is the subject of legal professional privilege within the above framework, must be produced for examination by the parties involved in litigation. The whole purpose of the relevant legislation is to assist in the administration of justice and, particularly, to speed a process which is often intolerably prolonged.

Current statute law is contained in the Administration of Justice Act 1970, ss.31 and 32 and the Administration of Justice (Scotland) Act 1972, s.1. Under s.31 of the 1970 Act, a person who intends to be a party to an action for personal injuries or death can apply for a court order to the effect that anyone else likely to be made a party to the action should produce for inspection any documents which may be relevant in the case. Once an action is in progress, s.32 empowers the court to order production of relevant documents in the possession of persons who are not likely to be a party to the action and this may involve a doctor who is unconcerned with the case—for example a general practitioner who is peripheral to a case against a hospital authority. Documents may be produced without waiting for a court order but we would strongly advise that any doctor under pressure to do so should refuse until he has received specific advice from his defence society.[11] It is to be noted that unreasonable delay in the production of notes and the like could conceivably lead to the resulting costs being laid against the practitioner.[12]

The problem of medical confidence has, inevitably, caused concern within the profession but the administrative rules are now laid down by statute.[13] Disclosure must now be made to the applicant's legal advisers, or to his legal and medical advisers or, in the absence of any legal advisers, to his medical or other professional advisers. The legal trend is consistently towards more openness in actions for personal injury. Thus, the court will exercise its power when: 'Its exercise would help to achieve the purpose of the Act, which is the proper administration of justice'.[14] It is perhaps of greater importance to the medical profession as a whole that, whereas judges were at one time very reluctant to order the disclosure of records and experts' reports in cases of personal injury involving medical negligence,[15] this dispensation will apply no longer.[16] Mustill L.J. said in *Wilsher*:

It seems wrong that in this area of the law, more than in any other, this kind of forensic blind-man's buff should continue to be the norm. [17]

This direction has been followed in the important case of *Naylor* when the Master of the Rolls explained rather succinctly the difference between medical advice, which attracted legal professional privilege, and experts' reports which should be disclosed. He said:

The general rule is that, whilst a party is entitled to privacy in seeking out the 'cards' for his hand, once he has put his hand together, the litigation is to be conducted with all the cards face up on the table. Furthermore, most of the cards have to be put down well before the hearing. [18]

The exchange of reports has now extended to the criminal courts, authority for the court to order such disclosure being contained in the Police and Criminal Evidence Act 1984, s.81. [19] This development is clearly of great importance to pathologists but the rules are so recent that there is virtually no experience of their effect.

The format of the expert's report

The format of the report can now be discussed in the light of the foregoing. There will be differences depending upon whether the matter is one of criminal or civil litigation. The former is the easier to consider as, by and large, all criminal trials pose much the same problem—only the severity of the consequences varies.

Here, we are prepared to take the risk of being regarded as unreasonably controversial and suggest that much depends on whether the report is prepared for the prosecution, that is the Crown, or for the defence. We are on record as firmly believing that the ideal should be the preparation of a report agreed by the experts from each side in which points of disagreement are clearly indicated and which should then be subject to examination in front of the court. This is an unlikely development and, as noted above, the provisions of the Police and Criminal Evidence Act, s.81 have not yet worked themselves into the system. As things stand, we believe that a report for the Crown should be factual both as to findings and to opinion; in the great majority of cases the reporter will be a paid servant of the State—and the State consists of the Crown and its subjects, both good and bad. It is no part of the medical expert's remit to *seek* the conviction of the accused. Special pleading is to be avoided and the potential importance of acknowledging alternative views in the body of a report is discussed later (p. 152). The defence expert, by contrast, is employed specifically in order to obtain an acquittal and we see nothing unethical in framing a report with that object in mind; nothing can stop the defence expert being on one 'side' and, in playing by the rules, he is under no obligation to score 'own goals'.[20]

It is to all intents impossible to suggest a format for a report in a civil action—the diversity of actions in which an expert opinion is requested is such that each report is unique to the particular circumstances. All reports must start with personal identification, a summary of one's expertise in the particular field, and the nature of the instructions which led to the preparation of the report. Medico-legal reports are often required by the increasing number of quasi-judicial or judicial tribunals which are being established; quite often, these relate to a person's fitness. This is, perhaps, the simplest type of report to write and can be looked upon as a template for all others; a suggested format is shown as Fig. 1. The two matters most likely to lead to a court appearance are those of personal injuries sustained as an admitted result of someone else's actions and secondly, the problems of negligence resulting in injury or death—of which the most difficult in the terms of the medical witness is medical negligence.

In essence, the concern in the first of these is the quantum of damages to be awarded and the report must be directed to that end. We suggest the following as a basic formula:

1. The nature of the injury
2. Its causation
   any alternative causes
   any contributing factors on the part of the injured person
3. The current extent of the disability
4. Its affect, now and in the future
   on the way of life
   on employment
   special considerations
5. The prognosis
   the likelihood of future complications
6. Supporting bibliography
   contrary bibliography to be noted

The courts are deducting a specified proportion of damages in a growing number of personal injury situations by reason of contributory negligence on the part of the injured person. These are typified by the attitude to compensation in vehicular accidents. Thus, failure to wear a seat-belt may attract a deduction of up to 25 per cent; however, this depends on proof that the injuries would have been prevented by the use of a harness—the mere failure to attach a seat-belt oneself is not, in itself, sufficient grounds for penalty.[21] A report on injuries sustained in vehicular accidents must include such assessments.

These considerations will also apply in cases in which negligence is alleged but additional expert opinion will then be sought as to the *fact* of negligence. Industrial injuries are a common area where this will be the case. Automatic compensation for injuries sustained at work is available under the Social Security Act 1975 and precise levels of remuneration are laid down in the secondary legislation;[22] these are matters for Industrial Tribunals and their Medical Boards. There is nothing to stop the injured person simultaneously suing the employer for negligence, this, very often, including an allegation of inadequacy or non-provision of safety equipment. These considerations will, accordingly, form a major part of the report. In this respect, we cannot overstate the advantages to be gained from a visit to the scene before reaching a conclusion; practical experience is infinitely superior to theory as a basis for opinion. On occasion, industrial injury will involve the general public—particularly so in the public transport sector—when many others may be seeking damages for negligence. The state of health of the injured employee will then become a matter of great importance, whether an opinion derives from clinical examination or from post-mortem dissection. A further important extrapolation is whether or not any disability was identifiable by the employer—nine figure settlements may depend on the answer. We place particular emphasis on this aspect with the pathologist in mind. 'Moderately severe atheroma of the left main coronary artery' may seem like a throw-away line in a report on a post-mortem following accidental death; its importance may be transformed in the subsequent litigation. Every pathologist should consider, and consider deeply, whether or not he should retain objective evidence of such subjective statements in the form of histological slides; much anxiety would be avoided by adopting the practice.

The question of medical negligence is addressed more specifically from the point of view of the defender in Chapter 11. Here, it need only be said, that difficult as it may be, an innate distaste for appearing on behalf of a plaintiff against a colleague should be sublimated to the needs of justice; it is far better that a really good opinion should be given rather than that of a poor substitute which was provided mainly because the 'expert' who was eventually obtained had no qualms about appearing in the guise of 'accuser'.

Clearly, the most important additional feature of the report beyond those described above, will be to demonstrate *why* a given treatment was unsatisfactory. The following check-list seems to us to cover most of the necessary points:

● Why was there a bad effect? Was it due to
   a wrong choice of treatment or
   a lack of skill in diagnosis or treatment
● What distinguished the treatment given from the norm?
● Was the normal routine operated? If not
   was the deviance a matter of omission or commission
   what extenuating circumstances can be adduced
   were there any positively culpable factors?
● Would any other practitioner have adopted the practice?
● What precautions were omitted?
● Has the patient contributed to his/her disability?
   e.g. by refusing remedial action

Fairness to both sides is critical in this situation. In few others is it so important to appreciate that the report is put forward as a matter of opinion, not of accusation. Of its very nature, it is likely to support the plaintiff's case but partisanship is limited by two factors. The report will be read and villified by the opposing experts if it falls short in objectivity and secondly, the court itself will comment adversely on any report which smacks of undue subjectivity.[23]

The expert preparing a report of this third type must prove his expertise to the satisfaction of all who will read his opinion.[24] Rather than detail one's experience in the body of the report, it is often best to produce a curriculum vitae as an attachment. A good C.V. is a finely balanced document; innate modesty must be resisted but, at the same time, only those attributes which are relevant to the current issue should be included—there is very little point in expanding on one's experience in aircraft accident investigation if one is dealing with an allegedly negligent radiological diagnosis.

The body of the report should contain a minimum of hearsay and should depend as nearly entirely as is possible on personal observation; the basis for any statements must be detailed. It is particularly important that the report does not contain reference to information which is, itself, subject to legal professional privilege. The writing of the report is very much a personal matter. We recommend taking points of controversy in turn and discussing them individually; an opinion should be backed, whenever possible, by precedents which have been verified personally and a bibliography must be attached— the opposition is entitled to know of and to be able to approve one's sources. The report must end with a detailed list of conclusions which will be maintained in the process of giving oral evidence. As we emphasize later, few occasions are more damaging to a case than the unexpected conversion of an expert during the course of trial. An opinion which cannot be sustained should not be in a report; the existence and limitations of a doubtful position can be discussed in the pre-trial conference.

The importance of strict professionalism in the preparation of all medico-legal reports can scarcely be overstressed. Scrawled added comments or asides are more than likely to be picked up by the opposition and used to one's disadvantage.

The pre-trial conference

There is nothing immoral in a pre-trial conference—indeed, within the current style of adversarial hearing in which the expert evidence is led by a non-expert, we believe it to be essential lest vital evidence be either omitted or misrepresented during the trial stage (see Chapter 10). It provides a forum in which the advocate and medical experts can ensure their mutual understanding of the facts and where the experts themselves can air their agreements and differences. It is not, as is so often believed, a secret gathering in which underhand moves are plotted but rather, a positive move towards achieving the ends of justice.

In our experience, insufficient use is made of the pre-trial conference in the criminal field. The medical witness will almost always wish to be 'in the picture' so as to be able to give his evidence more appropriately and to be spared unnecessary embarrassment. However, he is in the hands of counsel and the solicitors—two groups that seem to be chronically short of time.[25] We can only reiterate that the best witness is the best prepared witness and we would caution against accepting instructions which begin: 'We are sorry to give you so little time; the trial is, in fact, tomorrow'; if for no other reason, the warning signals should be flashing to the effect that a possible explanation is that no one else would take the case.

Civil actions are far more leisurely affairs (many would say far too leisurely) and a pre-trial conference is almost invariable. The difficulty here lies in its timing. The regular conference will be early in the case when the legal advisers are assessing the conduct of the case and the likelihood of success. Several months, or even years, may then elapse before the case is actually heard and, by that time, the expert may have forgotten many of the details. He will, certainly, have his report but the documents—for example the hospital notes—on which he based his report may well have been returned to the legal advisers. The clear recommendation is, therefore, to ensure that copies of the primary evidence are made and retained. There is, of course, no reason why the witness should not be selective in this; indeed, the volume of paper associated with a major civil action is such that indiscriminate storage becomes a logistic impossibility. The expert must, however, be adequately prepared against the chance that no further conference will be called.

The pre-trial conference is subject to legal professional privilege and thus to strict confidentiality both as to verbal communication and as to notes made at the time.

It is, perhaps, worth mentioning that this does not apply to the American pre-trial deposition. It may well be thought that this is a matter which is, at best, marginal to the purposes of this book. None the less, in these days of disasters involving international travel and multinational industry, a comparatively junior pathologist may find himself involved in US litigation and a word on the subject is not out of place. The deposition is, in effect, an examination of the potential witness by all the legal advisers involved—either singly or *en masse*. Evidence is taken on oath and a transcript can, and will, be read back in court if there is any discrepancy. The examination is often intensive. It is very little use referring to 'a branch of the left anterior descending coronary artery', you need to know, and be able to name, the precise branch. We would caution very strongly against taking any documents containing personal notations to a deposition; every item in one's files is liable to scrutiny and duplication and the explanation, say, of a pencilled underlining or question mark may prove extremely embarrassing. All in all, we would class the American deposition as being among the most unnerving experiences to which the forensic expert may be exposed.

Precognition

Precognition is a procedure peculiar to Scots criminal practice and one which is, similarly, directed to the equitable administration of justice. Under it, witnesses who will be called to give evidence in court are subject to examination by both sides prior to trial—the intention being to avoid the snap, ill-considered decisions which may be forced in examination and cross-examination and which so often result in unintentional misrepresentation. The precognition is normally taken orally but a doctor's factual report may form the basis of his statement and may, indeed, comprise the whole of his precognition.

A statement in precognition is not, save in exceptional circumstances, given on oath and the transcript is not signed by the witness. Moreover, the witness is not subsequently bound by his statement in precognition and discrepancies between precognition and evidence in court cannot be commented upon.

In a sense, therefore, precognition retains an adversarial element in so far as, while a witness for defence is bound to answer any questions put to him truthfully and fully, his conscience is still liberated by the 'own goal' principle. If the defence witness has a really good case, however, it may well be advantageous to put this strongly at precognition; he may, in this way, convince the Crown that a prosecution is impractical. Evidence given at precognition is as privileged as is that spoken in court to the extent that the doctor cannot be accused of breach of medical confidence in answering questions put to him (see Chapter 8).

References

1. *R* v. *Sang* [1980] AC 402.
2. Anonymous 'Medical reports not to the lawyers' liking' [1979] 2 *Brit. Med. J.* 1376.

3. Supreme Court Act 1981, ss. 33 & 34; Police and Criminal Evidence Act 1984, s.81.
4. Law Reform Commission *Privilege in Civil Proceedings* (1967) (Cmnd 3472) London: H M S O.
5. Legal Correspondent 'Disclosure of documents by doctors' (1985) **290** *Brit. Med. J.* 1973.
6. *Balabel and another* v. *Air India* [1988] Ch 317.
7. *Lask* v. *Gloucester Health Authority* (1985) Times, 13 December; *Waugh* v. *British Railways Board* [1980] AC 521, discussed in (1982) **284** *Brit. Med. J.* 519.
8. Havard, J. D. J. 'A question of privilege' (1985) 25 *Med. Sci. Law* 242.
9. [1989] 1 All ER 1089, ChD; [1990] 1 All ER 835 CA.
10. *Harmony Shipping Co SA* v. *Saudi Europe Line Ltd* [1979] 1 WLR 1380; *R* v. *King* [1983] 1 WLR 411.
11. Dyer, C. 'Disclosure of medical records in litigation' (1986) 293 *Brit. Med. J.* 1298.
12. *Walker* v. *Eli Lilly & Co* [1986] ECC 550—so stated by Dyer, ref. 11 above, although this is not included in the report of the judgment.
13. Supreme Court Act 1981, ss. 33 & 34.
14. *O'Sullivan* v. *Herdmans Ltd* [1987] 3 All ER 129 per Lord Mackay at 136.
15. *Rahman* v. *Kirklees AHA* [1980] 1 WLR 1244.
16. Consultation paper 'Expert evidence in actions for personal injuries' (1987) London: Lord Chancellor's Department; see also Dyer, C. 'Ending "forensic blind man's buff"' (1987) 294 *Brit. Med. J.* 1407.
17. *Wilsher* v. *Essex AHA* [1986] 3 All ER 801 at 830.
18. *Naylor* v. *Preston AHA and other appeals* [1987] 2 All ER 353 at 360.
19. Now brought into force by Crown Court (Advance Notice of Expert Evidence) Rules 1987 (SI 1987/716).
20. Mason, J. K. 'Expert evidence in the adversarial system of criminal justice' (1986) 26 *Med. Sci. Law* 8.
21. *Froom* v. *Butcher* [1976] QB 286; *O'Connell* v. *Jackson* [1971] 3 WLR 463 (for safety helmets).
22. The most recent of which is Social Security Benefits Up-rating Regulations 1989 (SI 1989/455).
23. *Whitehouse* v. *Jordan* [1981] 1 All ER 267 per Lord Wilberforce at 276.
24. Blair, D. 'Assessment of a doctor as a forensic witness' (1973) 13 *Med. Sci. Law* 211.
25. Brownlie, A. R. 'The presentation of scientific evidence in court' (1974) 14 *J. Forens. Sci. Soc.* 183.

7

The art of persuasion

We propose discussing the ways in which the witness can control his own destiny in the next chapter. Here, we wish only to draw attention to the art of the lawyer and to how this affects the quality of the testimony that is given. The hazards encountered in this way vary in their complexity; some are obvious, while others are so well concealed that many witnesses can pass the whole of their professional lives without ever appreciating their existence. The reasons for this lie in the fact that the lawyers practising within the court take a different view of its objectives, and of their own function, from that adopted by the scientific witnesses. This has been stated many times by several authors; it is clearly understood by the lawyers but only with difficulty and often not at all by their witnesses. [1]

Scientific inquiry

The scientist is accustomed to the rules of scientific inquiry, to making observations, forming hypotheses from them, conducting experiments to check the hypotheses and, thus, formulating theories. The object is to establish the truth—there are no compromises. The court, on the other hand, is there to resolve a dispute between two parties, either between two persons in a civil action or between an individual and the state in a criminal action. There may be an absolute answer to the dispute, with clear facts supporting one side only but more often, the issues are clouded—there are views in favour of both sides and facts which can be adduced in support of either point of view. The court procedure then takes the form of a debate, in which the opposing points of view are espoused by the lawyers for each side who try to present their client's case in the most favourable light.

Thus, although the scientific witness may propose to tell the court only the facts which he has observed, and his deductions from them, so as to assist the court to arrive at the truth, each lawyer wishes to put questions to him in such a way as to draw out those points and deductions which are most favourable to his client. Although many of the questions appear to relate only to known facts and to require straightforward answers, they are usually being asked in a deliberate sequence, building up a series of answers from which the lawyer may draw a logical conclusion. The technique is essential to lawyers and textbooks are written on the subject. Stone,[2] for example, describes several techniques of cross-examination, such as the direct and indirect tactics. In the former, the witness is confronted with a conflicting fact or opinion; in the latter, the aim of the lawyer is concealed by questions circumventing the topic. The modes may be either constructive, emphasizing points favourable to the client, or destructive, challenging the fact, or the witness. Other authors explore the many other techniques. A doctor about to give evidence would find perusal of Napley's *The technique of persuasion* a most enlightening exercise.[3]

Logic and rhetoric

In fact, an argument advanced by a lawyer on behalf of his client is based on rules that are as well-established as are those of scientific inquiry—they are embodied in the philosophy of logic. The oldest disciplines taught in many universities are those of logic and rhetoric. Logic enables the lawyer to formulate an argument and is the basis of the questions asked. Rhetoric is the art of oratory and eloquent persuasion, which is particularly used by lawyers when making their closing speeches designed to elicit the sympathy of the judge or jury.

What then of logic? It is not a subject which scientists are normally taught as part of their training; it has relevance in medicine[4] but is seldom, if ever, taught to budding doctors. It is a major tool of the trade of the lawyer but not all agree on its importance. Some take the view that, although it is certainly the mode of reasoning underlying legal argument, it has no role in making decisions based on the facts nor of reaching verdicts.[5] Nevertheless, Williams has said:

From time to time judges and even Law Lords tell us that logic is not compulsive in legal reasoning. In this they merely betray a lack of under-standing of what logic is.[6]

It is, therefore, wise for the embryo expert witness, who intends to spend much of his professional life giving evidence in court, to have at least a nodding acquaintance with a subject which is funda-mental to the way lawyers act. We can do no more here than give a brief introduction to the subject and indicate a few of the ways in which it influences the lawyer's strategy when questioning the witness. Anyone wanting a more accurate and detailed account of the subject is referred to any of the small books on the subject, examples of which appear in the references.

There are two branches of logic—deductive and inductive (see also Chapter 12). The latter is concerned with the type of thinking which scientists use in reaching conclusions. From observations made, an opinion is reached which, while not being absolutely certain, is the best possible explanation for the known facts. The conclusion goes further than the observed facts. Further facts which cause the conclusion to be altered may, of course, be discovered and this happens frequently within the disciplines of science.

Deductive logic, however, is the variety which may be used by lawyers and is that which we need to consider here. This branch of logic studies the rules that control good arguments. It is the form of the argument that is important rather than its content.[7] An argu-ment is a set of statements, or premises, which are designed to support a final statement—the conclusion. Thus:

(a) All whales are mammals. (Premise)

(b) All mammals are warm-blooded. (Premise)

(c) Therefore all whales are warm-blooded. (Conclusion)

If you accept the first and second statements, then you must accept the third, the conclusion. A simple medical example would be:

(a) Respiration is essential to human life. (Premise)

(b) Lungs are the organs of respiration in humans. (Premise)

(c) Therefore lungs are essential to human life. (Conclusion)

or:

(a) Oxygen is essential for the life of any tissue. (Premise)

(b) Oxygen is carried to the tissues by blood. (Premise)

(c) Therefore failure of the blood supply to a tissue will cause it to die. (Conclusion)

Most arguments of this type are so generally accepted that they are never stated in this form, though they had to be in the early days of a medical student's training. We are concerned that such arguments should be true for if they were not, much of the practice of medicine would be based on fallacious principles.

Logic, however, is not concerned with truth but rather, with validity. An argument is valid if the conclusion follows from the premises. Whether it is true or not is irrelevant. Hence:

(a) A cancer is a fatal disease.

(b) A rodent ulcer is a cancer.

(c) Therefore a rodent ulcer is a fatal disease

is a valid argument, since the conclusion follows logically from the premises. But it is obviously not true, since a rodent ulcer can be removed by surgery and metastasizes very rarely. Although the argument is logically valid, it cannot be accepted as proof that rodent ulcers are fatal. A proof must start with a premise that is accepted as true by all parties to the argument and must continue with true premises in order to reach a true conclusion. This is not necessarily so as to a valid argument in which the essential point is that anyone who accepts the premises adduced during an argument must, logically, accept the conclusion which follows from them.

The art of the lawyer

The skill of a lawyer lies in asking questions carefully so that he advances a series of premises which the witness accepts. This is facilitated if the crucial premises are concealed within a verbiage of obvious and simple facts; the lawyer may then spring the conclusion, which he has been circumspectly approaching, on the unsuspecting witness. Sometimes he may not put the conclusion at all during the questioning of the witness but will reserve it until he is addressing the jury in his closing speech. He can then put it that the doctor agreed that this and that matter were likely, from which it followed that such and such a situation was the most probable—and that that was one which favoured his client. The doctor may then be surprised to read of an unexpected result of the trial when he was sure that he had clearly explained to the court that the facts pointed in another direction; in fact, he was unaware of the significance of certain answers which he gave during cross-examination.

An experienced witness may have learnt to detect the direction that the lawyer's questions are taking him. He can be put on his guard if he can spot the intended conclusion well in advance knowing that it is unreasonable; he can then resist the line of questioning or can respond in such a way as to prevent the conclusion being reached. Indeed, he may, simply by experience, have absorbed some of the techniques of logical argument; but the relatively inexperienced person in the hands of a skilful lawyer is unlikely to be forewarned.

There are many well-known traps in logic by way of which a fallacious argument can be presented as being apparently sensible. One of these is known as 'affirming the consequent'. Two examples are offered. One can say:

If the heart is weak, the pulse is feeble. The heart is weak. Therefore, the pulse is feeble.

This is an entirely valid argument; the conclusion follows from the premises. In classical logic this form of argument is known as 'affirming the antecedent, the "if" '. But take an argument which appears very similar:

If the heart is weak then the pulse is feeble. The pulse is feeble. Therefore the heart is weak.

On a quick inspection this looks like the previous statement and it could easily be accepted as correct under the pressure of cross-examination. But it is not a valid argument. The feebleness of the pulse is not the 'if' but is consquent upon the 'if' and the conclusion does not follow from the premise which relates to one possibility only. There may be other reasons for the pulse being feeble: for instance, a fall in blood volume due to haemorrhage in a young man whose heart is particularly strong; or there may be an obstruction to the artery above the point where the pulse is being felt. At all events, the statement cannot be taken at its face value.

Indeed, a scientific conclusion may be wholly founded on a false argument. In his book *Logic and its limits*,[8] Patrick Shaw uses a passage from the Sherlock Holmes story, *The Boscombe Valley mystery*, to illustrate a fallacy of this form:

It was about ten minutes before we regained our cab ... Holmes still carrying with him the stone which he had picked up in the wood.
'This may interest you, Lestrade,' he remarked, holding it out. 'The murder was done with it.'
'I see no marks.'
'There are none.'
'How do you know, then?'
'The grass was growing under it. It had only lain there a few days. There was no sign of a place whence it had been taken. It corresponds with the injuries.'

This, though lengthier and more wrapped in colourful dialogue, is similar to the previous example. The conclusion that the stone is the murder weapon does not follow from the premises. It may be entirely coincidental that it is at the scene of the murder. There needs to be some other evidence to link it with the murder victim. All that this type of argument does is to indicate one possible explanation, not a valid conclusion.

There are other well known forms of argument. One is known as 'denying the consequent'. Thus:

If cancer is infectious then relatives of victims would often develop it as well. Relatives do not often develop the same cancer. Therefore it is not infectious.

This is valid. The conclusion follows from the premises by way of a series of denials. The antithetic form of argument is known as 'denying the antecedent'. This might run:

If cancer is infectious, then relatives of victims would develop it as well. Cancer is not infectious. Therefore relatives do not develop the same cancer.

This is not valid—the conclusion does not follow. A relative could develop the same cancer either by coincidence or perhaps, by being exposed to the same carcinogen. The conclusion is not true and cannot be accepted yet, when stated quickly, it seems to be similar to the previous, valid argument.

These are very simple examples and are not likely to confuse people as they have been stated here. A potential witness, studying them at leisure, would probably reflect that he would be able to distinguish valid from invalid statements of the types given without difficulty. But, it is unlikely that such a simple and obvious pattern of argument would be used during cross-examination. A longer train of reasoning, during which the witness might be unable to analyse each step, would be more probable. Again, the rules of logic include such a pattern of argument which is known as a hypothetical syllogism. This is often expressed in textbooks of logic by the use of symbols. Thus:

If p, then q;

If q, then r;

Therefore, if p, then r.

For example:

(a) If a patient is immobilized, the circulation in his legs will be slowed.

(b) If the circulation in the legs is slowed, there is a likelihood of venous thrombosis.

(c) A patient is immobilized, therefore there is a likelihood of venous thrombosis.

This is a valid argument but, clearly, the number of stages in the argument can be increased. Moreover, not all the premises may be true or acceptable. But, if one untrue premise passes unnoticed, then the ultimate conclusion will be invalid. Alternatively, a different conclusion would have been reached had there been more time for careful scrutiny of each point by the witness.

It is possible to imagine a line of questioning in a case of alleged child abuse:

Q1   Is it true that this child had a fractured skull?

A1   Yes

Q2   Where was it?

A2   At the top of the head.

Q3   How old was this child?

A3   3 months

Q4   So relatively recently born. Is it true that a young baby's skull is thin?

A4   Yes.

Q5   Can you tell the court how thin?

A5   Not precisely.

Q6   No, of course not, but approximately?
A6   About a sixteenth of an inch.
Q7   Is it true that a skull is made up of several separate bones, but whereas in an adult these are joined together, in a baby they are still separated?
A7   Yes.
Q8   Quite widely separated at the top of the head?
A8   Yes.
Q9   Is that the area called the fontanelle, or the 'soft spot'?
A9   Yes.
Q10   Is it true that a baby's skull can fracture during birth?
A10   Yes.
Q11   Which part of the skull usually fractures then?
A11   The top.
Q12   So it is true that a baby's skull can fracture in the course of a natural birth, without colossal force?
A12   Yes.
Q13   Tell me doctor, how much did this child weigh?
A13   12 pounds.
Q14   If it had been held in a woman's arms, level with her waist, how high would it have been above the ground?
A14   It depends on the height of the woman.
Q15   Yes, of course, but approximately, for an average woman? About 3 feet?
A15   Yes, perhaps.
Q16   If a weight of 12 lbs travels through a distance of 3 feet to impact, the force exerted would be 3×12 or 36 foot-pounds, would it not?
A16   Yes.
Q17   Yes—36 foot pounds. Thank you Doctor.

Thus, a series of premises, each of which would, on its own, be acceptable as true, leads to the unstated but implied conclusions that a baby's skull is very fragile, easily fractured, and that a fall from waist height would generate a large amount of force to be measured in double figures. These conclusions can either be left to the jury to reach for themselves or they can be elaborated in the closing speech. The witness has not made any comment as to the elasticity of the skull, the effect of the coverings on a floor, or as to the known statistical incidence of skull fractures following falls. It is likely that the questioning would be even more protracted in a real court situation, that the relevant premises would be more discretely concealed and that the doctor would be less able to anticipate the conclusion. A re-examination by the lawyer for the other side might, or might not, remedy the situation.

The good medical witness should therefore be aware of the technique, clear in his mind as to his own opinion, and must anticipate what is to him, the forced conclusion—and this, as we have stressed already, involves adequate 'homework' before entering the witness box. In the example given above, there are, in fact, several points at which the chain of argument could have been broken. Thus, A9 might well have read: 'Yes. It is there to facilitate moulding of the skull to changes in pressure'; or, later at A12, 'But the forces is imposed on the skull at parturition *are* colossal'; or, at A16, 'Yes—something less than had it slipped from the arms while being breast fed'. And, at the end of the day, the re-examination is likely to be just as skilful.

None of this can be easy even for the experienced person and the true expert witness, in addition, knows when he may be wrong. It is, essentially, a matter of preparation. The offside trap is a perfectly legitimate ploy but the winger who understands it also knows how to avoid it.

References

1. See, for example, Brownlie, R. 'The role of the expert witness' (1983) 51 *Med.-Leg. J.* 85; Jones, C. G. 'Men of science v men of law' (1986) 26 *Med. Sci. Law* 13.
2. Stone, M. *Proof of Fact in Criminal Trials* (1984) Edinburgh: W Green & Son, pp. 315–345.
3. Napley, D. *The Technique of Persuasion* (3rd edn, 1983) London: Sweet and Maxwell.
4. See Phillips, C. (ed.) *Logic in Medicine* (1989) London: British Medical Association.
5. Stone, ref. 3 above, p. 379.
6. Williams, G. *Learning the Law* (11th edn, 1982) London: Stevens, p. 236.
7. Salmon, W. C. *Logic* (2nd edn, 1973) Foundations of Philosophy Series, Englewood Cliffs: Prentice-Hall Inc.
8. Shaw, P. *Logic and Its Limits* (1981) London: Pan Books, p. 37.

8

On giving evidence

So far we have discussed the doctor's role in court in relatively academic terms. The actual giving of evidence is, however, a practical matter *par excellence*. Experience is one's only guide and, for this reason, this central chapter is anecdotal. Nevertheless, although we write from the position of emeriti, we would admit that going to court to give evidence is always an ordeal. No matter how often you have acted as a witness, the adrenalin still flows on every occasion— there is a feeling of anxiety, the mouth is dry, and the stomach uneasy. This is no bad thing. The role of the expert witness carries considerable responsibility; a person's liberty or financial stability may be at stake and it is an activity which should never be undertaken lightly. The nerveless expert who 'knows it all' is not necessarily the best suited to the distribution of justice. Neither is the role of expert witness an activity which you should vow to avoid at all costs nor one which should cause you to panic when it is inevitable. Unpleasant experiences can be avoided by taking relatively simple precautions.

Preparation

Many simple and obvious problems arise out of matters of procedure which we will enlarge on later. To start with a rebuke from the judge or coroner for being late is no way to improve one's professional image; nor is frequent recourse to one's notes in order to verify the simplest facts likely to help. A lawyer rising to cross-examine a witness who appears vulnerable may anticipate some benefit to his client from probing weaknesses and demonstrating a lack of competence. The harassed witness who, as a consequence, loses his temper as the questions become more difficult to answer, is playing into the lawyer's hands—and hasty answers, made without thought or care, only stoke the fires of discomfort.

Giving evidence is, in many respects, similar to lecturing. Everyone is nervous when giving their first lecture and most continue to feel so on subsequent occasions. Few people are naturally gifted lecturers, but almost anyone can reach an acceptable and competent level at which the anxiety is slight but is just sufficient to produce the necessary stimulation for a good performance. The secret lies in acquiring basic techniques, and in careful preparation—exactly the same applies to attempts to become a competent witness. Confidence depends upon knowing the details of the case thoroughly, having the appropriate documents and reports available for reference and having a sufficient knowledge of the literature relevant to the case. The witness who has taken the trouble to think of some possible questions and to have considered the answers will usually be pleasantly surprised to find that the examination and cross-examination are on a relatively untaxing level.

Competence naturally increases with experience but, whatever one's status, one's performance in the witness box will be open to comment by the court which may be relayed in the press. In a recent case, a newspaper reported a judge as saying that:

he found Dr X an 'unimpressive witness' persistently refusing to address his mind to the questions being asked. Sometimes . . . he had to be asked questions up to four times before giving an answer.

Referring to a later medical witness in the same case, the judge said that he had:

. . . been impressed with her impartiality and objectiveness, the hallmarks of an expert witness. [1]

The first, and most important, step towards competence is taken at the time of the original incident. Any event which is likely to lead to subsequent legal proceedings should be recognized as such. Obvious examples include the examination and treatment of an injury, particularly when caused by another person, an untoward occurrence during the course of medical treatment which may lead to suggestions of negligence, the examination of a person intoxicated by drink or drugs, or an autopsy examination which reveals some unsuspected injury. The notes made at the original event must form the basis of the final report. As we have emphasized in Chapter 6, memory is far too fallible an agent for this purpose. A simple sketch or diagram, saves much written description and can incorporate a few approximate measurements. The minutes spent on such notes or diagrams at this stage will be repaid handsomely if the matter later goes to court—their use, then, is considered in greater detail below.

Many years ago, one of us had made an autopsy examination on a victim of murder. When this had been completed, the police requested a quick inspection of the hands of the suspected murderer in order to confirm that there was a fresh cut on one of his fingers. This was done, but the circumstances were such that no detailed examination of the rest of the hands was made nor were any notes taken of the position of the cut. The wound on the suspect's hand was mentioned, without detail, at the conclusion of the autopsy report. The trial took place nine months later. The evidence was completed and the cross-examination began. The defence had noticed that, when the accused was admitted to prison, the medical officer had made a full examination of his hands and had kept detailed records. So the witness was asked to leave the witness box, walk through the court to the dock, and confirm that there was a scar on another finger. Back in the witness box, it had to be conceded that this corresponded with the position of another fresh wound described by the prison medical officer in his original notes but which was not recorded in the autopsy report. A second request followed to return to the dock and note that there was another scar on another finger, and the performance was repeated. One's stature diminished with each journey across the courtroom and almost vanished when it had to be conceded that the size of the only wound which *had* been seen was not recorded. After that, the jury was likely to view the autopsy findings with a degree of scepticism. The witness left the box a much humbler man. Care in the early stages is vital—for a mistake made then cannot be corrected later.

In a similar vein, we have already noted (p. 68) the importance of the correct procedure when taking samples and, particularly, of the 'continuity of evidence'. A vaginal swab taken at the examination of a case of suspected sexual assault must be labelled adequately by the practitioner at the time so that, when it is passed back in the witness box months later, it can be said: 'that is the sample which I took from this person' and that: 'when it left my hands it passed to . .'. This may seem pedantic but, in reality, it is no more elaborate than the precautions which are adopted in hospital to ensure that the correct cross-matched blood reaches the right patient.

The probability is that a doctor who is likely to be concerned in a court case involving personal injury—be it in the criminal or civil jurisdiction—will be asked to make a statement. The writing of a statement has already been discussed in Chapter 6. Here, we only re-emphasize that it will form the basis of evidence given in court which is the subject of this chapter.

The pre-trial hiatus

Once the statement has been given, there is liable to be a long interval before the witness hears anything further. Trials in magistrates' courts may be expected to come up in a few weeks, but cases going to Crown Court may take several months and a period of one to two years is not unusual in civil actions. Civil cases in Scotland are likely to take even longer to reach the Court of Session; however, serious criminal cases are often expedited by reason of the rule that an accused cannot be held in custody for longer than 110 days before being brought to trial. The danger, during the longer periods, is that the doctor will forget about the case and will fail to keep track of the relevant notes, documents, X-rays, and the like. It is wise to keep one's personal notes securely in one's possession and, particularly, to ensure that records and X-rays are returned for official storage in the appropriate departments. Given that a summons to attend court comes with little warning it is astonishing how many anxious hours can be spent in feverish search for documents which are finally discovered in a disused pending tray.

Further contact by police or lawyers may be made during the period of waiting; the purposes of this will be to clarify points made in the original statement and to discuss new aspects of the case which may have come to light recently. Such action is more likely in the relatively unhurried atmosphere of civil cases.

The landmark occurrence is the arrival of a witness order. This usually comes by post but may be delivered by a policeman. It is a printed form, the appearance of which may differ between one court and another. In England and Wales, it is usually issued by a magistrates' court in a case going on to the Crown Court; it bears the name of the accused, and the location where the trial is to take place, but the date of the trial is not mentioned and, at this stage, is often not known. Arrangements for fixing the date are made by an official, known in the Crown Courts as the listing officer. The comparable procedure in Scotland is the serving of the witness citation which, again, may arrive via recorded delivery post or by way of the Sheriff's officer when originated by the Procurator Fiscal; witnesses for the defence will be cited through the responsible solicitor. The citation specifies the place and time of attendance which, as will be appreciated later, is not necessarily the same as the time of the trial. In the case of inquests, or Scottish precognitions, witnesses are usually notified by telephone by the coroner's officer or by a police officer acting on his behalf or on behalf of the Fiscal.

A professional or expert witness who has important reasons for not being called to court at a particular time—such as absence abroad—is advised to contact the listing officer, or the police officer dealing with the case, as soon as possible. The name of a person to contact is often stated on the order. Such dates may also be mentioned at the time of making one's statement and the official stationery on which the statement is typed bears a small calendar for recording these matters. The officials are generally very obliging in trying to avoid difficulty for witnesses; but the pressure on them to obtain a satisfactory flow of cases through the courts is great and they can be expected to be helpful only if they are given the longest possible notice.

Be that as it may, the court has the last word and it can, if it so wishes—and it may well do so—compel a witness's attendance, no matter how inconvenient this may be. Tales are told of professional witnesses being recalled even from honeymoon! Moreover, sickness may not be an absolute bar to a summons to attend court. One of us was once immobilized by a slipped disc. The court chose to instruct the witness's general practitioner that he must issue a certificate stating that travel to court was quite impossible and applied the subtle pressure of insisting that he, himself, attend the court to give evidence to that effect. In the event, the witness attended, travelling cautiously in a police car. Such attitudes are rare nowadays; it would be more likely that the hearing would be postponed to another day.

A witness who is called to any court, whether it be a coroner's or a Crown Court, is bound to attend. Refusal of a normal request would provoke the issue of a warrant to arrest and bring to court; indeed, in the absence of a sufficient reason for his failure, he could be found guilty of contempt of court and consequently fined or imprisoned. A rather nice example of an exception was reported in 1988 when a witness stated that his non-attendance was due to lack of money but that, nevertheless, he was walking to London from the North of

England; the judge adjourned the hearing.[2] In fact, of course, a court requiring the attendance of a witness may pay his expenses which are known as conduct money. In passing, and although we have never heard of a case in point, there seems no reason why a doctor convicted of such contempt should not be, in addition, statutorily reported to the General Medical Council. Punishment for non-attendance is not confined to witnesses for the prosecution; witnesses for the defence who fail to appear are also liable to a fine.

Going to court

The court administration is now becoming increasingly organized and helpful and it is customary to receive a week or more's notice of the actual day on which one is required to attend. This means that several days are normally available for the final preparations for appearance in court. This is a boon of modern times and the interval should be well used. Yet many doctors still fail to take advantage of the opportunity and arrive in court unready for their duties. It reflects little credit on the abilities of a qualified and highly trained professional man if he arrives in court and, in response to simple questions, is unable to recall the time or date on which he saw his patient, whose condition is the subject of the legal action. It may also encourage the opposing lawyer, who previously saw little point in cross-examination, to feel that so unprepared a witness may make mistakes easily and is, therefore, worth interrogating at length on the off-chance that he will make a damaging admission.

It is wise always to take some trouble over preparation at this stage, no matter how trivial the evidence appears to be. First, a check must be made that all the relevant notes, reports, documents, X-rays, and any other material that relates to one's evidence is available. It is dangerous to leave this until last thing on the night before—the records department may well be shut.

Next, the notes must be rechecked and the report or reports restudied. It is unnecessary to try to commit the reports to memory, because the court will almost always allow reference to them in the witness box, but it is as well to have the principal facts in mind. A lawyer who is leading one through one's statement is quite likely to misread a measurement or similar fact; a polite and immediate correction will demonstrate good control of the situation and will indicate that attempts to discredit one's knowledge of the facts are likely to be unsuccessful.

Finally, a reasonable knowledge of any medical conditions which have a bearing on the case is essential. An hour spent reading through the relevant chapter of a textbook will greatly improve one's confidence. We would also strongly advise including a small book on the subject in the contents of a briefcase. There is a lot of waiting time in court work and, during it, many ideas arise in the head or are put there by others. Taking the oath to a mental background of: 'I wish I had looked up Da Costa's syndrome' starts one off badly; to be able to do so in the waiting room during an adjournment can be a useful sedative.

All this talk of careful preparation probably sounds unnecessary to those anticipating a brief appearance in a lower court or at a simple coroner's inquest. The truth is that no court appearance can ever be relied upon to be a trivial matter as any experienced witness may have found many times to his cost. Moreover, since most simple and uncontroversial cases are dealt with nowadays by the use of written evidence, a summons to appear at court in person should always raise warning signals of storms ahead. Someone must want you there in person for a good reason—and that reason is unknown. Cautionary activity is called for.

Arrival at the court

All writings on this subject stress the importance of a standard of dress. There are several reasons for this. In the first place, the officials and lawyers whose daily professional lives are conducted in and about the court have codes of appropriate dress; put at its lowest, it is discourteous for another professional person from a different discipline to attend in casual clothes, open-necked shirt, and the like.

Secondly, there is no doubt that your appearance influences the opinion that people have of your abilities and competence. In the criminal context, this is, perhaps paradoxically, of greatest importance in the lower courts of summary jurisdiction such as the magistrates' or sheriff courts where decisions will be taken by one or two persons who almost certainly have conservative views as to appearance. It is difficult to be so dogmatic as regards a jury but, no matter what may be the current standards of dress in the lay public, they still *expect* their professionals to look the part—we would hazard a guess that, given opposing medical experts, one in a pin-stripe suit and the other in jeans, a jury would be biased in favour of the former's opinion. In America, it has even been intimated to one of us that the 'jury would expect a club tie, not a floral one, from a Britisher'. There can be no doubt on this point in the civil court where a single judge is adjudicating on the 'weight' of opposing evidence. The side engaging an expert deserves his maximum effort which applies just as much to putting on a suit as it does to the preparation of a report. Finally, although we speak from senescence, we believe that the professional who has taken some trouble with his attire will feel more competent and confident—at least, it will have focused his mind on the importance of the occasion.

We have mentioned the importance of knowing the location of the court in Chapter 4, from which it is apparent that the rule should be to arrive before the time for one's appearance in the witness box. This may often be enforced and every doctor engaged in court work will be dismayed at the apparent waste of time and of public money that the process involves. Yet, while everyone complains, no one has the answer. The pressure on the courts is such that they cannot be left unused. But the court officials have no way in which to know how long a given trial will last and, especially, they cannot budget for the sudden plea of guilty or for the equally sudden withdrawal of evidence against the accused; in the civil courts, last minute settlements are almost the rule. The inevitable result (and it is a particular hazard of the lower courts) is that all witnesses will be called at the same time, some for trials which will not even start on the day in question. Most courts are very sympathetic to the problems thus posed for the doctor whose patients may also be waiting and will do their best to make specific arrangements; alternatively, the solicitors instructing the doctor may undertake to notify him of the precise time of his appearance. It has to be admitted that such discrimination depends in large part on the witness's position in the medico-legal hierarchy but, in any event, *some* waiting time is unavoidable. We have discussed above how this may be employed usefully in refreshing one's memory but even this may pall. We would strongly recommend the professional to take some work with him, particularly work which can be done in short bursts—many an examination script has been corrected in the surroundings of the criminal courts!

With this in mind, court ushers will often make arrangements for the medical witness to be accommodated elsewhere than in the busy waiting room. This, again, is not an unmixed blessing as the tendency is to site one some distance from the actual courtroom. At its best, this results in increasing concern as to the impatience of the court as one's journey following summons takes longer and longer; at its worst, the court ushers have changed and the witness's whereabouts are unknown. Getting 'lost' draws attention to the essentially practical problem of dealing with one's natural bodily functions. These should be attended to well in advance of an expected call to the witness box, something that may not be easy for the inexperienced witness. Not every witness room has adjacent toilets and it is well to tell someone where one is going; one of us has developed the theory that the most effective way to end a tedious period of waiting is to go to the men's room—almost invariably, and within a matter of seconds, this results in a knock on the door and a peremptory summons to the stand. It is, however, recommended only as a recourse of last resort.

In certain circumstances, a professional or expert witness may be allowed to sit in court. This is invariable at a coroner's inquest. It may happen in criminal cases, with the agreement of both sides and by leave of the court, particularly when the witness is giving evidence which may be of value to both sides and which may be modified if the evidence given as to fact varies during the course of the trial. In civil cases, in particular, he may be present to advise his solicitors and this will normally be the case in arbitrations, public inquiries, and the like. This may be time consuming and something one might not want to do as a routine but it certainly adds to the interest of a case.

Once the witness is giving evidence he is on his own and may not consult with other principals in the case. Thus, if his evidence is interrupted by the lunch-time adjournment, he must expect, and take, a lonely meal. The cut off point for isolation is the oath which, generally speaking, will comprise the first action on entering the witness box.

Going into the witness box

We can only advise the witness to be ready when the long awaited call comes. Have all the relevant notes and documents in one brief-case remembering that the witness box is seldom designed for the professional and that there is very little room for extraneous material. It is a very good idea to have available the minimal tools of the trade. We have both made a habit of including in our 'witness kit' a six inch ruler and a small magnifying glass. It always adds an air of professionalism to have the means of checking the size and appearance of any exhibit that is proffered for examination. Similarly, as many younger doctors will be involved in 'drink-driving' cases, the possession of a measuring cylinder greatly improves the answer to the question: 'how much drink do you think is present in that glass?' To be seen to confirm a measurement with precision, rather than to guess at it, adds weight to the value of one's evidence. Perhaps not least in importance, undertaking a meticulous examination may provide a few much needed moments for reflection.

By the same token, all unnecessary items, such as umbrellas, overcoats, and the supermarket shopping should be left with the court usher or a friendly fellow-witness before going into the court. Such things get in the way, the witness becomes flustered when, as is almost invariable, they are dropped, and they do nothing to enhance his standing in the eyes of the court. Moreover, there is a strong possibility that something will be left behind when the box is vacated.

To return to more serious matters, the first positive action will be the taking of the oath. The witness will be handed a Bible, usually a New Testament, on the principle that all witnesses are practising Anglicans until proved otherwise. Holders of other religious persuasions can ask for the appropriate holy book whether this be an Old Testament for Jews or a Koran for followers of Islam; it is unnecessary, and it may cause an irritating delay, to ask for a Roman Catholic missal. If the witness has a particular objection to taking an oath, which is essentially a theistic procedure,[3] he may affirm or state in a set form his intention of telling the truth;[4] the consequential effects are the same. Nearly all evidence in litigation is taken on oath. The only common exceptions which spring to mind are in Scottish precognitions and, generally, in arbitration proceedings.

The oath

In England and Wales, the oath is administered by an official of the court usually by offering the witness a printed card from which to read or by asking him to repeat his words while the witness holds the Testament or its substitute in his right hand. In Scotland, the procedure is more solemn, the oath being administered by the judge himself while the witness affirms his intentions by raising his right hand.

A measure of solemnity is appropriate as it impresses the importance of being 'on oath'. If a witness subsequently: 'wilfully makes a statement material in that proceeding, which he knows to be false or does not believe to be true, he shall be guilty of perjury'.[5] Making up false evidence with the intention of confusing the court is an offence at common law. The punishment for such offences may be severe and it is important to remember that the oath has a similar significance irrespective of where it is administered—the witness should not be misled by the apparent informality of, say, the coroner's inquest; the oath is just as binding there as it is in the Crown Court.

The witness to opinion may have doubts as to the appropriateness of the oath to his evidence and we return to the question in rather more detail in Chapter 10. For the present, it may be said that it is probably best for the expert to look upon the oath in a somewhat negative fashion—that is, that he will *not* tell an *un*truth, that he will not deliberately hide a truth, and that he will not intentionally answer any question untruthfully.

Evidence in practice

Initial evidence

Questioning begins as soon as the oath has been taken. This first stage of the evidence is known as the 'examination-in-chief'. It brings out the evidence which the witness came to court to give and is based on what has already been said about the matter, either by way of a statement or as evidence in a lower court.

The questions are put by whoever has called the witness. Thus, in a coroner's court, it will be the coroner himself; in the magistrates' court it will be the solicitor of the witness' side; and in the High Court, it will be the barrister appearing either for the prosecution or defence—or for the plaintiff or the defendant—depending upon who has instructed him.

The first thing that the lawyer has to do is to introduce his witness to the court. The temptation to regard all this as fatuous must be resisted. To be asked one's name by a man with whom one has been in deep conversation a few hours previously may seem absurd but, quite clearly, the witness is a stranger to the judge and/ or the jury; and the lawyer can no more ask 'leading' questions— that is, those which, of themselves, answer the question—as to one's identity than as to one's interpretation of a medical finding. However, it is well to remember that there *will* be routine questioning. One of us had his head so full of knowledge as to the intricacies of strangulation by ligature on first contact with the full panoply of the Scottish High Court of Judiciary that his mind went into a total blank when asked his age—a vacuum which was filled only by a kindly judge! The doctor will be asked his qualifications and these should be given in full—'I am MB, B.Ch., F.R.C.Path.' is likely to be meaningless, whereas 'I am a Bachelor of Medicine and Surgery and a Fellow of the Royal College of Pathologists' gives some intimation of one's expertise even to the least medically conscious juryman. We feel it is advantageous to be selective; it is probably wise to omit one's B.Ch. unless one is a practising surgeon and the fact that one holds a Diploma in Tropical Medicine and Hygiene is scarcely relevant to a road accident in the Pennines in winter. Similarly, the witness will be asked what his present position is, which is always important, but, when questioned as to his previous appointments, he need only, unless specifically asked, include those which are relevant to the matter in hand.

Next, the lawyer will establish how the witness fits into the rest of the picture which is being unfurled before the court. Quite how this is done will, of course, depend upon the type of court in which the case is being heard and on the status of the witness. For the relatively young doctor, it may consist of eliciting the fact that a person involved in the case, for example the victim or the accused, was examined, and when and where that examination took place. For the more senior consultant, it may well be directed through establishing the circumstances in which a report, based on documentary and other evidence, came to be written. The information is, in fact, just what appeared at the beginning of the original statement.

The questioning will then lead to what was found. Very often, and provided that the lawyers for the other side do not object, the examiner will go directly to that statement, a procedure which is known as 'leading the witness'. It saves time and has become the usual practice. The line of questioning is, then, likely to run: 'Is it true that when you first saw the patient he was in a state of shock?' or 'I believe that you found that he had injuries to the head, lacerations, and bruises. Would you describe them to the court, please.' Samples taken, say, of blood or as swabs, will be handed to the witness for identification and, if necessary, for comment. The label must be carefully noted and the attention of the court drawn to any discrepancy (see p. 68).

Factual matters having been dealt with, opinion evidence will be sought when this is appropriate. When were the injuries sustained? Do you think a weapon was involved? and, if so, of what kind? Are the injuries consistent with their having been caused by the use of the object now being passed to you? And so on.

Matters of medical knowledge may also be brought up. 'Since this man is suffering from diabetes mellitus, would he be likely to be affected by alcohol in a manner different from a healthy person?' Once the questions move into this area, care must be taken to remain within one's sphere of competence—the area in which one can speak with authority on the grounds of training and experience. A fine line may be drawn here and one which is difficult to identify. At what point does professional knowledge (or that knowledge which a layman will expect a competent doctor to possess) pass into expert knowledge—or that which requires specialist training within the medical profession? Thus, a pathologist who has performed an autopsy following a case of peri-operative death may be fully capable of expressing an opinion as to the general nature of the effects of an overdose of a given anaesthetic agent. He would, however, be very unwise to pontificate on precisely *how* that anaesthetic should have been administered. To do so would be to invite a difficult cross-examination and a sharp rebuke from the legal representatives of any anaesthetist concerned in the case, asking how often the pathologist gave anaesthetics and how many years ago he had last given one. The probably apocryphal story is told of the late, and great, pathologist Professor Keith Simpson, describing the clinical effects of alcohol. 'When, doctor', came the question 'did you last see a live patient?'

Such transgressions from one's field of competence are particularly important in the lower tribunals, for example in a coroner's court because only one doctor may be called to give evidence at an inquest. It is then easy to feel rather flattered when being asked to advise the court on a range of medical matters; an unguarded comment made at this stage may mislead the coroner and the interested parties and, thus, set in train a long and purposeless process of costly litigation. Any doctor is expected to have general basic knowledge over the full range of the medical field but, once the questioning moves into detail in a particular area in which he does not have special knowledge and experience, he should say so, and indicate that he does not feel competent to express an opinion. To say this is no disgrace; the court will have a better regard for the doctor who shows that he is trying not to mislead it nor waste its time opining on matters for which he has had no special training.

Technique

Giving evidence involves a technique which, in the end, can only be perfected by way of experience—and some of us never achieve an ideal. There are, however, some basic ground rules to be kept in mind. First, it must be remembered that a verbatim record is being kept of what is said. Tape-recorders are increasingly being used for this purpose but most courts still rely on typed or handwritten notes. So there is usually a shorthand secretary, or a court stenographer, writing down what is said at the time. The good witness must remember this and speak clearly and not too quickly; the alternative is being stopped by the judge or other person in charge and reminded of the fact. This can be disconcerting when one is in full flow. It is good practice to glance at the stenographer from time to time; not only does this give the opportunity to see how he or she is managing with one's method of presentation but it serves also to explain to the court what might otherwise be taken as unnecessarily pedantic diction. It must also be remembered that the judge may wish to make notes of particular points, and he will be forced to write very slowly in long hand. One must not place too much reliance on gestures or indications on one's own body—such demonstrations cannot be reproduced on a typewriter; visual demonstrations may be effective but remarks such as 'as long as my hand' must be qualified by '—seven inches'.

Secondly, although it is the lawyer who is asking the questions, it is the jury, judge, sheriff, or magistrate who need to know the answers. The witness must, therefore, speak clearly and loudly enough for them to hear and do so directly to them, especially if the matter is complicated; it is often surprising how useful a listener's facial expression can be in judging whether or not the message is getting across. In doing so, however, it is important to select the correct audience. One of us will not forget the moment when he was explaining a technical nicety to an American judge and was admonished: 'Don't talk to me, son' and, pointing to the jury, 'You're putting on your act for them'.

Finally, we must consider the general mode of presentation of the evidence. This is often considered in terms of the use of jargon which is but one example of the several special relationships between the expert and the court on which so much often depends. Every discipline has its own jargon—indeed, the legal profession is one of the worst offenders. Many practitioners become so used to using their own jargon as a working tool that they forget there is a more normal form of speech which is used by ordinary people. The unnecessary use of complex medical terminology is to be deprecated. A lay person, called to serve on a jury, may either be hopelessly lost among the strange words or, worse, may be led to form a wrong impression. There are many obvious examples such as saying that a person was febrile when a layman would say that he had a temperature, or talking of a haemarthrosis when the phrase 'bleeding into a joint' would be more easily understood. Almost all technical terms in anatomy and pathology can be translated into simple, everyday language and it is wise to have considered this before going into court. Some selectivity must, however, be applied. To use the word *prominentia laryngea* would, at best, be regarded as demonstrating condescending superiority but this is because the majority of *medical* persons would prefer to speak of the Adam's apple. On the other hand, some conditions or anatomical landmarks can only be expressed properly in medical terms; these should be used with an appropriate explanation appended: 'there was a comminuted fracture—that is, the bone was broken into several fragments'. While this may be essential in front of a jury, it may well not be so before a single judge who was probably trying personal injury actions when the witness was in rompers; such an authority may be irritated by the unnecessary translation, say, of 'femur' to 'thigh bone'. In some cases, it may be appropriate to have with one an anatomical model or a large chart by which to demonstrate a particularly complicated point—practically every one appreciates a visual aid to understanding.

A common example arises when describing the course of a fracture of the skull, particularly of one involving the base. There may well be autopsy photographs by which to illustrate the injury but judges are usually reluctant to require jurors to look at such exhibits. X-rays may be available but the untrained eye may find these extremely difficult to understand. As a result, judges are increasingly prepared to allow the use of charts and/or diagrams, especially if these can be photocopied and distributed to lawyers and jurors. Facilities for the projection of slides in court are rare and, even when available, are usually far from ideal. The introduction of a skull or skeleton to the witness box would rarely find favour and lifelike anatomical models, which could upset the jury, are also likely to be eschewed by the court. In appropriate cases, the witness would be well advised to prepare simple and clear diagrams beforehand and to ask if these may be used in the course of the evidence. He is unlikely to have the facilities said to have been afforded one medical witness who was allowed to draw the course of a fracture on an usher's bald head!

But there are aspects of medical terminology which cannot be illustrated easily. For example, it is difficult to describe the condition of 'asphyxia'. The court may need to understand the different varieties—mechanical, pathological, and the like. It may be necessary to draw a distinction between asphyxia, on the one hand, and anoxia on the other. Hypercapnia may have played a part in the condition. All these need to be explained simply. The problem may be compounded because the lawyer questioning the witness may have met some of the terms before, may think that he understands them, and may even try, himself, to clarify matters for the jury. On one occasion, a judge spent some time explaining to the jury how sudden death was caused by pressure on the thyroid gland; since the area of the body involved and the effect were right, the witness forebore to correct him. Even so, ensuring that the jury truly understand what is being said may make a substantial difference to the outcome of the trial. Only if they fully appreciate the distinction between such entities as 'asphyxia' and 'vagal inhibition of the heart beat' can they grasp the differences in the length of time a person took to die and, thus, gain insight into the intentions of the assailant.

Additional problems creep in as the concepts to be explained grow more difficult. Thus, a victim may sustain a head injury but, die, in the witness's opinion, from a cardiac condition. How that condition caused death, in the presence of apparently severe trauma, will require clear and careful explanation, especially if the victim did not have a gross and obvious heart lesion; the significance of the time intervals between injury and death needs to be made clear.[6]

Demeanour

The points outlined above illustrate the importance of demeanour or of forming a rapport with the court and we confess ourselves to be at a loss to advise on what can only be a matter of experience. The balancing of attitude can be difficult. One is present as an expert or, at least, as a professional but one cannot be condescending; on the other hand, to appear submissive will, at best, set up doubts as to one's expertise and, at worst, may frankly annoy the court. One gets on badly with some judges and well with others and, very often, the reason for the difference is beyond one's own control. No one is *entitled* to prejudices but it is a fact of life that everyone has them.

Many apposite examples could be given but the words, say, of Gorman J.[7] are useful in setting the overall scene:

... one has from time to time to prefer the evidence of one group of witnesses or one witness to another. I have had to pay regard to witnesses, not merely to what they have said, but to the impression which they have given to me, not merely by their words, but by their whole demeanour as witnesses even or their experience, and I have had to try to form a view as to which witnesses I prefer where there has been a conflict of fact.

If relations are clearly bad, it is worth giving a moment's thought to analysing the reason. It may well be that one is forgetting the golden rule of 'When in Rome . . .'; it may seem unfair but we feel it impossible to escape the conclusion that life is easier on one's home ground and, when playing away, it is important not to antagonize the local supporters—particularly if they are jurors.

If we cannot give any positive advice, two examples from judgments within our knowledge may be useful and are particularly informative because we know that the principals in each case were good, honest men doing their level best but failing to adapt. The first is from the Australian case of *Chamberlain*[8] where a judge in the Federal Court of Appeal referred to: 'an unbecoming arrogance' in some of the experts called for the defence at the trial. Whether this had any effect on the outcome of the appeal is, of course, unknown but it was clearly in the mind of the court. The second comes from an unreported Scottish case in which it was said of an expert witness:

Most judges, I imagine, dislike being lectured to in their own courts and I count myself among the majority.[9]

Such comments indicate that the witnesses had, albeit unwittingly, over-assessed their position. It must never be forgotten that, although one is a professional and, perhaps, an expert, one is in the presence of other professionals. The ideal to be sought is one of mutual respect; in the main, it is up to the witness to establish that relationship. We would particularly suggest that a witness, especially one who is inexperienced, would be well advised to avoid trying to appear clever at the lawyer's expense. Very occasionally, a careless question may be asked that elicits a spontaneous response which ranks as a winning return volley, but such occasions are rare. A colleague, giving evidence in a road traffic accident case, was questioned about the fragility of a victim's bones. The lawyer, seeking to diminish the expert's evidence, asked whether he had really made an adequate inspection of the skeleton. The pathologist's instant response was that so many bones had been broken by the accident that he had, indeed, been able to examine the skeleton very extensively —not at all the response the lawyer was seeking.

However, lawyers have a maxim: 'never ask a question unless you already know the answer'—and most follow it carefully. The witness is very unwise to attempt to manufacture such opportunities or to set out to be condescending to the lawyer. The former has probably been in court only a few times and is hopelessly outclassed. Nor is the witness advised to attempt to introduce humour into his answers or to make a joke of a reply. The cases in which a medical witness gives evidence are serious affairs having serious consequences. One of us was asked whether a shoe landing on a child could have caused the abdominal injuries discovered; the powerful temptation to answer 'not unless it had a foot in it' was, wisely, resisted. Humour is generally best reserved for describing one's experiences later and out of court.

In respect of demeanour, some young witnesses are often concerned as to what they should call the various persons in court. It may, at times, be difficult for the witness to know the correct address—a judge, for example, is nearly always referred to as 'My

Lord' but, in some circumstances—and certainly in the county court—he may be 'Your Honour'. The best rule is to follow the lawyers. A county court judge is 'Your Honour' and a magistrate 'Your Worship'. All judges in Scotland, whether in the High Court or Sheriff Court are referred to as 'My Lord'. In many instances, the repetition of such titles becomes tedious and a reversion to 'Sir' or 'Madam' is always permissible—the main concern being to establish a polite deference to authority. It is always politic to refer to the lawyers as 'Sir' or 'Madam'. At the least, such courtesy makes it more difficult for them to be rude in turn! Which is not a bad continuity line to take us to cross-examination.

Cross-examination

When the examination-in-chief is completed and 'one's own' lawyer has established all the points that he wished to make, he will simply sit down and it will be the turn of the opposition to cross-examine. There may, of course, be no such examination in the event that the evidence has been uncontentious; it may even be that the opposing lawyer realizes that a telling point has been omitted and does not want to give the witness a second chance—it is for this reason that a witness who is sure of his facts and his opinion often welcomes cross-examination. Alternatively, there may be several lawyers, representing different parties to the procedure, who wish to clarify points or, perhaps, obtain modification of the evidence to their advantage. This situation arises particularly often in the coroner's court where the evidence-in-chief is taken by the coroner himself; having done so, he will ask any lawyers who are present whether they wish to put any questions, and *any* examination by a lawyer then takes on the nature of cross-examination. Multiple cross-examinations will occur in the criminal court when there is more than one defendant and the same may, of course, happen in the civil courts when, for example, a doctor and a Health Authority may be separately represented in an action for medical negligence.

The duty of a cross-examining lawyer is to test the evidence on behalf of his client, to make sure that the facts were given accurately and to probe for any alternative interpretations of the facts which would be more beneficial to his client's case. This is his function and the most difficult concept which the inexperienced professional has to accept is that there is no attack on the witness *per se*; if an expert can be cajoled into modifying his view, it does no more than demonstrate the existence of a doubt and, if he has omitted some important point, it is in the interests of justice—not of demonstrating incompetence—that it be brought out. The vast majority of lawyers approach this task with courtesy and consideration for the honest witness and only become overtly hostile towards one who is clearly prevaricating. The days of the legal primadonnas, endeavouring to coerce witnesses by force of rhetoric or character, have gone; but, although the Marshall Halls and Sergeant Sullivans of famous legal battles are figures of history, there are few of us who have not, at one time or another, been floored by charm or subtle methods.[10]

The witness who has nothing to hide also has nothing to fear. The questions posed by the lawyer must be listened to carefully and attentively and answered politely and in full. If it is impossible to agree with a proposition which is put, this should be politely so stated; attempts by the witness to humilate or condescend to the questioner will fare badly in the eyes of the court. Similarly, the witness must take care not to lose his temper if the lawyer should attempt to hector him but, rather, to answer firmly but politely and courteously; the sympathy of the court will then be attracted.

The lawyer may advance a proposal or idea which has not been considered previously but which is possible. This must be answered. Merely to say: 'I had not thought of that' is to invite the judge to interpose: 'Then, think of it now'. Given that it is a quite novel suggestion—which, as we have seen, it ought not to be—it is far better to say: 'I would like a moment to consider that'. The judge will almost certainly allow it and might, indeed, find it an opportune moment for mid-morning coffee. The alternative of an ill-considered snap decision may lead the witness into perilous waters. A genuine possibility must always be admitted although the witness should state firmly the *degree* of possibility which he would place on the suggestion; an impossibility should be equally firmly rejected and the reasons for so doing should be stated at the time—these may, in fact, be very obvious to a medically trained person. Such a ploy on the part of the opposition need not be entirely to the witness's disadvantage; being new material, it is open to re-examination during which it may be possible to voice one's doubts even more forcibly. The witness must, of course, be on guard against being manipulated so as to appear to support a view which does not accord with the actual facts. But this is a more advanced aspect of giving evidence such as we have considered in Chapter 7.

Re-examination

Any new material, including modification of the original, which has come to light during cross-examination is open to re-examination by the lawyer who first took the evidence; the coroner is similarly entitled in the coroner's court. The advantages and disadvantages of being re-examined will be obvious from the foregoing but it is to be emphasized that, in the nature of things, one's own 'side' will now be attempting to counterbalance any points conceded in cross-examination; it follows that a genuine change of opinion will have to be defended with the same impartiality as was the original—and that is a stance which requires some moral courage. It is, however, reiterated that new material cannot be introduced for the first time in re-examination which is, essentially, a tidying-up exercise.

Finally, the judge may ask some questions to clarify his own mind or if he thinks that there are some points which a jury, when present, may find it hard to understand. Indeed, the judge may interrupt at any time during the evidence; these asides are generally pertinent and helpful but if, at any time, the witness finds them disconcerting, it is some, if only cold, comfort to know that they are equally so to the lawyer conducting the examination.

Evidence for the defence

If evidence is to be given for the defence, the same order as to 'sides' will be maintained although, of course, the lawyers concerned will reverse their roles. We discuss the problem of partisanship elsewhere (pp. 143–6). Here, we need only point out that the professional in the role of defence witness is, in essence, criticizing the evidence of a peer; defence evidence must, therefore, be soundly based and the underlying reasons must be particularly well explained to the court. It has to be remembered that the expert for the prosecution or the plaintiff has already presented his evidence and has, almost certainly, left a good impression; the production of unsupported, carping criticism is, therefore, not only useless but is likely to be positively counter-productive.

Evidence concluded

When the questioning is completed, the judge, magistrate, or coroner will invite the witness to 'stand down' from the witness box. In theory, this only permits retiral to the benches reserved in court for witnesses who have given evidence. However, it is probable that the professional man will want to be 'released'—that is, allowed to leave court altogether and return to normal duties. It is best to indicate this to one's lawyer before the trial begins and he will then, normally, put the request to the court. Otherwise, it is reasonable for the doctor to ask the court's leave personally stating, for example, that hospital or practice duties call. Such a request is almost invariably treated sympathetically but, if it is refused, there is no option but to remain in the courtroom.

Once out of court, friends or colleagues are likely to ask for a report on the experience. Such conversation is, of course, quite acceptable although we would, in principle, strongly suggest that the urge to discuss the case is resisted until the court proceedings are completed; it can be very embarrassing to be reported in the newspapers at third or fourthhand. It is just possible that reporters outside the courtroom may seek a statement and, again, we would strongly advise on silence. The correct answer, if one has to be given, is: 'I am sure your colleague in court has a note of my evidence'.

What is essential is that the trial is not discussed with anyone who is also a witness in the case—and especially one who has yet to give evidence. This could be regarded as collusion and could raise the risk of being accused of contempt of court. It could also mean that the judge would have to stop the trial and order a retrial—something which could seriously damage a promising medico-legal career.

Financial considerations

The financial arrangements for giving evidence are complex and depend on whether the action is in the criminal or civil courts. As to the former, there are various rates of payment for different classes of witness, some of which are negotiable as to amount and all of which are increased periodically. It is relatively pointless, therefore, to detail the amounts payable but, nevertheless, we attach at Appendix B a list of the fees which are payable at the time of writing; they can be taken as index-linked to inflation. Those for the professional witness are fixed by the Crown Prosecution Service; fees for expert witnesses are, theoretically, negotiable but it will generally be hard to achieve higher remuneration than that agreed between the CPS and the British Medical Association. Fees in the Scottish criminal court are laid down by the Crown Office and are reproduced in Appendix C. In England and Wales, an expert witness is also entitled to a 'preparation fee', which is paid at a certain rate per hour (currently recommended as £40–58) and is remuneration for the work involved in preparing the evidence; however, it is only paid if that evidence is given in person, not if a report is accepted and read out in court. In Scotland, the preparation fee is included in that paid for the report to the Procurator Fiscal; a standard remuneration for precognition is also payable. Travelling expenses for attending court can be claimed as a fare or a mileage allowance and, in certain circumstances, a doctor can claim for expenses involved in having to provide a locum during his absence. Any loss of pay is reclaimable. It is wise to see about these fees before leaving the court building; it is unlikely that anyone will issue a reminder.

Fees for giving evidence for the defence are negotiable with the solicitor concerned but, in general, should follow those available to the experts for the prosecution. Certainly, it will be hard to convince those dispensing legal aid of the need for an excessive increase—as a result, solicitors are disinclined to agree a higher figure and may make the contract 'subject to taxation' which, effectively, means that the witness is responsible for any shortfall between the agreed and the allowed amounts.

Civil actions are a different matter and fees for preparation of reports and for attendance at court are a matter for negotiation whether one is acting for the plaintiff or the defendant. In either case, we believe that the doctor should, so far as is possible, tailor his account to the financial status of the principal—for a person in a medico-legal quandary should be seen as one requiring medical care within his means. In practice, about one third of civil actions are legally aided; in the event of costs being awarded, the 'taxing officer' will allow only a fee which he regards as reasonable—which usually means those payable in criminal cases.

Summary

It is said that witnesses in America are coached before their appearance in court[11] and we would not wish this chapter to be interpreted as some sort of 'grooming' exercise. Moreover, we have deprecated elsewhere (p. 145) the concept of the 'expert witness' as opposed to the 'witness to expertise'. The former is often to be distrusted and is the subject of increasing scrutiny; a fascinating American court decision has held that it is competent to question an expert on his annual income from testifying and on the frequency with which he provides testimony for plaintiffs.[12] We would hope that such a 'trade' does not develop in the United Kingdom.

Nevertheless, within the confines of the adversarial system, *how* a witness to expertise presents his evidence can be important and injustice may be done if the right evidence is presented in the wrong way. It is to that end only that we have presented the simple guidelines above.

References

1. Davenport, P. 'Doctor condemned as judge returns children' (1987) *The Times*, 19 August, p. 1.
2. (1988) *The Times*, 23 January, p. 6.
3. Reynolds, M. P. and King, S. D. *The Expert Witness and his Evidence* (1988) Oxford: BSP Professional Books, p. 73.
4. Oaths Act 1978, s.5.
5. Perjury Act 1911, s.1(1).
6. For a very good example, see *Hendry* v. *HM Adv* 1987 SCCR 394.
7. *Osgood* v. *Thames Stevedoring Co and another* [1953] 2 Lloyd's Repts 134 at 142.
8. *Chamberlain and another* v. *R* (1983) 46 ALR 493 per Bowen C.J. at 520.
9. *Rolland* v. *Lothian Health Board* (1981) 27 August, Unreported, per Lord Ross.
10. See Appleby, L. 'Doctor in the witness box' (1988) 297 *Brit. Med. J.* 1982.
11. Tanton, R. L. 'Jury preconceptions and their effect on expert scientific testimony' (1979) 24 *J. Forensic Sci.* 681. Miller, T. H. 'Non-verbal communication in expert testimony' (1983) 28 *J. Forensic Sci.* 523.
12. *Trower* v. *Jones* 520 NE 2d 297 (Ill., 1988) at 302.

9

Some specific medico-legal situations

The number and variety of cases in which medical evidence will be of major importance is almost limitless. However, there are some scenarios which are not only recurrent in themselves but in which the script is also remarkably repetitive and these merit individual consideration. A description of the evidence in even such a limited series of actions would occupy a whole book and we have selected only a very few for discussion. The choice is obviously limited by our own interests but we hope the following are adequately representative of various medical specialties and of the likely level of expertise of the medical witnesses.

Alcohol and the Road Traffic Act 1988

There are, essentially, two possible alcohol associated offences covered by the Road Traffic Act 1988. Section 4(1) specifies the offence of driving or attempting to drive a motor vehicle on a road or other public place while unfit to drive through drink or drugs. Section 5(1)(a) proscribes the offence of similarly driving or attempting to drive after consuming so much alcohol that the proportion of it in the breath, blood, or urine exceeds the prescribed limit; the prescribed limits are 35 µg/100 ml breath, 80 mg/100 ml blood and 107 mg/100 ml urine (s. 11(2)). Failure to supply a specimen when properly asked to do so carries the same penalties as being found to be above the prescribed limits. There are parallel offences related to being in charge of, as opposed to driving, a motor vehicle on a road or other public place.

It will be seen that s.4 embodies clinical and discretionary interpretations. Different people respond to drugs in different ways while doctors, for their part, will elicit and interpret findings according to their own particular expertise and knowledge. For these reasons, it is often not difficult for the defence to challenge the opinion of the police surgeon successfully and, today, it is very uncommon for a charge to be laid under s.4 other than when the use of drugs is suspected. It is to be noted that the word 'drugs' is interpreted liberally—it can, for example, include non-medicinal substances such as toluene and other active principles related to solvent abuse, [1] in addition, of course, to the non-medicinal hallucinogens such as cannabis or lysergic acid. A doctor who is asked to examine a patient in respect of a s.4 offence is, therefore, being asked to exercise his clinical judgment and must do so according to his own lights. Some measure of objectivity is, however, essential and, accordingly, many police surgeons will make use of a standardized protocol, one form of which is reproduced as Appendix D. Similarly, tissue samples, most likely to be of either blood or urine, will obviously be taken for analysis but the interpretation of any positive findings as to their effect on driving is, again, a matter of opinion which is subject to confirmation or rebuttal by other experts.

By contrast, an offence under s.5 is one of strict liability. The section is unconcerned with the effect of the level of alcohol that is detected—it is the level itself which is significant. The amount by which the level exceeds the prescribed limit may be reflected in sentencing but is irrelevant as to guilt—the principle of *de minimus* does not apply. [2] None the less, there are some exceptions. A level of alcohol in the breath of less than 40 µg/100 ml will not be prosecuted—at least not in Scotland where, additionally, the driver must be informed of the fact. [3] A comparable concession is laid down in statute (s.8(2)) whereby an accused person whose breath alcohol is less than 50 µg/100 ml is entitled to a substituted blood or urine test. The decision between blood and urine is vested in the police officer, who may take the advice of the police surgeon, and not in the 'patient' who does not have to accept the offer; the police must put the option to him fairly[4] and must inform him of the alternatives available. [5]

The object of this exception is twofold. First, it allows for the possible inaccuracies of an automatic measuring and recording device. [6] Secondly, it circumvents, at least in the marginal case, the inequity imposed by the use of breath as a definitive measuring medium whereby an accused person is deprived of the right to an independent check on his specimen. Even so, the driver's major analytic hazard stems from the fact that an arrest under s.5 need not be coincident with the offence but can be delayed indefinitely;[7] during the interval, he may have consumed more alcohol and, certainly, some of the alcohol in the body will have been metabolized—and, as to this last, it has now been decided that the deletion of the words '[the level] as ascertained from a laboratory test' from the Road Traffic Act 1972 by the Transport Act 1981, Schedule 8 allows for 'back calculation' in order to establish the level at the time of the incident.[8]

Prior to 1981, the consumption of *any* alcohol after the relevant incident was held, in England, to nullify the result of the laboratory test.[9] It may be noted that this was never the case in Scotland where a steady line of decisions[10] indicates that the common law has always approximated to what it is now by statute. Section 15(3) of the Road Traffic Offenders Act 1988 now reads:

The assumption [that the proportion of alcohol in the accused's breath . . . at the time of the alleged offence was not less than in the specimen] . . . shall not be made if the accused proves—
  (a) that he consumed alcohol after he has ceased to drive, attempt to drive or be in charge of a motor vehicle on a road or other public place and before he provided a specimen; and
  (b) that had he not done so the proportion in his breath, blood or urine would not have exceeded the prescribed limit.

This defence is not a 'hip flask' defence as it is pejoratively known but is an essential safeguard for the driver who, unaware that he has committed an offence, is engaged in the perfectly legitimate occupation of having a drink in his own house.[11] It clearly, however, demands back calculation and this was noted, in *Gumbley*, as being further evidence of Parliament's intentions.

One further statutory defence is to be noted. Sections 4(3) and 5(2) allow it to be a defence to prove that there was no likelihood of the accused driving the vehicle while he was unfit to drive or while the proportion of alcohol in his body remained likely to exceed the prescribed limit. This defence may be established as a matter of common sense in respect of an offence under s.4; in the case of a s.5 offence, however, it obviously involves back calculation and the use of medical expertise.[12]

Thus, there is widespread evidence both from statute and from case law that Parliament and the courts intend that back calculations should become an integral part of road traffic law. The difficulties attending the exercise are immense; there is a large literature on the subject which has been ably summarized by Lewis[13] who, even so, believed, with considerable reservation, that back calculations made within two to three hours of drinking are likely to be right. Medical iconoclasm is unhelpful in the face of such legal determination and it is up to the doctor who is involved to make the best of what is, admittedly, a bad job.

Ideally, any back calculation should include provision for a number of biological variables—the individual's sex, weight, and height, the interposition of food, the 'normal' absorption of alcohol from the small intestine, and the personal rate of metabolism. Short of an experiment involving the particular subject, none of these can be known and, in our opinion, to introduce large numbers of corrective factors is to imply a spurious degree of scientific accuracy which is simply unattainable. It is far better—and fairer to all concerned—to admit to the inaccuracies and to claim no more than a broad impression of the true nature of affairs. Nevertheless, the two most important variables *in practice* are the subject's weight, suitability modified for sex difference as to fat distribution, and the rate of metabolism. All in all, we see no advantage in using basic data other than those originally prepared by the British Medical Association in 1960.[14] If nothing else, these are the only statistics which have recorded judicial approval.[15] Only blood and urine values are given but the breath value is easily obtainable from the formula: breath = blood/2.3×10^3. The major proviso is that the values given for beer are based on the rather weaker beer at the time (3.2 per cent v/v) whereas most modern drinking beer varies between 3.5 and 4.5 per cent v/v;[16] it is also to be noted that the ubiquitous vodka has a strength of 37.5 per cent alcohol v/v as opposed to the standard 40 per cent of good quality gin and whisky.

Undoubtedly, the most important biological variable is the metabolic rate—indeed, for back calculation in *Gumbley* terms, it is the only significant figure. The different rates that may be manifested by different persons and by different categories of person are well known. Lewis gives the figures of between 19 and 11 mg alcohol/dl blood/hour (4.1 and 2.4 mmol/l/h) for social drinkers, between 16 and 8 mg/dl/h (3.5 and 1.5 mmol/l/h) for non-drinkers and between 39 and 21 mg/dl/h (8.5 and 4.1 mmol/l/h) for alcoholics. Individual variations have been reliably estimated experimentally as lying between 9 and 27 mg/dl/h (1.9 and 5.9 mmol/l/h).[17] There is, thus, scope for considerable error in back calculation. Perhaps the most important figures in the present context are those accepted by the House of Lords in *Gumbley*—that is, between 10 and 25 mg/100 ml blood/h (2.2 and 5.4 mmol/l/h). The House, however, agreed that the most likely elimination rate was 15 mg/100 ml blood/h (3.3 mmol/l/h). What, then, is the position of the doctor required to give evidence in such cases?

Although the issue has not been tested in the courts, it seems to us that back calculation intended by the prosecution to establish a level at some previous time must, in equity, be based on the lower limit accepted by the House of Lords in *Gumbley*. If such a rule (a metabolic rate of 10 mg alcohol/100 ml blood/hour) is accepted, no motorist can claim to have been discriminated against. Moreover, given the fact that such an analysis showed the driver to have been above the prescribed limit at the relevant time, the court could reasonably hold that it was following the House of Lords in accepting back calculation only when it *clearly* [our emphasis] established the presence of excess alcohol at the time when the accused had been driving.

On the other hand, the driver himself must prove the necessary alcohol loss when a defence is run under s.4(3) or s.5(2). [18] Here, in fairness to the driver who is, by definition, of no danger to the public at the time, the maximum acceptable rate (25 mg alcohol/100 ml blood/hour) should be accepted although, again, this proposition has not been tested.

We are left with what might be termed the middle ground—and certainly the commonest form of back calculation—that is, the defence under the Road Traffic Offenders Act 1988, s.15(3) which has two limbs: first, as to credibility (*was* drink consumed) and, secondly, as to calculation (was it sufficient to reduce the analytical result to a level within the prescribed limit). In such circumstances, it seems to us that the 'scientific' evidence must be equally 'fair' to both sides; this involves accepting the 'most likely' value as defined in *Gumbley* (15 mg alcohol/100 ml blood/hour) which converts to 6.5 µg alcohol/100 ml breath/hour. This method clearly has been applied in the English courts [19] and its use in the Scottish ambience has been described by one of us. [20]

The essential features of this type of evidence must be to accept and to admit the limitations, or the unscientific aspects, of the 'science'. Any suggestion that it can discriminate between 34 and 36 µg alcohol/100 ml breath must be resisted. Offences under the

Road Traffic Act 1988, ss. 4 and 5 are criminal offences; proof of guilt thus has to be beyond reasonable doubt. The evidence must, also, be interpreted and presented in a reasonable manner.

Sexual offences

There are few criminal prosecutions that are easier to defend than are those related to sexual offences. One major reason for this is the difficulty of obtaining and presenting the necessary medico-scientific evidence. It is convenient to take a charge of rape as an example. For a prosecution of rape to succeed, there must have been sexual intercourse and lack of consent to such intercourse. At one time it was relatively easy to obtain the necessary evidence; public attitudes and mores are, however, changing so that it is becoming increasingly difficult to do so.

By common law definition, sexual intercourse in respect of the criminal law involves no more than penetration of the vulva. It is clear that medical examination is very unlikely to demonstrate vulval penetration only—there must, in general, be deep penetration before signs are evident. Yet the classic signs of a ruptured hymen are now the exception rather than the rule in other than paedophilic rape; the victim may well be married, and have had children, while virginity above the age of sixteen years is now less likely than was once the case.

In practice, therefore, proof of penetration is likely to rest on proof of emission. But emission is incidental, not essential, to sexual intercourse[21] and vasectomy is now relatively common—although perhaps less so among rapists; in any event, reliance on the demonstration of ejaculate would undoubtedly lead to a number of true cases of rape being missed. Which is not to say that a search for spermatozoa need not be made; rather, it is an essential part of the examination and must include swabs from both the vagina and the vulva—the latter being, possibly, the only evidence available of rape involving minimum penetration.

The difficulties are not yet exhausted for, even if there has been ejaculation, it is still not certain whether spermatozoa will be identified satisfactorily. Several commentators have described the ready recovery of spermatozoa from the vagina three or more days after intercourse.[22] Others have not been so fortunate[23] and it is our

experience that morphologically perfect spermatoza are often difficult to find more than twelve hours after a rape—which raises the
possibility that the vaginal environment is more hostile to the sperm
in such conditions than is the case in normal consensual intercourse.
In the event that only imperfect forms are discovered, it is better, in
our opinion, to pre-empt cross-examination by describing these in
terms such as 'appearances indistinguishable from those of degenerat-
ing spermatozoa'.

The problems in demonstrating lack of consent are equally frustrating. The days of a woman being required to resist penetration 'to
the utmost' are long since gone; most women would now prefer to
see the whole terrible experience ended quickly rather than risk the
possibility of serious injury, and the law itself has recognized that a
state of what might be called 'resigned submission' does not indicate
consent to sexual intercourse.[24] Non-consent may, of course, be
overcome by fear or fraud as well as by force. The end result is that
the victim may show surprisingly little evidence of injury yet,
nevertheless, have been legally raped; injuries in the form of bruises
and abrasions may be found but, in practice, that is in a minority of
cases.

It follows that the medical examiner must ensure that any positive
findings relate to the instant case. Victims of rape *do* make consensual love and that, itself, may be relatively violent; the finding of a
bite mark in either the victim or the suspect is not *necessarily*
evidence of forceful rape. One case of suspected rape in which
extensive bruising was found on the suspect is imprinted in the
mind of one of the authors; the relatively serious injuries had all
been inflicted several days before by the girl's paramour. Again, the
importance of attempting to age bruises and abrasions cannot be
over-emphasized; a very useful aid is often provided by re-
examination twenty-four hours after the original inspection—
bruises, in particular, which have been inflicted very recently may
well show marked changes in shape and extent which can be demonstrated by serial photography.

It also goes without saying that a rape victim may well have had
normal sexual intercourse shortly before the incident and it is
essential that every effort be made to distinguish such a possibility.
This aspect of evidence in the investigation of sexual offences may be
revolutionized now the so-called DNA 'fingerprinting' technique is
becoming more readily available;[25] such tests will be able to identify

positively the origin of biological material such as spermatoza. Until DNA profiling becomes routine, the identification of tissue fluids, sperm, and the like must depend upon the relatively negative blood group evidence which is predominantly, but not exclusively,[26] associated with the secretion of A, B, and H substances. It is, perhaps, too obvious to point out that a group A man could have passed on the group A substance discovered—but so could some 40 per cent of the male population. Such evidence is, therefore, of negative value—it may demonstrate that a given suspect could *not* have donated the material discovered. Clearly, such evidence becomes more 'positive' the more systems that are tested (see Chapter 12) but this is possible only in respect of blood itself; in general terms, the doctor must be cautious as a witness to this form of identification. Even more important, from the point of view of both prosecution and defence is the adequacy of controls in such tests, not only as to the sensitivity and specificity of the laboratory procedures but also to distinguish, if possible, between the secretions of the victim and the suspect. The example of *Preece* v. *HM Adv*,[27] in which the distinction was not made, and which is discussed in greater detail in Chapter 10, is particularly cautionary.

We have concentrated here on the rape trial but it is obvious that similar difficulties will be encountered, say, in a case of sodomy or incest. It has been suggested[28] that there are practical as well as conceptual reasons for reducing the sexual element in 'sexual offences' and concentrating more on the concept of an aggravated assault[29]—the safety of women might thereby be greatly improved.

The battered baby

Few medico-legal conditions are subject to more fluctuating changes of public interest, and assessment of professional evidence, than is child abuse. Physical signs within the non-accidental injury syndrome are particularly susceptible to subjective interpretation and it is clear that the history of the case is open to fabrication both by the potential perpetrators and by the injured subject.

The 'incidence' of child abuse has escalated in recent years in a fashion which is inexplicable on the simple premise that there has been a real increase in violence against children. Thus, reportings of such incidents in South Wales increased from four in 1973 to thirty-seven in 1975;[30] in Scotland, a comparable trend has been seen which corresponds to an annual increase of 40 per cent between 1985 and 1986.[31] The reasons for this are probably multiple.

1. The diagnostic envelope of child abuse is steadily widening; the simple concept of the battered baby, or non-accidental injury, has now been extended to include not only sexual abuse but also emotional abuse.[32]
2. There is not only an increasing awareness of the condition among more recently qualified doctors[33] but clinical signs of lessening severity are being identified and reported.
3. Public awareness is influenced by the publicity given to particularly infamous cases and physicians are not above being swayed by public opinion.

Thus, the doctor faced with an injured child has to steer a difficult and narrow course. On the one hand, he must operate for the maximum benefit to the individual child patient and he must do so in the knowledge that the essence of the management of child abuse is early recognition and intervention; on the other, he must recognize the very severe effects of misdiagnosis[34]—perhaps the most important of which is that, should it become overt, parents will be discouraged from bringing accidentally injured children for treatment.[35]

The characteristics of non-accidental injury can be summarized as obscure lesions which are repetitive in nature and which are inflicted by a caring agency—the baby-sitter is as likely to be responsible as are the parents; there is indecision in bringing the child for medical attention and, when this is done, the history provided is, almost inevitably, deceptive.

It is this last attribute which is probably the most diagnostic. Cameron published an interesting resumé of false explanations given in his series of cases.[36] These included not only such common excuses as 'I tripped while carrying the baby' but also bizarre explanations such as 'he must have strayed too near the fire'. Such statements are likely to be repeated in court. The function of the doctor acting as expert witness is then to decide whether or not the injuries discovered are compatible with the account of events. Often enough, this is relatively simple, particularly if the significance of recognizable patterns is kept in mind—a child cannot, for example, fall into a hot bath and scald only his feet and buttocks. At the same time, the expert must be prepared to admit the possibility of accidental injury as described. To avoid a miscarriage of justice is as important as it is to obtain a conviction.[37] The sequence of events may border on the surreal. Wecht has recorded an incident in which a woman was charged with homicide resulting from child abuse.[38] The true sequence of events elicited included the child tripping over his shoe lace, being dropped in the bath while his injury was being washed, the carer falling over another child who was trailing a towel, and finally being bowled over by a sheep dog with the child still in her arms! Nearer home, we have a child diagnosed as being sexually abused when, in fact, she had fallen over a bench and injured her vulva[39]—a circumstance that is fairly typical of an 'unlikely' story. Indeed, it has been found that the greatest difficulty arises in cases of sexual abuse; here, the major considerations are that individual signs should not be taken as diagnostic and that the doctor should not be averse to seeking other opinions[40] particularly, perhaps, that the clinician should co-operate with the police surgeon and vice versa.

Care must also be exercised in interpreting the force involved in causing injury. An exasperated slap delivered to a child's head will normally result in no more than slight abrasion with or without minor bruising; however, if the child falls over on to the outstretched hand, the clavicle may be broken. The results are quite different and will provoke different emotional responses; but the motivation and the violence used have been identical in both cases.

The repetitive element in child abuse results in injuries which can be shown to be of differing age. The importance of distinguishing between old and recent bruising is discussed on p. 73 and cannot be over-emphasized. Serious abuse is typically associated with fracture; thus, radiology not only forms an integral part of the investigation but also provides permanent evidence of obscure, repetitive, and untreated injury. Some patterns are virtually diagnostic: the 'string of pearls' fractures of the posterior ribs associated with shaking, the spiral fractures and separation of epiphyses which is pathognomonic of twisting, and the periosteal lesions associated with delay in treatment are good examples. Dating fractures is possible and provides good objective evidence but repair is influenced not only by the metabolic state of the victim but also by the anatomic position of the fracture—for example fractures of the skull may not heal for several months. Moreover, there are several disease states which may precipitate natural fractures or which may mimic the results of fracture.[41] For these reasons, we believe that radiological evidence in cases of suspected child abuse should not be regarded as being a mere fragment of the clinical examination; it should be evaluated and presented by a specialist in diagnostic radiology.[42]

Some common defences to murder

'He ran on to the knife'

Stabbings constitute the largest category of homicides in the United Kingdom. Knives, other than flick knives,[43] are readily available. Certainly, their possession in a public place is now illegal, other than in the case of small pen-knives, and the police powers to stop and search (under the Police and Criminal Evidence Act 1984, s. 1) have been extended to pointed weapons of all sorts;[44] nevertheless, it is difficult to discover such weapons and not all stabbings occur in a public place. Stabbing injuries and deaths are mainly the result of drunken pub-brawls or domestic violence when, not at all uncommonly, a wife takes up a kitchen knife, usually as a deterrent rather than for deliberate defensive use. In either event, the defence may well be that the 'stabbing' resulted from movement of the victim rather than movement of the knife. The medical evidence eventually turns on the interpretation of force and direction of the wound or wounds.

For obvious reasons, it is difficult to provide experimental data on the force involved in stabbing injuries; stabbing human cadavers is aesthetically and ethically complicated save for the purposes of essential, basic research. However, such studies as are available are unanimous in emphasizing that once the point of a knife has penetrated the dermis, the remainder of the weapon is likely to penetrate deeply in the soft tissues with the addition of surprisingly little force.

Thus, the interposition of clothing makes a considerable difference, particularly if there are multiple layers[45] although a single shirt, for example, makes little difference. The most important feature of the instrument used, usually a knife, is the sharpness of the point.[46] Green[47] has established the rather surprising fact that the length of the knife also matters; long knives such as bayonets, require more force to penetrate the skin than is the case with short, rigid weapons. Once the skin is penetrated, it is extremely difficult for the assailant to 'hold back' the knife. However, conversely considerable force is often needed to withdraw a knife and this is exaggerated with long weapons. Therefore the defence of accident is readily acceptable in the event of a single wound being reasonably placed; it is unacceptable when multiple wounds are present not only because of the general indications of intent but also on the grounds of biodynamics.

The suggestion that more force must have been used if the knife has penetrated to the hilt is not necessarily true. It might be held that extensive bruising due to the impact of the hilt indicates a vigorous, homicidal intent rather than accident but this interpretation should be adopted with care. Falling on to a knife held in the hand *could* cause bruising but the contrary implication, that the absence of bruising suggests little force, is equally suspect. Bruising requires compression of the blood vessels. It is therefore unlikely in any circumstances if the wound is, say, in the abdomen; even allowing for such obvious variables, hilt bruising is relatively uncommon and appears to be virtually confined to the chest wall.[48] It is also to be noted that the lengths of the blade and of the wound track are often disproportionate. A track which is shorter than the blade is obviously compatible with incomplete penetration; a wound that is deeper than the length of the blade is explicable on the basis of compression of the tissues by the knife—an apparently longer track is actually to be anticipated, say, in the abdomen where the measurements are made after the elastic abdominal wall has realigned itself.

Finally, it should be noted that the time taken for the victim to die and for the victim's potential for movement after the attack are functions of the structures that are penetrated rather than of the force used. Johnson[45] recommended caution in evidence on this point and a recent study has shown that 50 per cent of those stabbed in the chest or abdomen will survive for more than 5 minutes;[49] however, the greatly improved survival times in recent years[50] may be due to no more than improved facilities for treatment.

Interpretation of the position and direction of the wound in relation to accidental stabbing may be easy, for example at the extreme it is very unlikely that a wound in the back can be attributed to accidental self-infliction, or it may be difficult and dependent on subjective assessment. The witness can only say that the direction of the track is or is not compatible with the account given and this may involve comparison of the size of both victim and assailant. It is important to remember that the relative positions of the viscera as seen in a supine body on the post-mortem table need not necessarily be the same as they were in a standing body in life. A wound which appears at autopsy to be upwards may have been inflicted horizontally; comparison with damage to any clothing may be very helpful in this context.

'I only touched her neck'

A certain amount of violence is a natural part of 'love play' and this quite often takes the form of mock strangulation. It is almost commonplace for a man who is charged with the murder of his wife or lover by strangulation to contend that she died suddenly when minimum force was applied to the neck. Death, in these circumstances, is due to reflex cardiac arrest or, as it is sometimes known, to vagal inhibition of the heart. The precise mechanism is uncertain but is probably triggered by stimulation of the sympathetic system—in this case, through the carotid bodies; reflex parasympathetic reaction then results in cardiac arrest. Quite how often this occurs is open to argument. It is noted in Gradwohl[51] for example, that it is rare 'and certainly does not happen with the frequency that defence counsel would have a jury believe'. While this last observation is certainly true, we would not be quite so sceptical. It is certainly the common mode of death in accidental self-strangulation and there is no reason why it should not occur when two persons are involved, particularly as the autonomic nervous system is hyperactive in the presence of emotionally induced hyperadrenalinaemia. Autonomic activity is also enhanced when cerebral cortical control is inhibited by the action of alcohol—and moderate acute alcoholism is to be expected in the circumstances envisaged.

The diagnosis and the evidence to be derived is entirely negative in character. The signs of hypoxia—congestion, petechial haemorrhages, and pulmonary oedema—are completely absent, bruising and excoriation of the neck is improbable and there are no fractures of the laryngeal structures; it must be remembered that reflex cardiac arrest can result from such fractures and their presence will give strong evidence in favour of homicide rather than accident. However, given wholly negative findings and that the appearances at the locus are consistent with the story, the medical witness can support the defence with few qualms.

'The gun went off'

While suicidal gunshot wounds are relatively easy to identify, there are few criteria which can indicate with certainty the distinction between homicidal and accidental shooting. The Firearms Act 1968 stringently controls the availability of rifled weapons; thus, in Great Britain, the main medico-legal concern as to gunshot injuries is with those due to shotguns.

In considering the defence of accidental fatal discharge of a shotgun, the best the medical witness can usually do is to assess the correlation between the account given and the physical signs which are usually surprisingly well defined. The defence of accident is raised both as a result of a struggle and of inadvertent discharge from a distance. Thus, the following must be considered: the bruising, burning, and explosive damage of a contact wound; the singeing and tattooing of the close injury; the absence of wads from the wound inflicted from beyond two metres or thereabouts; and the spread of pellet wounds in the approximate ratio of 2.5 cm diameter for each metre of distance must all be considered in relation to the history of the event.

The most suggestive evidence often derives from the direction of the shot. A homicidal discharge is, by definition, aimed and it commonly shows evidence of purpose in its distribution. Thus, an aimed shot is likely to show a circular distribution of pellet marks; the more tangential, and suggestively unaimed, it is, the more the pattern will approximate to that of an apostrophe. Similarly, an aimed discharge from close quarters will result in a symmetrical entrance hole, whereas a random, oblique shot will show tapering of the surface wound. Obviously, an accidental shot which results in death, will involve some vital part but the resultant wound may well not have the premeditated appearance of the homicidal injury which is, often, characterized by symmetry. In a case seen by one of us, an avowed accidental shot had penetrated the anus and rectum of a man who was said to be kneeling; the perfect symmetrical pattern of injury cast very great doubts on the explanation given. Such evidence can never be other than suggestive; our only recommendation in this context is that the medical witness keeps an open mind.

Psychiatric evidence

There are few experts who face such difficulties in giving evidence as psychiatrists. No other specialty is so dependent upon the history provided and, in the forensic context, this is particularly likely to be distorted; psychiatry depends in a special way upon a good doctor/patient relationship and this is conspicuously absent in the medico-legal context. As Chiswick has put it:

The defendant, not the patient, is referred not by a medical man but by a lay man, on behalf of the prosecution, defence, or sentencer. Whether he is a willing, an indifferent, or a reluctant attender, he attends not at his own initiative but at the suggestion of somebody else. [52]

Psychiatry is a difficult science for the layman to understand. Diagnosis and assessment may be perfectly clear to the specialist concerned but may elude even the most intelligent lay audience. The words of Lord Normand are now part of medico-legal folklore. Having listened to a description of the symptomatology of psychopathy, he remarked: 'it is, to my mind, descriptive rather of a typical criminal than of a person . . . regarded as being possessed of diminished responsibility'. [53] As a result of this 'mystique', psychiatric testimony is seldom controverted except by other psychiatrists and few experts are called upon to assist the court in a comparable manner. On the other side of the coin, and to quote Chiswick again:

[Giving] evidence provides opportunities for the unwary and the unscrupulous to produce psychiatric testimony on demand in a stereotyped and unthinking manner, because experience dictates that such evidence relieves the court of its difficulties and is therefore welcomed.

The list of circumstances in which psychiatric evidence will be called is long and includes opinion evidence in respect of fitness to plead, the insanity defence, diminished responsibility, and appropriate sentencing; moreover, the psychiatrist may be called to give evidence before Mental Health Tribunals and to give advice to parole boards. In either case, he will be required to advise on the subject's disposal, including return to the community; in effect, a prognosis as to dangerousness is called for. It is not possible here to discuss all these in detail; greatest interest, in our view, focuses on diminished responsibility and dangerousness.

The concept of diminished responsibility is of particular importance in relation to the fixed penalty for murder. It is one which has always existed at common law in Scotland and which is subject to statutory definition in England and Wales. The Homicide Act 1957, s.2, states:

Where a person kills or is party to a killing of another, he shall not be convicted of murder if he is suffering from such abnormality of mind (whether arising from a condition of arrested or retarded development of mind or any inherent causes or induced by disease or injury) as substantially impaired his mental responsibility for his acts or omissions in doing or being a party to the killing.

Immediately, therefore, the psychiatrist, whose testimony is essential to the defence, is in some difficulty. He is being asked to look into an accused's mind whereas his expertise is directed to establishing his or her mental condition. Diminished responsibility is a legal, not a psychiatric, term[54] and the defence has no basis in psychiatric theory.[52] Its introduction into English law stemmed from a societal impulse and, in effect, psychiatry broke with its own practices in its response to social attitudes and to the needs of the court in attempting to find a route to leniency in apparently deserving cases. This is, perhaps, best seen in the context of 'mercy killing' and in the statutory offence of infanticide.

In the case of 'mercy killing' the decision to kill out of kindness to the victim has almost always been taken after considerable reflection and the act of killing marks the acceptance of a heavy responsibility. Yet such cases attract great sympathy and some means must be found to apply the Homicide Act 1957, s.2. The simple ruse is to accept a diagnosis of depressive neurosis, something which Walker[55] described as psychiatric perjury, albeit a harmless misinterpretation of the legal term. This move towards interpreting the defence of diminished responsibility in accordance with the morality of the case 'rather than as an application of psychiatric concepts'[56] is being extended. A case has recently been reported in the news media, though not in the law reports, in which a woman battered her mother to death two months after giving birth; a conviction for murder was set aside in favour of manslaughter with diminished responsibility on the grounds of postnatal depression combined with premenstrual tension at the time of the killing—a probation order was imposed.[57]

The question of post-partum psychosis arises in the specific environment of the Infanticide Act 1938 under which a mother who kills her child aged less than twelve months old may be punished as if for manslaughter if it can be shown that the balance of her mind was, at the time, disturbed by reason of her not having fully recovered from the effects of giving birth to the child or of lactation consequent upon that birth. It is now almost impossible to find a case of infanticide that has been punished by imprisonment[58]—and the same can be said of Scotland where the Act does not run and where there is no such offence as infanticide by that name; indeed, the strange situation arises in a trial for infanticide in England that the prosecution must adduce evidence of extenuating mental disturbance. Nevertheless, it has been consistently shown that the majority of women who kill their infants within the first 24 hours of life are psychiatrically normal.[59]

Clearly there is an anomaly and this is of such proportion that it now seems almost redundant to discuss the precise meaning of 'diminished responsibility'. Suffice it to reproduce, first, the original description, one version of which reads:

... there must be a state of mind which is bordering on, though not amounting to, insanity; that there must be a mind so affected that responsibility is diminished from full responsibility to partial responsibility—in other words, the prisoner in question must be only partially responsible for his actions.[60]

However, this view has been greatly modified, at least in England, where it has been held inappropriate to direct a jury in terms of partial or borderline insanity; chronic reactive depression amounting to mental illness is properly characterized as an abnormality of mind which is sufficient to impair a man's mental responsibility.[61]

The courts and psychiatrists seem to be reaching common ground but, in the confusion engendered, it is not surprising that expert evidence is sometimes ignored, for the final decision is that of the judge or jury.[62] This was typified in the celebrated case of *Sutcliffe*.[63] Sutcliffe pleaded not guilty to the murder of thirteen women. Both the prosecution and the defence were prepared to accept a plea of guilty to manslaughter by way of diminished responsibility but the trial judge was unwilling to do so; the case went to trial and, despite the evidence that he was a paranoid schizophrenic, Sutcliffe was found guilty of murder. Analysis of the case throws some light on the difficulties surrounding psychiatric testimony. It may be that, as was suggested at the time, the psychiatrists were bad witnesses—but the definition of a bad witness is discussed in Chapter 8. On the other hand, a respected legal opinion points to the fact that psychiatrists are in something of a cleft stick; unedited expression of what they are told in consultation is likely to lead to disbelief, while to choose which items to present may be taken as arrogating the function of both judge and jury.[64] Prins[63] has succinctly pointed out that, despite the importance which was attached by the court to uncontested medical evidence in the case of *R* v. *Matheson*,[65] there was nothing necessarily inconsistent in the apparently perverse verdict; the jury could well accept the diagnosis of paranoid schizophrenia but, at the same time, reject the supposition that this substantially impaired the accused's responsibility.

The second assessment—that of dangerousness—is one which the psychiatrist is frequently called upon to make, not only in the criminal courts in order to assist in sentencing but also in such forums as the Mental Health Tribunal or the Parole Board. His precise public accountability in this respect has not been tested in the United Kingdom but there are ominous signs from the United States. In *Tarasoff*,[66] a case based on negligent failure to warn individuals that they were at risk from a released patient, it was stated:

Predicting whether a patient presents a serious danger of violence is comparable to the judgment which doctors and professionals must regularly render under accepted rules of responsibility.

Similarly, in *Lipari*[67] the court was:

not persuaded that the inherent difficulties in predicting dangerousness justify denying the injured party relief regardless of the circumstances.

While we do not believe that British courts would expect so much of the psychiatrist, it is worth taking a brief look at the current status of such evidence.

Perhaps the most important factor in the prediction of dangerousness is that it is a prediction of probability (see Chapter 12) and this holds despite the fact that the outcome is absolute; it has been pointed out that a person cannot, for example, be 75 per cent imprisoned or released.[68] Moreover, the contribution of mental illness to an individual's dangerousness—which is the preserve of the psychiatrist—may be of minor statistical importance; once again, therefore, the psychiatrist may be forced into making judgments based on social and other non-medical factors, the significance of which cannot be accurately predicted or assessed. Finally, no matter how many statistics are collected or from what angle, it is impossible to transfer them to the individual. The simple fact that 10 per cent of those discharged from special hospitals may be involved later in serious or homicidal acts of violence[69] does little to assist in the prognosis for a single person and, in any event, not all observers would agree on such a figure. If, as seems likely, the main predictive index of dangerousness is the number of previous convictions for violence and if subsequently the most important determinant is the degree of community care, it seems that the criminologist rather than the psychiatrist is the appropriate expert opinion. The major lesson to be gleaned is that the limitations of prediction should be acknowledged and that the psychiatric evidence should not be stretched in order to accommodate the courts. The psychiatrist's usefulness may, then, be undermined but Chiswick's warning—to the effect that usefulness as an expert witness may be attainable only at the cost of disregarding the ethical obligations—should be kept very much in mind.

One associated issue has recently come to the fore—the nature of the confidentiality of psychiatric information that is obtained in a medico-legal context. Such evidence may be of particular sensitivity to the individual but, equally, may be relevant to the public interest. The problem has been highlighted recently in *W* v. *Egdell*.[70] In this unusual case, a consultant psychiatrist was commissioned to make an independent assessment of an inmate of a top security hospital who sought transfer to a regional secure unit; the report was adverse and the application for review was, accordingly, withdrawn. When Dr Egdell found that his opinion was not recorded in the patient's notes, he sent a copy to the medical director of the hospital and pressed that it be further copied to the Home Office, a process which was effected. W claimed that his cause had been undermined by a breach of confidentiality. The court held that the public interest in disclosure prevailed even though that conclusion placed W and persons like him in a position where the duty of confidence owed by psychiatrists to them was less extensive than that owed to ordinary members of the public—which W was not.

The balance of public interest as between disclosure of information obtained and the protection of medical confidences may, at times, be difficult to assess;[71] in the present case, the Court of Appeal found Dr Egdell's action to be fully justified.[72]

Psychiatric testimony is a matter *par excellence* for the specialist. Indeed, we feel that the most important comment we can make is to advise casualty officers and pathologists against venturing into that field. Bizarre, violent, and unusual behaviour *may* indicate a mental illness but there may also be other explanations. In any event, the diagnosis and assessment are for the psychiatrist who has access to all the facts; the traumatologist—be he clinician or pathologist—would do well not to try to cross the line on the basis of relatively isolated findings.

References

1. *Bradford* v. *Wilson* [1983] Crim LR 482.
2. *Delaroy-Hall* v. *Tadman (and associated cases)* (1968) Times, 9 November.
3. *Lockhart* v. *Deighan* 1985 SLT 549; *McConnachie* v. *Scott* 1988 Scotsman, 3 June.
4. *Benton* v. *Cardle* 1987 SCCR 738; *Anderton* v. *Lythgoe* [1985] RTR 395.
5. *Hobbs* v. *Clark* [1988] RTR 36.
6. *Cracknell* v. *Willis* [1987] 3 All ER 801, HL.
7. *Blake* v. *Pope* [1986] 3 All ER 185.
8. *Gumbley* v. *Cunningham* [1989] RTR 49, HL.
9. *Rowlands* v. *Hamilton* [1977] 1 WLR 647.
10. From *Wood* v. *Brown* 1969 SLT 297 to *Campbell* v. *Mackenzie* 1982 SLT 250.
11. He need not even have been driving a car for the request to provide a specimen to be legitimate: *Bunyard* v. *Hayes* [1985] RTR 348; *R* v. *Ashford and Tenterden Magistrates Court, ex parte Wood* [1988] RTR 178; *DPP* v. *Redling* (1988) *The Times*, 11 October, p. 2.
12. *Pugsley* v. *Hunter* [1973] RTR 284; *DPP* v. *Frost* (1988) Times, 27 June.
13. Lewis, K. O. 'Back calculation of blood alcohol concentration' (1987) 295 *Brit. Med. J.* 800.
14. British Medical Association *The Relation of Alcohol to Road Accidents* (1960) London: BMA, Appendix A.
15. *R* v. *Somers* [1963] 3 All ER 808.

16. Some very specialized non-draught lagers may contain as much as 8 per cent alcohol v/v.
17. Oliver, J. S. 'Forensic Toxicology' in Mason, J. K. *Forensic Medicine for Lawyers* (2nd edn revised, 1988), p. 284.
18. *DPP* v. *Frost*, ref. 12 above.
19. *Lloyd* v. *Knight* (1985) Times, 13 February.
20. Mason, J. K. 'Section 10 defence to charges of driving with excess alcohol' (1984) 128 SJ 539.
21. Sexual Offences Act 1956, s.44. For civil authority, see *Baxter* v. *Baxter* [1947] 2 All ER 886; *R* v. *R (orse F)* [1952] 1 All ER 1194.
22. David, A. and Wilson, E. 'The presence of seminal constitutents in the human vagina' (1974) 3 *Forensic Sci.* 45.
23. Sharpe, N. 'The significance of spermatoza in victims of sexual offences' (1963) 89 *Canad. Med. Ass. J.* 513.
24. *R* v. *Olugboja* [1981] 3 WLR 585.
25. Jeffreys, A. J., Wilson, V., and Thein, S. L. 'Individual-specific "fingerprints" of human DNA' (1985) 316 *Nature*, London 76.
26. Davies, A. 'The appearance and grouping of mixtures of semen and vaginal material' (1982) 22 *Med. Sci. Law* 21.
27. [1981] Crim LR 783. See Brownlie, A. R. 'Medical evidence in the light of *Preece* v. *H M Adv*' (1982) 22 *Med. Sci. Law* 237.
28. Mason, J. K. and McCall Smith, R. A. *Law and Medical Ethics* (2nd edn, 1987) London: Butterworths, p. 28.
29. Very much the direction taken in several Commonwealth jurisdictions. E.g. Canadian Criminal Code, s.246; Crimes (Sexual Assault) Amendment Act 1981 (NSW); Acts Amendment (Sexual Assaults) Act 1985 (WA). For discussion, see Temkin, J. 'The radical solution to the rape law crisis' (1987) 1(12) *Law Magazine* 30.
30. Jenkins, J. and Gray, O. P. 'Changing incidence of non-accidental injury to children in South Glamorgan' (1987) 294 *Brit. Med. J.* 1658.
31. Scottish Education Department, Social Work Services Group Statistical Bulletins CH10/1986, Ch11/1987.
32. Gath, A. 'The emotional abuse of children' in Mason, J. K. (ed.) *Paediatric Forensic Medicine and Pathology* (1989) London: Chapman and Hall.
33. Boyter, E. M., MacLean, D. W., Zealley, H. E., and Mason, J. K. 'Non-accidental injury to children: a survey of professional attitudes' (1983) 33 *J. R. Coll. Gen. Pract.* 773.
34. Kirschner, R. H. and Stein, R. J. 'The mistaken diagnosis of child abuse: a form of medical abuse?' (1985) 139 *Amer. J. Dis. Child* 873; Wheeler, D. M. and Hobbs, C. J. 'Mistakes in diagnosing non-accidental injury: 10 years' experience' (1988) 296 *Brit. Med. J.* 1233.

35. Editorial Comment 'Child abuse: the swing of the pendulum' (1981) **283** *Brit. Med. J.* 170.
36. Cameron, J. M. 'The fetus, neonate, infants and children' in Camps, F. E., Robinson, A. E., and Lucas, B. G. B. (ed.) *Gradwohl's Legal Medicine* (3rd edn, 1976) Bristol: John Wright & Sons.
37. But, for the standard of proof in wardship cases, see *In re G (a Minor)* [1987] 1 WLR 1461. An instructive Scottish case is *W and another* v. *Kennedy* 1988 SLT 583.
38. Wecht, C. H. and Larkin, G. M. 'The role of the expert witness in paediatric forensic practice' in Mason, ref. 32 above.
39. Davenport, P. 'Doctor condemned as judge returns children' (1987) *The Times*, 19 August, pp. 1 & 18. Though the actual injury may not be so uncommon as might be supposed: West, R., Davis, A., and Fenton, T. 'Accidental vulval injuries in childhood' (1989) **298** *Brit. Med. J.* 1002.
40. Valman, B. 'Implications of the Cleveland inquiry' (1988) **297** *Brit. Med. J.* 151. See, in particular, the government publications: Department of Health and Social Security and the Welsh Office *Working Together* (1988) London: HMSO; Department of Health and Social Security *Diagnosis of Child Sexual Abuse* (1988) London: HMSO.
41. E.g. Chapman, S. 'Child abuse or copper deficiency? A radiological review' (1987) **294** *Brit. Med. J.* 1370.
42. For a very full account, see Evans, K. T. and Roberts, G. M. 'Radiological aspects of child abuse' in Mason, ref. 32 above.
43. Strictly controlled under the Restriction of Offensive Weapons Acts 1959 and 1961.
44. Criminal Justice Act 1988, ss. 139, 140.
45. Johnson, H. R. M. 'Stabbing and other knife wounds' in Mason, J. K. (ed.) *The Pathology of Violent Injury* (1978) London: Edward Arnold.
46. Knight, B. 'The dynamics of stab wounds' (1975) 6 *Forensic Sci.* 249.
47. Green, M. A. 'Stab wound dynamics—a recording technique for use in medico-legal investigations' (1978) 18 *J. Forens. Sci. Soc.* 161.
48. Murray, L. A. and Green, M. A. 'Hilts and knives: a study of ten years of fatal stabbings' (1987) 27 *Med. Sci. Law* 182.
49. Levy, V. and Rao, V. J. 'Survival times in gunshot and stab wound victims' (1988) 9 *Amer. J. Forens. Med. Path.* 215.
50. Cf. Spitz, W. V., Petty, C. S., and Fisher, R. S. 'Physical activity until collapse following fatal injury by firearms and sharp pointed weapons' (1961) 6 *J. Forensic Sci.* 290.
51. Camps, F. E., Robinson, A. E., and Lucas, B. G. B. (ed.) *Gradwohl's Legal Medicine* (3rd edn, 1976) Bristol: John Wright, p. 333.
52. Chiswick, D. 'Use and abuse of psychiatric testimony' (1985) **290** *Brit. Med. J.* 975.

53. *Carraher* v. *H M Adv* 1946 JC 108 at 117.
54. Hamilton, J. R. 'Psychiatric aspects of homicide' (1988) **28** *Med. Sci. Law.* 26.
55. Walker, N. 'Butler v the CLRC and others' [1981] Crim LR 596.
56. Williams, G. *Textbook of Criminal Law* (2nd edn, 1983) London: Stevens, p. 693.
57. *R* v. *Reynolds* (1988) *The Times*, 23 April, p. 3.
58. *R* v. *Scott* [1973] Crim LR 708.
59. Resnick, P. J. 'Murder of the newborn: a psychiatric review of neonaticide' (1970) **126** *Amer. J. Psychiat.* 1414; Myers, S. A. 'Maternal filicide' (1970) **120** *Amer. J. Dis. Child* 534; d'Orban, P. T. 'Women who kill their children' (1979) **134** *Brit. J. Psychiat.* 560.
60. *H M Adv* v. *Savage* 1923 JC 49 per Lord Alness at 50. For a similar English definition, see *R* v. *Byrne* [1960] 3 WLR 440.
61. *R* v. *Seers* (1984) **79** *Cr. App. R.* 261 per Griffiths LJ.
62. Mackay, R. D. 'Diminished responsibility—some observations arising from three case studies' (1986) **26** *Med. Sci. Law* 60.
63. Prins, H. A. 'Diminished responsibility and the Sutcliffe case; legal, psychiatric and social aspects (a 'layman's' view)' (1983) **23** *Med. Sci. Law* 17.
64. Henderson, R. 'Criminal responsibility: a view of counsel' (1988) **28** *Med. Sci. Law* 31.
65. [1959] 1 WLR 474.
66. *Tarasoff* v. *Regents of the University of California* 17 Cal 3d 425 (1976).
67. *Lipari* v. *Sears, Roebuck & Co* 497 F Supp 185 (Neb., 1980). See also *Durflinger* v. *Artiles* 673 P 2d 86 (Kan., 1983); aff'd 727 F 2d 888 (1984).
68. Mullen, P. E. 'Mental disorder and dangerousness' (1984) **18** *Austral. NZ J. Psychiat.* 8.
69. Bowden, P. 'What happens to patients released from the special hospitals?' (1981) **138** *Brit. J. Psychiat.* 340.
70. [1989] 1 All ER 1089.
71. Dyer, C. 'Duties to society and patients: a conflict of interests?' (1989) **298** *Brit. Med. J.* 71.
72. [1990] 1 All ER 835. A very similar conclusion has been reported recently in *R* v. *Crozier* (1990) *Independent*, 11 May.

10

Failure of the expert witness

Everyone undertaking the role of a professional or expert witness is, or should be, acutely conscious of his or her own fallibility and the likelihood of being mistaken. Probably even more worrying is the thought of this being shown to have been the case in court and in the full glare of publicity. In most areas of medicine, it is possible to correct mistakes, or to remedy them, before they are noticed. However, this is not possible in the medico-legal arena, where the number of actions for medical negligence is ever-increasing and the proceedings in court are widely reported. A doctor has to live with the risk of being discredited every time he acts as an expert witness. Failure involves a tangible and painful experience, which few who go to court more than once or twice are likely to be able to avoid completely. For we all make mistakes in the course of a professional lifetime—most of us very many of them.

Occasional failures on the part of the experts are inevitable and do not reflect badly on the witness, nor bring into question the efficiency of the courts, unless they are frequent and gross. Some mistakes are not obvious and a witness may commit them without realizing what he has done nor, indeed, that he has made a mistake at all. Yet they are likely to be serious in that they can disrupt the processes of justice in a way that episodes of personal failure will not. Some of them are the result of lack of care on the part of the witness; some are due to the form of the legal procedure, in which the witness may be powerless, or relatively so, to prevent the error occurring. They all give reason to consider how the legal system could be changed so as to improve the reliability of expert evidence.

Partisanship

Many of these failures arise out of the fact that, as we have discussed in Chapter 3, the form of legal process in Britain is adversarial. There is, therefore, an inevitable tendency for the witness to identify himself with the side that has called him and, possibly without realizing, to deliver his evidence in such a way which lends support to that side. It has, indeed, been well said that the adversary system does not fit well with the use of experts to assist the court. [1]

It is always taught that the witness's role is not to 'play for' either side and that he must be objective and fair in all that he says so as to avoid any suspicion of partisanship. However, that is much more easily said than done. We have noted (at p. 34) that the expert should be convinced of the strength of his opinion and that his 'side' have chosen him for, and are depending upon, that confidence. The inherent dilemma has been summed up by Mr Justice Shaw:

One often hears it said that an expert witness should not appear to be an advocate in the cause. In one sense this is true . . . He must not contend for a verdict or judgment one way or the other. That is not his business. But he must be an advocate for the opinion he expresses about a matter which may have a bearing on the ultimate outcome of the trial . . . He must not be a protagonist of the party [for whom he has been called] but he is a protagonist of the opinion he expresses for he has come to support it and must seek to do so *as long as he believes in it* [our emphasis]. [2]

And, therein lies the rub for, under astute questioning, his confidence may be eroded; the dividing line between defence of one's opinion and defence of one's status, or loyalty to one's side, can then become strained.

Having once made a statement which supports one or other side, a witness is likely to feel a considerable need to maintain that position. Any change of mind or admission of an alternative interpretation may be seen as disloyalty or exposure of a lack of ability and something to be avoided if it is at all possible. There may be more subtle forces playing on the witness. Altering an original statement which supported a prosecution case so as to weaken or destroy the prosecution's chances will not endear him to the police, and good relations with the local police force are clearly important if a career as a police surgeon or forensic pathologist is intended. A consequent reluctance to make a change in his evidence may force the witness into adopting a partisan position. The results may be far-reaching.

If lawyers recognize him as a partisan witness, they are likely to find it that much easier to discredit his evidence by cross-examination. Indeed, books written to instruct lawyers on the skills of cross-examination give examples of tactics to be used in such circumstances. The value of his evidence may still be diminished even if the lawyers do not realize the witness's partisan stance and determinedly attack him. The subconscious alignment of the witness with a particular cause or point of view means that he will be preconditioned to ignore or reject alternative possibilities to those which support his side's case and, in this way, he may mislead the court. A forceful witness, with imposing manner and good credentials, may persuade the court to accept his side's view. This is very satisfactory for those calling him and he will become known as a 'good witness'. But this approach may lead to a miscarriage of justice for he will, in fact, only have been putting forward a hypothesis as to what may have happened. He may be wrong and laymen may then not realize that any alternatives exist. If, moreover, no other medical witness is being called, there will be no counterbalance to restore proportion to the expressed view; in succumbing to the subtle pleasure to be derived from convincing the court, the witness may not realize until much later, if at all, that, in so doing, he has not alerted them to any alternatives. Mr Justice Shaw, in another passage from his address quoted above, makes what is, to us, a chilling observation in respect of Sir Bernard Spilsbury: 'He could persuade a jury to accept a bad scientific proposition more readily than others could achieve acceptance of a right view'. [2]

The lure of the alternative position, of excessive compliance with every alternative put, must also be avoided. Few things will lower a witness in the eyes of courts and lawyers more than for him to maintain a particular position firmly with apparent conviction at all discussions with the party calling him up to the time of going to court, and then to have a sudden, and substantial, change of heart during cross-examination. The witness who agrees with one proposition after another as they are put to him is likely to cause the court to wonder if he has any expert knowledge or ability at all.

At the end of the day, the expert witness has to square his conscience with his oath—to tell the truth, the whole truth, and nothing but the truth; unfortunately, his position is not, thereby, clarified. Certainly, he will tell the truth as he sees it but there is no way in which he can tell nothing but the truth so long as his evidence is a matter of opinion. The 'other side' is certain to produce an alternative opinion and, logically, one or other expert is committing technical perjury within the existing framework of the oath. The eminent Scottish jurist, Gordon, interprets the expert's position in that: 'he fulfils his oath by giving his opinion frankly and honestly without minimising any difficulties it might cause or suppressing any doubts he has'.[3] This sounds very simple but still begs the essential question posed by the adversarial system as related to the expert witness—what is the whole truth if it is to be contained in answers to questions which are posed by parties who cannot, by definition, be experts in the witness's particular field? We will return to this central issue later; in the meantime, we would draw attention to the suggestion that there may be a distinct juridical difference between verbal evidence—which is, to a large extent, outwith the control of the witness—and written evidence by way of a report which is entirely of his own making.[4]

Isolation of the witness

It is particulary important, especially in a complex case, for the witness to have tried, at an early stage of preparation of statements and reports, to have stated his own opinion and deductions from the facts, to have indicated any alternative interpretations which are possible, and to have made it clear how he arrived at his conclusions. He should clarify any areas in which he would admit to alternative possibilities if they were put to him, even though he would prefer his own opinion as he has stated it. In this way, lawyers preparing a case know its possible weaknesses from an early stage and cannot claim to have been taken by surprise when the witness admits his doubts in court.

The normal practice for lawyers on opposing sides to guard their witnesses carefully, and to prevent them from being contaminated by contact with the other side, tends to force them into partisan positions. It is common for expert witnesses to be discouraged, or forbidden, to discuss any features of the case beforehand with experts on the other side and the consequent element of tactical surprise which the lawyer can introduce is considered to be valuable. This is, of course, excellent material for plays and films; the revelation of the unexpected evidence at the eleventh hour is the very stuff of drama. However, it does little to facilitate the careful consideration and reliable presentation of facts and possibilities to the court. Long, and sometimes bitter, experience has taught us that many of the expert witness's problems stem from a limited knowledge of the wider facts of the case.[5] Our antipathy to the practice is not, as has been suggested,[6] a matter of self defence, it is simply that the introduction of the 'surprise super-expert' is not the best way of assisting the court to reach the scientifically *correct* solution.

Most experienced witnesses can give examples of the poor presentation of evidence due to segregation of the experts for the two sides. On one such occasion, the prosecution expert had examined a badly decomposed corpse with a knitted woollen scarf wound round its neck which had, apparently, been used as a ligature. The results of various tests carried out on the corpse and the ligature, made to establish whether strangulation was the cause of death, were set out in his report. He supplemented these with reports of other investigations performed in the months before the case came to court. At the trial he was, for the first time, made aware that a colleague, who had been told not to contact him, had been called as an expert for the other side; he had independently carried out other tests which supported a different opinion. When giving evidence, each expert was asked to comment on the other's tests, which had neither been seen nor checked. Thus, the presentation of reasonable possible explanations to the jury was made that much more difficult. The result was a verdict for the prosecution which was reversed on appeal on the interpretation of the medical evidence. This was a waste of time and money which might have been avoided by proper consultation between the experts before the trial.

One of the best known examples of the problems caused by the isolation of experts concerned the trial of Dr Arthur in 1981.[7] The defendant, an eminent paediatrician, had been responsible for the care of a newborn infant with severe Down's syndrome whose parents 'did not wish it to survive'; Dr Arthur, accordingly, ordered nursing care only, which included the withholding of nourishment, and the administration of large doses of dihydrocodeine. The baby died sixty-four hours later. An autopsy examination was undertaken by an experienced forensic pathologist, aided by an equally senior paediatric pathologist. No evidence of congenital disease was discovered and, on the basis of an agreed report, death was ascribed to bronchopneumonia due to dihydrocodeine poisoning in a child with Down's syndrome. Dr Arthur was charged with murder. The forensic pathologist gave his evidence, and it was only while being cross-examined that he was made aware, by the defence, that the same paediatric pathologist had since discovered the presence of congenital natural disease in histological preparations made from the tissues removed at autopsy. The forensic pathologist was thus obliged to look at the relevant slides, and to reach a conclusion, during the lunch recess; he was then cross-examined further on his opinion. Not surprisingly, he was obliged to concede the possibility that natural disease contributed to the death; the prosecution case collapsed and Dr Arthur was found not guilty on the reduced charge of attempted murder.

It is worth considering the repercussions of such a case. Leaving aside the fact that the prosecution might well have demitted the case had the later paediatric report been available, it does the criminal legal process as a whole no good to hear the trial judge viewing with alarm, as he put it:

... the prospect of expert evidence being given in a charge of murder which turns out to be incomplete and inaccurate.[8]

Material facts become distorted, particularly when a case is not reported officially, and comments in the medico-legal literature such as: 'the prosecution evidence was found to be incomplete, inaccurate, conflicting, unclear and unsatisfactory regarding the cause of death'[9] reflect particularly hard on persons who are no more than victims of circumstance—or, as it has been rather well put: 'the "fall guys" for the lawyer and the legal system'.[10] Medically speaking, the case was an important one, having major implications for the practice of paediatrics and for medical ethics. It has been said that there are surprisingly few substantive issues in medical ethics that the Arthur case does not raise;[11] it deserved a more careful and thoughtful assessment of the facts than the conditions of the trial allowed.

Exchange of evidence in criminal cases

Such tactics had been described earlier by Sir Roger Ormrod, in his Kettle Memorial Lecture delivered to the Royal College of Pathologists in 1982, as being unhelpful. He advocated the removal, so far as is possible, of the element of surprise in regard to expert evidence:

Ideally there ought to be an exchange, well before the hearing, of the reports of scientific experts who are to be called to give evidence, so that each expert can see and consider the other side's evidence and, perhaps, even probably, modify his own views. [12]

The persuasive nature of this argument was acknowledged in the Police and Criminal Evidence Act 1984, s.81 which allowed the Crown Court to make rules requiring disclosure of expert evidence from each side before a criminal trial. These rules have now been formulated. [13] Rule 3(1) states:

Following the committal for trial of any person, or the making of an order for his re-trial, if any of the parties to the proceedings proposes to adduce expert evidence (whether of fact or opinion) in the proceedings (otherwise than in relation to sentence) he shall as soon as practicable, unless in relation to the evidence in question he has already done so:

(a) furnish the other party or parties with a statement in writing of any finding or opinion which he proposes to adduce by way of such evidence

The effect of this is to impose a duty of making an early decision to engage an expert; it will add urgency to pre-trial conferences between lawyers and experts. [14]

Rule 3(1)(b) states:

Where a request in writing is made to him in that behalf by any other party, provide that party also with a copy of (or if it appears to the party proposing to adduce the evidence to be more practicable, a reasonable opportunity to examine) the record of any observation, test, calculation or other procedure on which such finding of opinion is based and any document or any other thing or substance in respect of which any such procedure has been carried out.

Selfe [14] makes the further point that care must be taken to ensure the confidentiality of information which is subject to professional privilege (see p. 76). There is a strong chance that, in the absence of such precautions, lawyers will be even more reluctant to provide the expert with all the details of the case.

For some time, we have thought it right that experts in criminal cases who are sworn to secrecy should refuse to accept the commission; however, this is a purely personal view. A lawyer, for example, might well regard the unauthorized exchange of views between experts as collusion and reprehensible. Mutual assistance has become the increasing rule over the years, certainly between pathologists;

were they not to provide it, the job of the defence expert, called to make an examination some days or, often, weeks after an event, would be impossible to perform properly. The basic issue has been summarized by the American lawyer Belli: 'do the adversary proceedings conflict with the ethics of the medical profession and should the medical witness become an advocate for justice?'[15] Some experts for the defence have found moral consolation in the fact that the accused is in receipt of legal aid and that their duty is, then, to the public who provide that aid. In any event, it is comforting now to have some degree of statutory approval for what was undoubtedly unofficial practice.

The Police and Criminal Evidence Act 1984 follows in the wake of the Supreme Court Act 1981 which dealt with the exchange of reports in civil actions. This is discussed at greater length on p. 78.

Neither of us has any experience of the operation of 'section 81'—indeed, there are no anecdotal reports of its having been used. It is, of course, not fool proof in the sense that the dedicated adversarialist can omit what he wants from a written report—just as the witness subject to Scottish precognition, which is not taken on oath, need not disclose his full hand unless he believes, as we do, in the concept of neutral expert evidence. But this reservation leads directly to a further hazard of partisanship, that is limitation of disclosure.

Limitation of disclosure

The function of the expert witness as seen through legal eyes is summed up in the words of Lord Cooper:

> ... [he] shall give his evidence to the best of his ability on his special subject in a fair and unbiased manner, making a full and frank disclosure so as to provide the Court with the material necessary to enable it to come to a reasoned decision on the merits of the scientific issue.[16]

Again, this is, apparently, a simple exposition of the facts but it is, none the less, a precept which it is almost impossible to maintain. Brownlie[17] has pointed out that no expert is under an obligation to do his opponent's job for him—or, as we have put it previously, it is quite irrational in the ambience of a team game for the other side to *expect* a witness to score own goals.[18] Yet it is obvious that failure to draw attention to adverse factors can result in perversion of justice and the courts may or may not take a serious view of such behaviour.

In a case pursued by one of us in the form of a 'prisoner's friend', some importance attached to the origin of some blood on the trousers of the accused. The ABO system was the only blood group polymorphism which could make a distinction; equally, it was the only common blood group system which was omitted from the serological report. However, the omission was not regarded as a matter involving sufficiently new evidence by which to justify a review by the High Court under the terms of the Criminal Procedure (Scotland) Act 1975, s.263

We can contrast this with the widely publicized case of *Preece* v. *H.M. Adv*[19] which resulted in the public condemnation of a distinguished forensic scientist. In that case, the accused was convicted in 1972 of the murder of a woman who was said to have been strangled in the cab of his lorry just north of the border between Scotland and England.

Much of the evidence against the accused was in the form of scientific 'transfer evidence' relating to grass, hairs, and the like. In addition, the woman's pants were stained with vaginal fluid and with semen containing group A substance; since Preece was a group A secretor, this added to the evidence against him. His appeal against conviction was refused. However, in 1981, disquiet arose as to the general neutrality of the forensic scientist, Dr Clift, and the case was reviewed in the High Court of Edinburgh. There it was revealed that Dr Clift had failed to disclose to the court at the original trial that the deceased was also group A and was probably a secretor. Despite Dr Clift's protestations of his ability, the majority opinion of serological experts was that the apparent seminal grouping result could have been due to contamination by vaginal secretion.

The court was extremely critical of the way in which the evidence was presented and held that Dr Clift had deprived the trial court of the means whereby his confident opinion could be called into question; his conduct, it was said, fell far short of the standards of accuracy and objectivity to be expected of an expert witness. The High Court then extrapolated Dr Clift's failure in the tissue grouping field so as to assume that it cast doubt on all his other scientific evidence; the trial verdict was, accordingly, quashed.

Brownlie,[17] who has made a particular study of the case, concludes that the outcome must fill every past and prospective expert witness with alarm. Perhaps the most important practical lesson to be learnt is that it is now unsafe to throw away one's notes relating to *any* important criminal trial of which a review is likely—a somewhat chilling thought for those about to seek the sanctuary of a small retirement home! Secondly, the importance of a written report which will be used in evidence is re-emphasized. It would seem that, certainly in Scotland, a written report must include disclosure of the weaknesses as well as the strengths of the evidence whether or not this is asked for and there is every reason to suppose that *Preece* would be followed in this respect in England. But from the academic viewpoint, the case demonstrates again the difficulty of the expert in the witness box. Brownlie points out that the yawning gap in the evidence was there for all to see. What is so strange, he says: 'is that no one [in court] asked a single question as to the victim's group'.

The *Preece* case is, undoubtedly, an object lesson which should be taken to heart by all expert witnesses. Nevertheless, it is possible to see Dr Clift as Jones's classic 'fall guy'.[10] The legal profession is not above criticizing itself for such shortcomings. Following a very comparable failure of the system in England—in the trial of *Lattimore and others*—Blom-Cooper asked:

Is it within the bounds of propriety for the Crown to content itself with what it has obtained, secure in the knowledge that any gaps in the case will be remorselessly exposed by the defence? This is extremely hazardous because there can be no guarantee that everything will be sorted out at the trial.[20]

Experts in error

This case brings one to a further hazard of partisanship—that is, error. The more convinced the expert is of the 'rightness' of his case, the greater may be the subconscious drive to sublimate the possibility that he is mistaken. The Australian case of *R* v. *Chamberlain*[21] is likely to remain the classic of its type.

It is scarcely necessary to recapitulate the circumstances of the case in detail. Mrs Chamberlain's baby disappeared from a tourist camp in the Northern Territories; some of the clothes were discovered but the body of the child was never found. Mrs Chamberlain maintained that a dingo dog had carried the baby off. This was accepted at the coroner's inquest but, at a second inquest, Mrs Chamberlain was indicted for murder. She was found guilty at trial and appeals to the Federal Court and to the High Court of Australia failed. Eventually, the case was referred to a Royal Commission of Inquiry which found that: 'if the evidence before the Commission had been given at the trial, the trial judge would have been obliged to direct the jury to acquit the Chamberlains on the grounds that the evidence could not justify their conviction.'[22]

Despite the opinion of the judges in the appeal courts, there is little doubt in our minds that two particular pieces of evidence must have had a powerful influence on the jury.[23] These were the identification of a spray of fetal blood on the inside of the Chamberlain's car and of a hand print in blood, of a small adult, on the clothing of the baby, both of which were said by the prosecution to support the theory of the murder of the baby in the car. By the time of the Inquiry, the scientific evidence indicated that the spray of blood was, in fact, a spray of bitumenous sound-deadening compound used in manufacture and that the hand-shaped staining was occasioned mainly by the red dust of the terrain. Morling J. summed up these remarkable discrepancies:

... with the benefit of hindsight, it can be seen that some experts who gave evidence at the trial were over-confident of their ability to form reliable opinions on matters that lay on the outer margins of their fields of expertise.[24]

For present purposes, we would isolate four lessons which should be learnt from *Chamberlain*. Firstly, there is the possibility, which was raised by Gerber,[23] and to which we have referred above, of bias—and, particularly, of the understandable pressures which can be directed to the non-autonomous forensic scientist towards what might be paraphrased as 'playing his or her part in the team'; the inevitable conclusion that there should be independent forensic science institutes, possibly based on uninvolved and academic university units, is beyond discussion in a book of this type. Secondly, and of far more practical importance, it was found that, by the time of the trial, all the plates and gels on which the 'spray' conclusions were based had been discarded; and, in addition, inaccurate footnotes had been added to the bench book. Thirdly, the Federal Appeal Court referred to the 'unbecoming arrogance' of two of the expert witnesses for the defence; clearly, we cannot comment on the propriety of this assessment. However, it does bear particularly on the *mode* of presentation of expert evidence to which we refer at p. 112. Finally, *Preece* and *Chamberlain* are on all fours in calling attention to the general *acceptability* of scientific tests. The immunologists in both cases relied on methodology which had not withstood peer assessment and which has been criticized on that account. However, neither case addresses the details of acceptable expertise. Should, for example, a technique have to have been reported in the scientific literature before it is acceptable to the courts—and, if so, what *quality* of reportage is necessary? Some form of 'established expertise' test may be desirable, although as Gerber points out, this may result in the courts 'constantly lagging behind the advances in science while they wait for novel scientific techniques to win general acceptance'. This proposition is, again, outwith the present discussion. All that it does is to reinforce the advice that an expert witness must be able to *prove* his expertise; and if his technique is novel, his methodology must be available to both sides of the action so that it is subject to specific evaluation.

The conclusion to be drawn is that the witness should indicate not only the factual findings of his original examination and any tests made subsequently but also any possible deficiencies in these examinations or tests, and what steps he took to obviate them. This clearly requires a high standard of preparation of evidence. But this is no more than should be due from an expert witness who, after all, expects to be treated with courtesy and consideration by the court— and such courtesy and consideration has to be earned. The difficulty lies in knowing what findings and alternative conclusions are relevant, since very often the witness is not in full possession of all the facts of the case when he prepares his report, or even when he gives evidence in court.

Limitations on information

The statements from many witnesses form bulky files by the time the case goes to court. The expert witness rarely sees them in criminal trials, although he is more likely to have been shown them, or an edited collection, in a civil action.

In a civil case, the doctor is likely to have had more than one conference with counsel. However, in a criminal case he may well not meet the lawyers calling him until he enters the witness box; if he succeeds in having a conference with them, it is most likely to be a hurried affair, designed solely to clarify some points in his evidence for the benefit of counsel, not to inform the doctor. There is little opportunity for the witness to obtain information as to what statements other witnesses have made, or what other features of the case there are which might affect his conclusions or deductions.

He is not even likely to hear all the evidence as it is given in court. In theory, an expert witness is entitled, with the permission of the bench, to be in court throughout the trial and to hear all the evidence save that of his fellow experts; but, in practice, he is almost always kept outside the criminal court and only enters when he is due to give evidence. He usually leaves the court as soon as permission has been given. No matter how great his personal interest in the case, his employer, usually the NHS or a university, will not take kindly to his wasting hours or even days sitting in court in order to listen to evidence which may well turn out to be irrelevant. It follows that an unsatisfactory aspect of criminal work is that the expert depends for his knowledge as to the facts, findings, and conclusions in the case on what he can glean from the lawyer in charge. It is an unfortunate result of the nature of criminal work that one can seldom *know* whether one is right or wrong; the pressure of work dictates that one often does not even discover the grounds on which one's opinion was challenged. As a result, the forensic expert may persist in the same mistake throughout his career without ever considering it as such. And once an opinion has been given in the individual case, it is extremely difficult to modify it in the light of subsequent knowledge.

In the *Preece* case, it is obvious that the expert was already in possession of the knowledge that could have modified the conclusions and he failed to communicate this to the lawyers. In cases such as this, where the information is known to the expert, he is clearly open to criticism if he fails to make the disclosure; but it is difficult to see how the witness can comply with the court's requirements for full and frank disclosure if the relevant information is external— possessed by someone else—and is not communicated to the expert.

Moreover, he is constricted by the system—perhaps, less today than in previous decades—by which a great deal of his evidence is given by way of answers to questions; and you cannot answer a question if you are not asked it. This is a hazard of which the witness should be wary. We would strongly advise that, given the fact that there is an important point to make, it should be made at the first opportunity—for a second chance may never come and there are few things more unsatisfactory than a game ending while one still has an ace in one's hand. A story against one of us illustrates the point. The question arose in cross-examination: 'could these injuries have been inflicted by a car travelling at 30 m.p.h.?' The trouble is that nothing in circumstances such as a vehicular accident is absolutely *im*possible although, in the instant case, it seemed very unlikely. A simple answer 'I don't think so' seemed unsatisfactory, but how to make the point with maximum impact? Disastrously, the following imaginary exchange flashed through the witness's mind: 'It's possible but improbable', 'how improbable?', 'as nearly impossible as you can get in a biological situation'. So he answered 'It's possible but improbable'. At which point, the far more astute counsel sat down. 'No matter', thought the witness, 'I'll say it in re-examination'; but there was no re-examination. Expert witnesses should remember that they *may* be mentally more agile than experienced counsel— but it is a remarkably rare relationship in practice.

A more worrying example of the effects of inadequate information is within our experience. An apparently clear-cut case of homicide by the infliction of a single stab wound occurred. A relative confessed to murder, giving full and convincing details of the events which were passed on by the police to the pathologist at the time of his examination. The relative was tried and convicted, the medical witness not being called to give evidence in such an uncomplicated case. About a year later, the prisoner indicated that the first story was untrue, that the victim had committed suicide and that the confession had been made in order to shield the deceased's memory from the stain of suicide. Since the victim's death was caused by a single wound in a situation which was accessible to self-infliction, this explanation was consistent with the facts and the appeal was successful. Had the pathologist been called to the original trial, he might have been cross-examined about the possibility of self-infliction of the wound, or some other aspect of the case might have raised a doubt. As it was, he was left wondering whether he could have done more at the time to emphasize the possibility of self- or even accidental infliction even though these suggestions appeared to have no relevance at all to the case as it had been described to him.

It would be foolish to suggest that this problem is a major one, bedevilling all court cases. Very often the case is, indeed, straightforward and the witness has no difficulty in deciding what to disclose. Even so, the danger of failures to do so lies in the fact that no one can foretell when such occasions will arise and the outcome, as in *Preece*, can be devastating.

Training for the witness

Of course, the more experienced the witness is, the more likely he or she will be able to foresee the problems inherent in a case. But nowadays obtaining the necessary experience is, itself, likely to present problems, as it is increasingly rare for young doctors to be called to court. Twenty or thirty years ago there was little cause for concern. Coroner's inquests provided an excellent training ground, as most cases were uncontroversial and straightforward, but the doctor was required to attend court and give evidence in all of them. Most young doctors gained their first experience of the court room, and the sensation of standing in a witness box, in the relatively common inquiries into deaths in hospital of old people following fractures, or suicides by carbon monoxide poisoning. However, the Coroners Rules 1984,[25] in a laudable endeavour to reduce delays and to spare relatives unnecessary distress, now allow for most medical evidence to be given in the form of written statements; physical attendance at court is rare, thus removing a major source of training. At a slightly more advanced level, the Criminal Justice Act 1967 also introduced the much more frequent use of written expert evidence at the committal stage in the magistrates' court and so reduced a further valuable training source for the embryo pathologist or police surgeon. It is now quite likely that a doctor may have had almost no experience of court prior to his being called to give evidence in a major and complicated case at Crown or High Court. The dangers attendant on this situation, both for him and for the court, are obvious.

The only solution would appear to be to train all doctors for their role in their undergraduate or specialist postgraduate courses—for all doctors are likely to be in the witness box at some time in their careers. Very little such training is carried out at present.[26] Yet, without it, the consequences are likely to be, at best, an uncomfortable experience or, at worst, a psychological disaster for the doctor and loss of credibility for the profession as a whole.

An alternative solution lies in the greater use of assessors, senior professional men in the appropriate field, whose opinions would be sought by the court, in the person of the judge, rather than by either side. Court experts are sometimes used now, but only in cases not involving a jury;[27] they are currently not looked upon with favour[28] but they could have a much greater role to play. However, such matters are for Law Reform Committees; in practical terms we can only hope that the standards of scientific evidence will be maintained through the efforts of those whose function it is to teach on the subject.

References

1. Kenny, A. 'The expert in court' (1983) 99 LQR 197.
2. Shaw, S. 'The law and the expert witness' (1976) 69 *Proc. Roy. Soc. Med.* 83. See Drife, J. O. 'Doctors, lawyers, and experts' (1989) 299 *Brit. Med. J.* 746 for a recent, succinct criticism.
3. Gordon, G. H. 'The expert witness' in McLean, S. A. M. (ed.) *Legal Issues in Medicine* (1981) Aldershot: Gower, p. 215.
4. Brownlie, R. 'The role of the expert witness' (1983) 51 *Med.-Leg. J.* 85.
5. Gee, D. J. 'The expert witness in the criminal trial' [1987] Crim LR 307.
6. Napley, D. 'Defend the accused not the expert witness' (1984) *The Guardian*, 19 March, p. 9. For a riposte, see Johnson, H. 'The pathologist as an expert witness' (1986) 54 *Med.-Leg. J.* 26.
7. *R* v. *Arthur* (1981) *The Times*, 6 November, pp. 1, 12.
8. Quoted in Brahams, D. and Brahams, M. 'The *Arthur* case—a proposal for legislation' (1983) 9 *J. Med. Ethics* 12.
9. Samuels, A. 'Death and the law—medico-legal problems' (1983) 23 *Med. Sci. Law* 183.
10. Jones, C. G. 'Men of science v. men of law' (1986) 26 *Med. Sci. Law.* 13.
11. Gillon, R. 'An introduction to philosophical medical ethics: the Arthur case' (1985) 290 *Brit. Med. J.* 1117.
12. Ormrod, R. 'Scientific evidence in the judicial process' (1982) *Bull. Roy. Coll. Pathol.* No. 40, p. 5.
13. Crown Court (Advance Notice of Expert Evdience) Rules 1987, r.3. (SI 1987/716).
14. Selfe, M. 'Attention forensic pathologists' (1988) *Bull. Roy. Coll. Pathol.* No. 66, p. 17.
15. Belli, M. M. 'Forensic medical experts, obligations and responsibilities' (1968) 8 *Med. Sci. Law* 15.

16. *Davie* v. *Edinburgh Magistrates* 1953 SC 34 at 40.
17. Brownlie, A. R. 'Expert evidence in the light of *Preece* v. *H M Advocate*' (1982) 22 *Med. Sci. Law.* 237.
18. Mason, J. K. 'Expert evidence in the adversarial system of criminal justice' (1986) 26 *Med. Sci. Law* 8.
19. [1981] Crim LR 783.
20. Blom-Cooper, L. 'A miscarriage of justice—English style' (1981) 49 *Med.-Leg. J.* 49.
21. (1983) 46 ALR 493 (FC); (1984) 153 CLR 521 (HC).
22. Report of the Commissioner (Mr Justice T. R. Morling) of the *Royal Commission of Inquiry into the Chamberlain Convictions* (1987) Darwin: Government Printer of the Northern Territory.
23. For an excellent medico-legal analysis, see Gerber, P. 'Playing dice with expert evidence: the lessons to emerge from *Regina* v. *Chamberlain*' (1987) 147 *Med. J. Austral.* 243.
24. Ref. 22 above at p. 340.
25. SI 1984/552.
26. Gee, D. J. 'Training the expert witness' (1988) 28 *Med. Sci. Law* 93.
27. Rules of the Supreme Court, Order 40.
28. Lawton, Lord Justice 'The limitations of expert scientific evidence' (1980) 20 *J. Forens. Sci. Soc.* 237.

11

The doctor as defendant

The scope and sophistication of modern medicine are advancing so rapidly that medical practice is outdistancing the law. So much is now possible and is increasingly expected by the public— particularly, perhaps, within the context of a 'free' health service. Conflicts may then arise when advanced treatments are *not* under- taken and these may occur irrespective of the basic reasons for the refusal of a particular therapy. Effectively, the public is asking that a feasibility test be applied to treatment/non-treatment decisions—'if it can be done, it should be done'; however, the medical profession will prefer a productivity test—'do it only if it is worth doing'— and the assessment of productivity may be balanced as much on a group or resource based argument as on the value of a particular treatment to an individual patient. Major decisions of this type are commonest at the extremes of life when they become, literally, those of life or death. Thus the doctor so engaged is exposed both to the civil law and to peer assessment of his methods; he may also be running perilously close to the criminal law and the pressures which are developing may operate so as to force him to sail ever closer to the wind.

We thought it would be useful to consider some selected ex- amples of 'grey areas' and then to recapitulate some of the ways in which the doctor may be called to account for his actions.

Care of the incurably or terminally ill

There is every sign that euthanasia will become the next focal point in medical law[1] and the pressures on the doctor to adapt his traditional attitudes will become severe. We believe it is important in this sphere to distinguish carefully between, on the one hand, the deliberate ending of a life because of its poor quality in terms of either of suffering or consciousness and, on the other, the manage- ment of terminal illness; the former generally requires some activity on the part of the doctor while withholding treatment from the dying may well be seen as a matter of not prolonging death unreasonably. Whether or not there is any *moral* distinction to be made between activity and passivity when the same result—death—is anticipated in each case is a heated argument beyond the scope of this chapter.[2] What is certain is that the law makes a very definite distinction. 'The Good Samaritan', wrote Lord Devlin, 'is a character unesteemed in English law'[3] from which it follows that causing death by omission is seldom regarded as criminal. Much depends upon the degree of duty to provide that which is omitted; the doctor certainly has a duty to care for his patient but 'care' will be liberally construed to imply a holistic approach to the patient's best interests.

By contrast, actively to kill any person must be, at least potentially, murder. The historic direction of Devlin J, as he was at the time, in *R* v. *Adams*[4] also makes it clear that the physical state of the victim is of no significance.

If the acts done are intended to kill and do, in fact, kill, it does not matter if the life of the victim is shortened by months or weeks, or even hours or minutes, it is still murder.

Mars-Jones J has restated the position more recently in *R* v. *Carr*:[5]

However gravely ill a man may be, however near his death he is, he is entitled in our law to every hour, nay every minute of life that God has granted him. That hour or hours may be the most precious and most important hours of a man's life. There may be business to transact, gifts to be given, forgivenesses to be said, attitudes to be expressed, farewells to be made, 101 bits of unfinished business which have to be conducted.

The law as it stands, then, has little or no sympathy with active euthanasia even in terminal conditions and consent by the patient would be immaterial. The central issue is that of intent. The Director of Public Prosecutions has remarked that action may be needed against doctors who 'deliberately speed death' and this has been taken as an unacceptable interference with clinical freedom.[6] But the DPP's use of the word 'deliberately' and Devlin J's expression of intent are crucial. There is no suggestion of delimiting the privilege to treat the patient as one sees fit; this was made clear in Devlin J's further direction in *Adams*:

The doctor . . . is entitled to do all that is proper and necessary to relieve pain and suffering even if the measures he takes may *incidentally* shorten life [our emphasis]

It is quite possible to apply the legal doctrine of necessity to treatment of the terminally ill and to justify this on the moral basis of double effect—that is, so long as there is no less injurious alternative, an action is permissible when its intended good effect can only be obtained at the expense of, and in the expectation of, a coincidental ill effect, provided that there is an adequate proportionate reason for allowing the expected ill to occur.

The means of justifying withdrawal or withholding of treatment, including withdrawal of intensive care support from a patient who is not brain-stem dead, depend on whether or not the patient is competent. It is emphasized that a competent adult patient is perfectly entitled to refuse treatment and perseverance by the doctor in the absence of consent could attract an action for assault. The problem of the incompetent patient in the United Kingdom is to be resolved simply on the basis of good medical practice backed, if necessary, by the moral distinction which is drawn between ordinary and extraordinary treatment—or, better, we believe, productive and non-productive treatment. There is no better definition of this than has been given by Pope Pius XII:

Man has a right and duty in the case of severe illness to take the necessary steps to preserve life and health. That duty . . . evolves from charity as ordained by the Creator, from social justice and even from strict law. But he is obliged at all times to employ only ordinary means . . . that is to say those means which do not impose an extraordinary burden on himself or others. [7]

The important concepts to be noted in this are, first, that the test is individual, not generalized—one cannot, for example, make a blanket statement that cytotoxic therapy either is or is not extraordinary treatment; secondly, it is permissible to include the effects upon others in the analysis—for example there is no ethical or legal reason why any problem as to the scarcity of resources should not be taken into consideration. We believe the two most important legal dicta in this connection to have been made in the United Kingdom are that of Lord Emslie L.J.-G. in the Scottish case of *Finlayson*[8] who claimed that he was not guilty of the culpable homicide of a man who was removed from intensive care:

... the natural consequence which the perpetrator must accept is that the victim's future depended on a number of circumstances, including whether any particular treatment was available and, if it was available, whether it was medically reasonable and justifiable to attempt it and to continue it.

and the later English statement, given in much the same circumstances, which reads:

where a medical practitioner using generally acceptable methods, came to the conclusion that the patient was for all practical purposes dead and that such vital functions as remained were being maintained solely by mechanical means, and accordingly discontinued treatment, that did not break the chain of causation between the initial injury and the death.[9]

The doctor's position in taking a non-prolongation of life stance is, therefore, well covered. However, there is no justification for the deliberate taking of life, whether it be by way of active voluntary euthanasia or of assisted suicide,[10] no matter how forcibly the patient may express the wish for such action—and in our experience, most patients wish to hold on to life for as long as possible once their pain or other intolerable condition has been mastered. There is something of a clamour for the United Kingdom to follow the lead of the Netherlands[11] but until now, the medical establishment has not supported this movement.[12] We believe that this resistance should be maintained and that doctors should be very wary of following any other course. There is no guarantee that all juries or all judges will be as forgiving as those that tried Dr Adams. We commend the words of Alexander Capron:

I never want to have to wonder whether the physician coming into my hospital room is wearing the white coat (or the green scrubs) of a healer—concerned only to relieve my pain and restore me to health—or the black hood of the executioner. Trust between patient and physician is simply too important and too fragile to be subjected to this unnecessary strain.[13]

Selective non-treatment of the newborn

Many of the same principles apply, although perhaps with added force, at the beginning of life. What is to be done with the defective neonate? On all logical grounds, given the wide availability of and public approval of abortion, the correct procedure would be to kill an infant that has slipped through the net of the Abortion Act 1967,

s. 1(1)(b). However, this course cannot be followed. It would be totally repugnant to the public and to the profession. The legal status of the developing human changes dramatically at birth; from being a fetus with virtually no rights as a person, it becomes a creature in being with full human rights—in particular, the right not to be killed. It is, therefore, impossible to see feticide and neonaticide as being on the same *legal* plane although it is perfectly possible to regard them as being *morally* indistinguishable. [14] How, then, can selective non-treatment of the defective newborn be justified in law?

We believe that the important feature here is to distinguish between the infant who is physically defective, of which the simplest example is the child with neural tube defect, and the one who is mentally subnormal as exemplified by Down's syndrome. The former case is readily covered by the concept of good medical practice. We all know what pain is, we can all evaluate the effects of severe physical disability—in short, prognosis is relatively simple and the objective selection is, in Lorber's words:

... not to avoid treating those who would die early in spite of treatment but to avoid treating those who would survive with severe handicaps. [15]

While many would say that it was, then, right to end the child's life actively and rapidly so as to minimize suffering, we have seen above that to do so would not be consonant with the existing state of the law. By contrast, the law seems content to accept medical decisions not to treat as expressions of medical good faith; so far as we are aware, no doctor who has failed to treat a severe case of neural tube defect after full consultation with the parents has ever been brought to the criminal or civil courts in the United Kingdom although there are many instances of both judicial and administrative involvement in such clinical decisions in the United States. [16]

The Down's syndrome baby, who is apparently making every effort to survive in his or her own internal environment is, however, another matter. The literature in this field has been dominated by the case of *R* v. *Arthur* [17] in which, it will be remembered, a doctor was acquitted of the attempted murder of an apparently physically healthy Down's syndrome neonate who died within three days of birth; the doctor had instructed in the case notes: 'Parents do not wish it to survive. Nursing care only.' and had prescribed large doses of dihydrocodeine in order to diminish the child's appetite.

The Down's syndrome infant with congenital physical defects which will be fatal in the absence of treatment falls somewhere within these two extremes and there is instructive case law in this area. The legal history of the child in *In re B*[18] was turbulent and began with the refusal of the parents to consent to the treatment of duodenal atresia in the Down's syndrome neonate. The case ultimately reached the Court of Appeal where Dunn LJ had this to say:

. . . she should be put in the same position as *any other mongol child* [our emphasis] and must be given the chance to have an existence

thus clearly excluding any thought of an uncomplicated case of Down syndrome being eased to death. By contrast Templeman LJ asked:

. . . was the child's life going to be so demonstrably awful that it should be condemned to die or was the kind of life so imponderable that it would be wrong to condemn her to die?

In our view, he indicated general approval of the exercise of clinical judgement in the management of severe *physical* defect.

It has been suggested that *Arthur* makes new law[19] but we agree with those who believe that the verdict has no precedental significance[20]—it does little more than demonstrate the reluctance of British juries to expose a doctor to the possibility of unmerited imprisonment. The law as it stands is to be found in *In re B*. After an initial period of approval, there is little doubt that professional opinion turned away from Dr Arthur's management regime and, as with a future Dr Adams, we suggest that a future Dr Arthur might well be less fortunate in his pathologists and his judge. Vincent J summed up the matter in the Australian case of *F* v. *F*[21] which concerned the withholding of feeding from an infant with severe spina bifida. He said:

No parent, no doctor, no court has any power to determine whether the life of any child, however disabled that child may be, will be *deliberately taken* from it. [our emphasis]

This is likely to be the current view of the courts in the United Kingdom.

The living abortus

Selective non-treatment of the newborn and the living abortus are connected in that a high proportion (17 per cent) of abortions performed after the twentieth week of pregnancy are justified on so-called 'fetal grounds'. A fetus 'capable of being born alive' is now defined[22] as one which is able to oxygenate its tissues through its own lungs with or without the aid of a ventilator—a physiological state that is achieved at approximately 23–24 weeks gestation. Such fetuses are, therefore, legally protected by the Infant Life (Preservation) Act 1929, a matter which was addressed by the Lane Committee in 1974:

If a live and apparently viable foetus emerges from the termination, there is a statutory duty to try and keep it alive, however unwanted or abnormal it may be, and for the mother and child to be cared for by the midwife for 10 days. Further, if after delivery a foetus shows signs of life, an offence is committed if the birth and death are not reported or if it is incinerated other than in a crematorium.[23]

Thus, the doctor performing a late termination may be in a dilemma; he has, on the one hand, contracted with the pregnant woman to relieve her of her fetus while, on the other, he may find himself confronted with a living human organism for whom he may well have to provide certificates of birth and of the cause of death. What is his position?

It is clear from the foregoing that the majority of living abortuses will be defective; the same practical rules then apply as in selective non-treatment of the neonate with the additional certainty in this case that the parents have abandoned the child. However, even in the best run practices some late abortuses will be apparently normal and, while there are no precedental cases on which to rely, the theoretical situation seems to us to be that the doctor who deliberately fails to care for such a baby, even if that is no more than to transfer the duty of care to the neonatal intensive care unit, is at risk of a charge of attempted or actual homicide.

Even if such transfer is effected, the situation is less than crystal clear as a proportion of very premature infants will sustain serious defect, including brain damage, simply by virtue of their prematurity[24] and the prognosis for the individual must be uncertain. We believe that this is an area of medical practice which requires urgent legislative attention while modern technology narrows the gap between prematurity and viability; the Lane Committee thought much the same some fifteen years ago. In the meantime, the doctor must take his chance with the law and with his peers. The law is certainly not anxious to proceed against doctors in this very difficult field. So far as we know, no further action has followed any findings in the coroner's courts—and a finding of lack of attention at birth in such circumstances is a rarity; moreover, the Director of Public Prosecutions has instigated proceedings in only one case[25] when the magistrates took the unprecedented step of deciding there was no case to answer.

These examples of hazardous areas for the modern doctor have, in the main, related to the criminal law. We now look briefly at some other ways in which his professional activity may be challenged.

Negligence

There are many who would hold that the cards are dealt too heavily in favour of the defendant in a case alleging medical negligence; vigorous campaigns backed, among others, by the British Medical Association[26] are being launched with a view to introducing 'no-fault' types of compensation for medical mishaps along the lines of schemes introduced in Sweden and New Zealand. Certainly, the law looks on doctors and other professionals very favourably. Thus, we have May LJ holding:

It would be to shut one's eyes to the obvious if one denied that the burden of achieving something more than the mere balance of probabilities was greater when one was investigating the complicated and sophisticated actions of a qualified and experienced [professional] than when one was enquiring into the momentary inattention of the driver of a motor car in a simple running down action[27]

or Lawton LJ:

In my opinion, allegations of negligence against medical practitioners should be regarded as serious[28]

from which it follows that the standard of proof of medical negligence is a high probability. Moreover, it is only recently that the early exchange of documents in cases involving personal injury has been extended to include those thought to be the result of medical negligence (see Chapter 5).

None the less, there are strong indications of a subtle change of mood. The days of Lord Denning MR, who said that a doctor ought to be held liable only if he falls below the standard of a reasonably competent practitioner in his field:

so much so that his conduct may fairly be held to be—I will not say deserving of censure but at any rate—inexcusable[29]

are now passed. Whether a doctor has been negligent is for the courts to determine and they will take a flexible view which is expressed in the words of Lord Fraser in relation to errors of judgment:

The true position is that an error of judgment may or may not be negligent; it depends on the nature of the error. If it is one that would not have been made by a reasonably competent professional man professing to have the standard and type of skill that the defendant holds himself out as having, and acting with ordinary care, then it is negligence. If, on the other hand, it is an error that such a man, acting with ordinary care, might have made, then it is not negligence.[30]

Doctors are being increasingly often sued for damages resulting from negligence; the reasons for this are complex but, to an extent, involve the availability of increasingly sophisticated means of treatment and resuscitation and, consequently, the quantum of damages awarded is rising steadily; subscriptions to medical defence societies are escalating[31] to the extent that the National Health Service now recognizes that the required financial outlay is beyond the capacity of its junior employees. On all counts, the doctor of today should have a working understanding of this route to the civil courts.

There can be no negligence unless there is a duty of care and the law does not insist that a registered medical practitioner, who has a right to provide care, should necessarily exercise that right; Lord Devlin's comments on the Good Samaritan have already been noted[3] and the law casts no opprobrium on the Levite. On the other hand, no formal contract is needed to establish a duty to care, a simple offer to assume a duty suffices. Negligence then evolves from a failure in the provision of care; even so, the patient must have suffered injury before damages can be awarded.

The fact and extent of a failure to provide care can only be measured against a standard and, here, the most important English case is that of *Bolam* v. *Friern Hospital Management Committee*.[32] The standard laid down in *Bolam* has been followed ever since; it runs:

The test is the standard of the ordinary skilled man exercising and professing to have that special skill. A man need not possess the highest expert skill at the risk of being found negligent. It is a well-established law that it is sufficient if he exercises the ordinary skill of an ordinary man exercising that particular art.[33]

This test is clearly open to question at each extreme, for both the specialist and the novice. As to the former, it has been confirmed that he will be judged on the standards of the 'ordinary skilled man' when he causes damage as a result of lacking some knowledge or awareness. However, if he has extra knowledge and he acts in a way which, having that extra knowledge, he ought to have foreseen would cause damage, then he would be judged at a higher standard.[34] The novice will continue to be governed by the 'ordinary' standard. This may seem harsh but the public has every reason to suppose that the treating doctor has reached a satisfactory standard of competence; it has been suggested that the inexperienced house officer will have discharged his duty if he asks for advice but it is unfortunate that the most recent Court of Appeal decision on the subject has been returned for review[35] and the matter, as a whole, remains unresolved.

The 'ordinary' standard is set by what is commonly known as the 'custom test' which, effectively, defines what is a normal practice in any given field. The matter was addressed in the Scottish case of *Hunter* v. *Hanley* which has been widely approved in the English courts. There, it was held that three facts have to be established before a doctor can be said to be liable for a deviation from 'normal practice':

First of all it must be proved that there is a usual and normal practice; secondly, it must be proved that the defender has not adopted that practice; and thirdly (and this is of crucial importance) it must be established that the course the doctor adopted is one which no professional man of ordinary skill would have taken if he had been acting with ordinary care.[36]

This was refined in *Bolam* as: 'a doctor is not guilty of negligence if he has acted in accordance with a practice accepted as proper by a responsible body of medical men skilled in that art'. Thus, the standard of normal practice is very much defined by the profession itself—if, for example, there are two schools of thought as regards management of a patient, the court is not entitled to prefer one to the other.[37] However, the court has always been empowered to assess the standards of its witnesses. Blatant partisanship is frowned upon and there is, in fact, evidence that increasing attention is being given to the quality of expert evidence in general—a good example being the amendment to *Bolam* introduced by the Master of the Rolls to the effect that the body of medical men appealed to should *rightly* be regarded as responsible:[38] 'The law', said the then Sir John Donaldson, 'will not allow the medical profession to play God'.

In practice, therefore, the fact of negligence lies not so much in making a mistake as in how that mistake was made. One could, for example, misdiagnose a case of malaria and that could be no more than mischance; however, it would be negligent to fail to consider the diagnosis in a person who has recently returned to the United Kingdom from Africa[39] because all responsible doctors, acting with ordinary care, *would* have appreciated the possibility given the signs and symptoms in such a patient. But, in existing circumstances, the onus is on the plaintiff or pursuer to prove his or her case on a balance of probabilities and the plaintiff must not only prove negligence in *Bolam* terms but, having done so, he must show that it was that negligence which caused the disability complained of. This may be an insuperable hurdle particularly, say, in actions concerning the negligent use of drugs or vaccines.[40]

Are there, then, any times when conditions are eased for the patient seeking compensation? In practice, of course, a high proportion of successful suits never reach court and are settled as being indefensible; in addition, the difficulties in recovering costs are, in some circumstances, such as to make it economically preferable for the defendant doctor to settle a claim which is theoretically defendable. Only rarely can the boot be placed on the other foot once the case reaches court. If the defendant can find no one to support his action, then clearly, it is up to him to explain his unique departure from customary practice. An important recent judicial opinion held that the onus of proof shifted if a doctor failed to take a precaution and the condition which that precaution was designed to obviate did materialize.[41]

On other, infrequent, occasions, the court will admit a plea of *res ipsa loquitur*, the effect of which is to give rise to an inference of negligence on the defendant's part. It can be applied particularly when the allegedly negligent practice was of a complicated nature which the patient would be unlikely to understand and when there is no particular person on whom to pin the blame. The doctrine can only operate when the injury is one which would not usually occur in the absence of negligence. Its classic expression is in the words of Lord Denning in *Cassidy* v. *Ministry of Health*:

> [The plaintiff is entitled to say] I went into hospital to be cured of two stiff fingers. I have come out with four stiff fingers and my hand is useless. That should not have happened if care had been used. Explain it if you can.[42]

The danger of *res ipsa loquitur* is that it tends to turn what is no more than mischance into assumed negligence and, as a result, the courts are very reluctant to allow the plea.

Consent-based negligence

A relatively new form of the tort of negligence has developed particularly in the United States and is gaining hold in the United Kingdom. That is the 'consent-based' suit which depends upon the principle that true consent to medical or surgical treatment involves the exercise of an informed choice on the part of the patient rather than a simple general agreement to allow the doctor to decide on his course of action. The latter is sufficient to protect the doctor from a charge of assault or battery[43] but it does not prevent the patient, in the event of mishap, pleading, in effect, that: 'but for your negligence in failing to inform me of the risk, I would not have consented to the treatment and I would not now have a disability'. The effect of the doctrine of informed consent is, therefore, to extend the compass of negligence to include the occurrence of mishaps which are a recognized hazard of the treatment even when this is carried out with due care; as such, it has been described as: 'a cloth from which [American] courts slowly have begun to fashion a no-fault system for compensating persons who have suffered bad results from medical treatment'.[44]

This opinion clearly influenced the Lords of Appeal in the very important case of *Sidaway*[45] which represents the present English law on the issue; the question is simply a matter of how much information is required and who is to decide upon that amount. This

is not an appropriate place to discuss the relative merits of the doctor-
or patient-oriented approach nor, in the case of the latter, whether this
should refer to the 'reasonable' patient—an objective assessment—or
to the particular patient—the subjective view. The argument is rather
sterile in the United Kingdom because the House of Lords in *Sidaway*,
with only one partially dissenting opinion, firmly applied the *Bolam*
principle to 'informed consent' as well as to diagnosis and treatment.
Thus, the standard of information to be given is the standard agreed as
proper by a responsible body of medical opinion.

Attempts to constrict this ruling have been consistently rebuffed;
thus, the giving of non-therapeutic advice such as that related to
social contraception is to be looked on in the same way as giving
advice as to treatment.[46] Nevertheless, *Sidaway* made some inroads
into the purely professional standard. In particular, Lord Bridge, in
a majority opinion, added the rider that there were certain risks, the
disclosure of which was so obviously necessary to an informed choice
on the part of the patient, that no reasonably prudent medical man
would fail to make it. It was further generally agreed that a doctor
must answer truthfully and fully such questions as the patient
specifically puts. However, the general obligation as to disclosure
was based on a balance between the likely occurrence of a known risk
and the severity of the resulting disability.

As to the latter, if one is to judge from the opinions in *Sidaway*
and in the significant Canadian case of *Reibl* v. *Hughes*,[47] a *significant*
occurrence is one pitched at somewhere between 1:10 and 1:100
which seems, on the face of things, to be unduly high. No standard
is available as to severity but it is remarkable that an Australian
Appeal Court did not consider a risk of blindness from a treatment to be
sufficiently severe as to dictate disclosure.[48] All Commonwealth,
and many United States, decisions have accepted the concept of
'therapeutic privilege' under which a doctor may withhold information
if it would be to the patient's disadvantage to divulge it, and this was
agreed even in Lord Scarman's minority opinion in *Sidaway*.

It is interesting to note that, despite the wide use of the term in
current medical writing, Dunn LJ[49] thought that: 'the doctrine of
informed consent forms no part of English law'. Indeed, in view of
the uncertainties of the limits of the existing law, there is much to
be said for the substitution of 'rational' consent based on the
patient's understanding in place of a rather obscure standard of
information to be given.

Action to be taken

The part of the allegedly faulty doctor in an action for negligence is relatively circumscribed and, at least in the early stages, may be difficult. Thus, the Medical Defence Union advises members to explain the facts to the patient and to strive to rectify the problem sympathetically when something has gone wrong.[50] This is clearly good advice and following it may well avert litigation in a number of cases; none the less, it is clear that the line between good ethical practice and an admission of liability is easily blurred. The doctor concerned will, of course, be required to give all relevant information to his legal advisers who will, normally, be provided by his defence organization; he will have to give his evidence in court and be subject to examination and cross-examination. However, policy decisions as to the disclosure of documents and the provision of supporting expert opinion will lie in the hands of his legal advisers. In practice, the Health Authority will be joined in an action with the doctor. This will not, of course, apply in the case of private practice where, in addition to a charge of negligence, the doctor may be sued in breach of contract. Since this book went to press, the government has introduced National Health Service indemnity for hospital and community doctors and dentists whereby many of the protective obligations of the defence societies are taken over by the State. The transfer of responsibility is by no means absolute—e.g. the government provides no indemnity for negligent emergency treatment given at an accident site—and practitioners should very definitely ensure that their reduced subscription to a defence society covers all such eventualities. Perhaps the most important lacuna within the present context is that 'Crown indemnity' does not extend to negligence arising from the preparation of medico-legal reports.

Some doctors who are asked to provide expert evidence against a defendant doctor in a case of alleged negligence are unwilling to do so on grounds of professional loyalty; reluctance on such grounds is generally ill-founded and the Medical Defence Union, for one, has counselled against it.[51] It is argued that a patient has just as much right to a second opinion when considering litigation as when agreeing to a course of treatment; moreover, if a highly skilled and experienced professional does not accept the invitation, the probability is that one who is less well qualified will do so to the detriment of the case on both sides. The most important caveat is that the evidence given must be objective and related solely to the standard of care provided; gratuitous personal criticism of a colleague may well attract the attention of the General Medical Council. The Medical Defence Union summarizes the position by saying that the lot of an expert, whether he be instructed by the defendant or by the plaintiff, is not easy but that the task is a necessary one.

The General Medical Council

Unlike many of the professional governing bodies which have been established by statute, the General Medical Council is not concerned with professional negligence *per se*. It is only when a doctor's technical standards fall so low as to bring the profession into disrepute that the Council will step in—and it is doing so increasingly frequently; disregard of professional responsibilities to patients which, admittedly, includes more than negligence, constituted the largest category of referrals both to the Preliminary Proceedings Committee and the Professional Conduct Committee in 1986.

The disciplinary function of the General Medical Council forms only part of its duties but it is the only one which matters within the title of this chapter. The Council itself cannot instigate an inquiry into the conduct of the doctor. Misconduct may be presumed as a result of conviction in a criminal court and this is the commonest way in which doctors face professional disciplinary proceedings; the clerk of the court must report the conviction of a registered medical practitioner and the verdict of the court is irrebuttable before the Council. One important result of this is that doctors should never plead guilty—say, to a motoring offence—if they believe they have a defence; the General Medical Council will not be influenced subsequently by a plea that: 'I did it to save time'. On the other hand, the Council is not bound by the quashing of a verdict on appeal, particularly if the success of an appeal depends upon a legal nicety. The case of Mr Abrol, who was a dentist appearing before the sister organization, the General Dental Council, is illustrative. Mr Abrol gave single-handed anaesthesia and dental treatment to a patient who died in the surgery, the cause of death being certified as asphyxia due to inhalation of gastric contents while under the influence of a general anaesthetic. Mr Abrol was convicted and sentenced on a charge of manslaughter; as a result, his name was erased from the dental register. Some time later, the cause of death was questioned and the conviction was set aside on the grounds that the verdict was unsafe in the light of the evidence. None the less, the erasure from the register stood because the disregard of all advice against such dental practice was, of itself, serious professional misconduct.[52]

Allegations of misconduct may be lodged by corporate bodies— including the administration of the National Health Service—by other doctors, or by individuals; in the last case, a complaint must be supported by declarations made by one or more independent persons. There is no limited definition of severe professional misconduct other than the generalization that it constitutes conduct which would reasonably be regarded as disgraceful or dishonourable by a doctor's professional brethren of good repute and competency.[53] The general public is unlikely to appreciate the meaning of this[54] and it is not surprising that a great many complaints are rejected by the Preliminary Screener of the Council; in the year 1985–86, about 70 per cent of relevant complaints, that is those which were not readdressed to the National Health Service disciplinary authorities (14 per cent of the total), were dismissed at this level. A small proportion of complaints (7 per cent) are dealt with on an informal basis but the remainder are referred to the Preliminary Proceedings Committee.

The Preliminary Proceedings Committee then has several options open: it can take no action; it can issue a letter of caution, advice, or admonition; it can defer the case for further consideration; it can place conditions on a doctor's practice for up to two months; finally, it can refer the case to the Professional Conduct Committee or, when the health of the doctor is in question, to the Health Committee. Just under 30 per cent of cases were referred to the Professional Conduct Committee (P.C.C.) in 1985–86. The P.C.C. consists of a panel of up to ten members of the Council and a majority of these must be elected.[55] Its hearings are conducted as if in a court of law and are public, although there are now discretionary powers which allow for parts to be held *in camera*. Thus, the doctor may be and almost always is, legally represented, this being arranged through the relevant defence society—the costs of such representation are not covered by the 'Crown indemnity' scheme (see p. 173). In the event of the doctor being found guilty of serious professional misconduct, the Committee may admonish, suspend sentence (effectively place the miscreant on probation), place conditions on his future practice, refer a case to the Health Committee, or direct that his name be erased from the register. In 1986, there were twenty-one decisions, including six of erasure, which affected a doctor's registration. Thus,

3 per cent of cases considered by the Preliminary Screener resulted in very severe action on the part of the Professional Conduct Committee.

When one considers some of the cases resulting in a 'guilty' finding, it is apparent that many of the culprits were foolish rather than knavish. It is almost impossible to conceive of a consultant psychiatrist being so immature as to pass confidential information about his patient to the 'other side' in a matrimonial dispute; but this is precisely what has led to admonishment. No anaesthetist would deliberately disregard the fact that his patient had failed to recover consciousness for three post-operative hours, yet it has been done and has been regarded seriously. In an ideal world, a doctor should ask himself if he could justify his action in front of the General Medical Council every time he makes a decision involving ethics and etiquette—and a considerable proportion of inquiries result from no more than a failure in this respect. It is, of course, impossible to specify the pits of misconduct into which a doctor may unwittingly fall. The General Medical Council is particularly concerned with the maintenance of professional confidentiality. Offences which may well be attributable to impetuousness include rudeness to patients and criticism of one's peers. We believe that the doctor should also be aware of the insidious lure of the television camera and the investigative reporter; what seems like a throw-away remark at the time can appear very differently on the video screen or in the next day's newspaper.

The figures show that the Council does not engage in witch-hunts; indeed, such criticism as it attracts is most commonly on account of apparent leniency—many of these resulting from misunderstanding of the Council's role. A doctor whose name is erased from the register may apply to the Council for reinstatement after ten months and, thereafter, every eleven months and a very fair proportion of such applications are successful. Appeal from the immediate determination is to the Privy Council but this is only available on the point of law; the Privy Council will not involve itself in professional standards and will protect the rights of the General Medical Council as sole arbiter in that field. For example, Lord Scarman has said, of the Tribunal on the Misuse of Drugs:

The Tribunal was concerned with the misuse of controlled drugs but not with the ethical standards of the profession. It would have been an impertinence for the Tribunal to make any findings as to professional misconduct.[56]

In summary, an appearance before the Professional Conduct Committee of the General Medical Council may well be more significant for the doctor than would be involvement in an action for negligence. Moreover, the writ of the Council extends indefinitely and there are some circumstances, particularly in the field of professional confidentiality, in which a patient may find restitution hard to obtain through the courts. A good case can be made out that the protection of the public is best served by peer review rather than by legislation;[57] however, it is obvious that compensation for damage resulting from professional misconduct remains a matter for the courts.

Discipline in the National Health Service

The great majority of cases of disregard of responsibilities to the patient are, in fact, breaches of the terms of contract with the National Health Service and are dealt with at that level. Serious cases may be reported to the General Medical Council but the objective of the two inquiries is different.

An essential element of dealing with complaints against general practitioners is to maintain informality so far as is possible. Thus, every complaint which reaches the Family Practitioner Committee (F.P.C.) or its Scottish equivalent, is dealt with first by the Chairman through his appointed negotiator, often on an oral basis. Should this fail, a local hearing takes place before the Medical Services Committee consisting of a lay Chairman, three lay members of the F.P.C. and three professionals from the relevant local committee; one lay committee member must be a woman if a woman or a child is concerned in the hearing. Again, the hearings are in private and paid legal representation is not allowed. In theory, the hearing could be conducted by correspondence but, normally, witnesses may be adduced who will be questioned and cross-questioned by members of the committee.

The issue is whether the professional was or was not guilty of a breach of his terms of service. In the event of a positive finding, the doctor may be cautioned or fined; the committee can recommend a compulsory reduction in the size of his practice or they may call for a Tribunal to assess his fitness to continue to work for the National

Health Service. An appeal against financial penalties is available to
an Appeal Board which consists of a lawyer, a doctor of the relevant
government department and a doctor chosen from a selected panel;
evidence before the Appeal Board is taken on oath and legal representation is allowed.

Doctors in hospital are direct employees of the Health Service;
the hospital is, therefore, vicariously liable for the actions of its
servants[58] and it may well be argued that it has a direct, non-
delegable responsibility in terms of care provision.[59] It follows that,
in addition to concern for the hospital doctor's personal conduct, the
hospital authority can rightly question his professional competence;
thus, complaints against hospital doctors commonly arise from
the authority itself or from colleagues—the latter may give rise to
particularly acrimonious proceedings.[60] Problems associated with
junior staff are generally self-regulating and may well be dealt with
informally; many would feel that this is unfair but it is a fact of
life. Short of acceptance of the allegations and resignation, the
case of the consultant demands an official approach and this is
usually subject to the conditions laid down in the Ministry of Health
Circular HM (61) 112 of 1961. In view of the serious circumstances,
the Chairman of the hospital authority will almost certainly have
suspended the doctor concerned from duty—though this will have
been on full pay. Preliminary inquiries of an unspecified nature must
be made by the Regional Medical Officer as to whether there is a
prima facie case. At least twenty-one days' notice that an inquiry is
to be held should be given to the doctor complained of and, during
that time, he should be given all the relevant documentary evidence.
Much depends on whether it is the doctor's personal conduct or
professional competence which is in issue. An inquiry into the
former is generally less formal and contains fewer safeguards for the
subject of inquiry. The difficulty is to distinguish between the two
heads particularly when, as is so often the case, the fundamental
cause lies in a clash of personalities. An inquiry under HM (61) 112
is conducted by a legally qualified chairman but the membership of
the committee may vary from being wholly professional—as when
professional competence is in dispute—to being equally divided
into lay and professional members, as when conduct is also being
considered. Evidence in this type of inquiry is not given on oath
but legal representation is allowed and witnesses for both sides
are subject to cross-examination; the hearings are generally in

private. In the event of a consultant being recommended for disciplinary action, an appeal is available to the Secretary of State who considers the evidence by way of a professional panel. There is the further possibility, common to all determinations by administrative tribunals, of obtaining a judicial review of the findings. All commentators regard this process as being intolerably drawn out and expensive; negotiations to improve matters are in progress at the time of writing.[61]

The coroner's inquest and the fatal accident inquiry

Many deaths which are the subject of a coroner's inquest will result from possible medical mishap. The doctor giving evidence in such cases must, therefore, feel himself to be at some risk of public obloquy.

It would be idle to deny that this may be so and particularly if the inquest is one in which the various parties are represented and the inquiry takes the form of an uneasy superimposition of an adversarial approach on what is, essentially, an inquisitorial system. Any person whose conduct is likely to be called into question must be given reasonable notice of the time and place of the inquest[62] and may, himself, be represented. In the event that the doctor so placed is summoned to give evidence, he is under no obligation to answer questions which may lead to his incrimination[63] and both the coroner and his legal representatives will protect him in this respect. Moreover, the coroner's 'verdict' may not be framed in such a way as to impute civil or criminal blame to any named person.[64] Finally, the distinction between the neutral finding of 'accidental death' and the faintly pejorative 'death due to misadventure' is now deprecated.[65] All in all, the doctor whose fault may have contributed to a death is reasonably well protected against persecution in the coroner's court.

The nearest approach to a coroner's inquest in Scotland is the fatal accident inquiry. A public inquiry must be held under the Fatal Accidents and Sudden Deaths Inquiry (Scotland) Act 1976 if a death has occurred while at work or while in custody. More importantly in the present context, such an inquiry *may* be held whenever the Lord Advocate considers it to be in the public interest and a relatively large proportion of such inquiries result from supposed medical mishap. The public hearing is before the Sheriff sitting without a jury although he may, and generally does, have the assistance of an expert assessor; evidence before the court is led by the Procurator Fiscal and his witnesses may be cross-examined by other interested parties.

The fatal accident inquiry following a medically associated death differs from the coroner's inquest in several important details. First, it is discretionary; the mere fact that an inquiry has been instituted suggests some particular gravity of medical fault. Secondly, while witnesses have a right to refuse to answer questions, this only extends to those which are likely to suggest criminal liability. Thirdly, it is an integral part of the Sheriff's determination that the cause of the fatality should be thoroughly investigated with a view to disclosing any defects in the relevant system and to preventing a recurrence; thus the doctor may find himself in the position of an accused without having, at the same time, the prerogative of mounting a specific defence. The findings following a fatal accident inquiry cannot be used as primary evidence in any subsequent civil or criminal proceedings. Nevertheless, there are many who would see such an inquiry as being potentially far more damaging to a professional reputation than is an action in negligence. It is an occasion which should be taken very seriously by any doctor who is directly involved—the recovery of any costs involved in representation remains subject to membership of a defence society.

References

1. Higgs, R. 'Not the last word on euthanasia' (1988) 296 *Brit. Med. J.* 1348.
2. Rachels, J. 'Active and passive euthanasia' (1975) 292 *New Engl. J. Med.* 78; Kuhse, H. 'A modern myth. That letting die is not the intentional causation of death' (1984) 1 *J. Appl. Philosoph.* 21.
3. Devlin, P. *Samples of Law Making* (1962) Oxford: University Press, p. 90.
4. Palmer, H. 'Dr Adams' trial for murder' [1957] Crim LR 365.
5. *The Sunday Times* (1986) 30 November, p. 1.
6. Havard, J. D. J. 'The legal threat to medicine' (1982) 284 *Brit. Med. J.* 612.
7. (1957) 49 *Acta Apostolicae Sedis* 1027.
8. *Finlayson* v. *H M Adv* 1978 SLT (Notes) 60.

9. *R* v. *Malcherek, R* v. *Steel* [1981] 2 All ER 422 per Lord Lane C.J. at 429.

10. Suicide Act 1961, s.2.

11. Hull, R. 'Euthanasia' (1987) 295 *Brit. Med. J.* 1052. For an exposition of the Dutch situation, which does *not* legalize unsupervised active euthanasia, see Sluyters, M., 'Euthanasia in the Netherlands' (1989) 57 *Med.-Leg. J.* 34.

12. Beecham, L. 'From the Council' (1988) 296 *Brit. Med. J.* 1408.

13. Capron, A. M. 'Legal and ethical problems in decisions for death' (1986) 14 *Law. Med. Hlth Care* 141.

14. See, for example, Kuhse, H. and Singer, P. *Should the Baby Live?* (1985) Oxford: University Press, Chapter 5.

15. Lorber, J. 'Ethical problems in the management of myelomeningocele and hydrocephalus' (1975) 10 *J. Roy. Coll. Physicians* 47.

16. Gostin, L. 'A moment in human development: Legal protection, ethical standards and social policy in the selective non-treatment of handicapped neonates' (1985) 11 *Amer. J. Law Med.* 31. For a recent, and rather special U.K. decision, see *In re C (a Minor) (Wardship: Medical Treatment)* [1989] 2 All ER 782.

17. *The Times* (1981) 6 November, p. 1.

18. *In re B (a Minor) (Wardship: Medical treatment)* [1981] 1 WLR 1421.

19. Kennedy, I. 'Reflections on the *Arthur* case' (1982) 59 *New Society* (999) 7.

20. Brahams, D. 'Putting *Arthur's* case in perspective' [1986] Crim LR 387.

21. *Re F, F* v. *F* (1986) Unreported, Supreme Court of Victoria, 2 July.

22. *C* v. *S* [1988] QB 135; see also *Rance* v. *Mid-Downs HA* (1990) Times, 15 February.

23. Report of the Committee on the Working of the Abortion Act (Cmnd 5579) (1974) London: HMSO.

24. De Garis, C., Kuhse, H., Singer, P., and Yu, V. Y. H. 'Attitudes of Australian neonatal paediatricians to the treatment of extremely premature infants' (1987) 23 *Austral. Paediatr. J.* 223.

25. *R* v. *Hamilton* (1983) *The Times*, 16 September, p. 1.

26. Smith, R. 'No stopping no-fault' (1988) 297 *Brit. Med. J.* 935.

27. *Dwyer* v. *Roderick* (1983) Times, 12 November; (1983) 127 SJ 805 at 806.

28. *Whitehouse* v. *Jordan* [1980] 1 All ER 650 at 659.

29. *Hucks* v. *Cole* (1968) 112 SJ 483.

30. *Whitehouse* v. *Jordan* [1981] 1 All ER 267 at 281.

31. Harland, W. A. and Jandoo, R. S. 'The medical negligence crisis' (1984) 24 *Med. Sci. Law.* 123.

32. [1957] 1 WLR 582.

33. Per McNair J. at 586.
34. *Wimpey Construction UK Ltd* v. *D V Poole* [1984] 2 Lloyd's Rep 499.
35. *Wilsher* v. *Essex AHA* [1988] 1 All ER 871. The Court of Appeal stage [1986] 3 All ER 801 is discussed in Dyer, C. 'Is inexperience a defence against negligence?' (1986) 293 *Brit. Med. J.* 497 and the House of Lords in 'Retrial ordered in "medical negligence case of the decade"' (1988) 296 *Brit. Med. J.* 855.
36. 1955 SC 200 per Lord Clyde L.-P. at 206.
37. *Maynard* v. *West Midlands RHA* [1984] 1 WLR 634.
38. *Sidaway* v. *Board of Governors of the Bethlem Royal Hospital and the Maudsley Hospital* [1984] 1 All ER 1018 at 1028.
39. Anonymous 'Malaria: a medicolegal hazard' [1975] 4 *Brit. Med. J.* 475.
40. *Loveday* v. *Renton and another* (1988) Times, 31 March.
41. *Clark* v. *MacLennan and another* [1983] 1 All ER 416.
42. [1951] 2 KB 343 at 365.
43. *Chatterton* v. *Gerson* [1981] QB 432.
44. Meisel, A. quoted in Robertson, G. 'Informed consent to medical treatment' (1981) 97 LQR 102.
45. *Sidaway* (ref. 38 above) [1985] 1 All ER 643.
46. *Gold* v. *Haringey HA* [1987] 2 All ER 888.
47. (1981) 114 DLR (3d) 1.
48. *Battersby* v. *Tottman and State of South Australia* (1985) 37 SASR 524.
49. In *Sidaway* ref. 38 above at p. 1030.
50. Medical Defence Union *Annual Report 1988*, p. 11.
51. Allsopp, K. M. 'Expert advice' (1988) 4 *J. Med. Def. Union* 25.
52. *Abrol* v. *General Dental Council* (1984) 156 *Brit. Dent. J.* 369.
53. General Medical Council *Professional Conduct and Discipline: Fitness to Practise* (1987), para. 6.
54. Laurance, J. 'How bad doctors stay in business' (1988) *The Sunday Times*, 6 November, p. A9.
55. General Medical Council Preliminary Proceedings Committee and Professional Conduct Committee (Procedure) Rules, Order of Council 1980 (SI 1980/858).
56. *Dasrath Rai* v. *General Medical Council* [1984] 1 *Lancet* 1420.
57. Jacob, J. M. 'Confidentiality: the danger of anything weaker than the medical ethic' (1982) 8 *J. Med. Ethics* 9.
58. *Roe and Woolley* v. *Minister of Health* [1954] 2 QB 66; *Hayward* v. *Board of Management of Royal Infirmary of Edinburgh* 1954 SC 453.
59. For discussion, see *Ypremian et al* v. *Scarborough General Hospital et al* (1980) 110 DLR (3d) 513 especially opinion of Blair J.A. at 579.
60. Anonymous 'The lessons from the Savage inquiry' (1986) 293 *Brit. Med. J.* 285.

61. Forsythe, M. 'Disciplining doctors: the need for better methods' (1988) **296** *Brit. Med. J.* 1421.
62. Coroners Rules 1984 (SI 1984/552), r.24.
63. Coroners Rules 1984, r.22(1).
64. Coroners Rules 1984, r.42.
65. *R* v. *Coroner for City of Portsmouth, ex parte Anderson* [1987] 1 WLR 1640.

12

Proof or probability

One problem which a doctor acting as witness is likely to encounter is understanding how the court evaluates his evidence and as a corollary, how it uses such an evaluation in reaching its decisions. He needs to understand not only why some things that he would wish to say are not acceptable to the court—a matter which has been addressed already (see Chapter 5)—but also how the standards of proof and methods of reaching conclusions, to which he is accustomed as a scientist, differ from those used by the legal profession.

The way in which the court decides whether something is established, or proved, differs even between different branches of the legal system and has been discussed already in Chapter 3. In summary, in matters involving the civil law, the necessary degree of proof is based on a balance of probabilities; there does not have to be a strong probability and in practice, cases in which there *is* a strong probability of one side being right are generally settled out of court.

On the other hand, when matters of criminal law are under consideration, the standard of proof required is that of proof beyond reasonable doubt. So that if, in the civil court, the doctor says it is more probable than not that a person's illness was contracted due to his employment, that is a sufficient standard for the court to accept his view in forming its judgment. But, in a case of homicide, he needs to say more than that it is probable that death was due to injuries inflicted by another, rather than to a co-existing natural disease. It is the lawyer's function to probe the degree of certainty and the courts are quick to emphasize this distinction of roles. Thus, the doctor cannot be asked if he is convinced 'beyond reasonable doubt' for this is a term of legal art to be addressed by the court, if necessary, under the direction of the judge. [1]

All of which raises the question of how certain *can* the doctor be of any opinion which he expresses; can he use the same processes that he uses in the course of his usual medical practice when demonstrating his certainty in court? Or will he have to adapt his mental procedures to the legal requirements?

Legal and scientific standards

As we have intimated in Chapter 7, there are some fundamental differences between the legal and scientific processes involved. In forming diagnoses and prognoses, medicine very largely uses the process of arguing from a group of cases to a single diagnosis. Thus if the profession, over the years, has noticed that a number of patients, who have the same symptoms at the start of their illness, all show the same progression of their condition and show the same pathological findings, then it infers that these patients all are suffering from the same disease, which it names; this is greatly corroborated if the same remedy alleviates the illness in each patient. When, therefore, an individual doctor observes these signs and symptoms in a patient, he decides that the diagnosis is the same as in all the predecessors and he treats them accordingly. If the treatment is successful, he will say that he is certain of the diagnosis. Only if it is unsuccessful will he have cause to reconsider his first opinion. There may, of course, be diseases which have similar beginnings, and relatively similar symptoms, which have to be distinguished as a matter of differential diagnosis; but the doctor will always be arguing from conclusions drawn from a group of cases and will focus these on the particular patient.

He may be in a position to investigate the condition further by experimental methods. In such an event, he will be dealing with groups of experimental subjects or patients and will need considerable numbers because his results will have to be proved by statistical methods. In essence, the more subjects the doctor studies, and the more often a particular result appears, the more likely it is that he is correct in his inference. This is even more certain when he uses control subjects—those in whom the studies are carried out with a particular ingredient, such as a particular drug, missing. In practice, few scientific studies can be considered valid without the use of controls.

However, the criminal court works differently. It considers the matters before it as isolated events, where guilt or innocence is not dependent on what other people may have done on similar occasions in the past, but on what can be shown to have happened in this particular instance (see Chapter 5). Indeed, the criminal court procedure goes to some lengths to prevent the hearing being tainted by infecting the minds of the jury with information as to how the accused has behaved in the past. Evidence of previous convictions must not be introduced until after the court has reached its verdict; only then may such evidence be produced in order to assist the court in sentencing. [2]

A scientist, aware that a man has twenty times in the past responded to the discovery of an unlocked motor car by stealing it, would deduce that on a twenty-first occasion he would do the same. The lawyer cannot follow the same mental process. The twenty-first occasion has to be treated as quite distinct since, on this occasion, the man may have been able, for a variety of reasons, to have resisted the temptation. By contrast, a man who has had an allergic reaction after eating strawberries on previous occasions and who, on this occasion, eats strawberries and becomes ill, will be diagnosed and treated as a case of allergy until the treatment proves unsuccessful.

Inductive and deductive reasoning

Such a thought process, whereby a conclusion is based on a sample of previous cases, is called inductive reasoning (see also Chapter 7). It is the usual basis for most peoples' methods of reaching decisions and may depend upon the observer's own past experience or on that of others. Thus, all medical education is a form of inductive reasoning. A student learns to diagnose appendicitis by using the distilled experience of many predecessors; he does not have to start afresh, and study a hundred cases before being able to pronounce on a particular patient.

Moreover, a doctor usually has the advantage of having time to confirm his conclusion—for instance, by doing various tests which may extend over weeks or months. For the lawyer, the process stops when the accused is arrested or when the case comes to court. You cannot confirm a verdict of attempted murder by putting the accused and the victim together and seeing whether, this time, murder actually results.

The alternative method of reasoning is known as deductive, that is the process of inferring a particular instance from a general law. This is the method used, in part, by the legal process, whereby laws and precedents which have been established over the years are applied to a particular case. Thus, the role of the court, as tribunal, is to ascertain the facts and, by applying well-established rules of law to these facts, to arrive at a decision on the case. Many rules exist either in the form of acts of Parliament or, more frequently, as precedents laid down in previous cases and the lawyers arguing a case will try to find rules which can be applied persuasively in the interests of their side. None the less, observation, analysis, inductive inference, and other scientific methods may also be used in legal reasoning.[3]

The division between inductive and deductive reasoning as a distinction between scientists and lawyers may not, however, be as simple as this. Stone, in his book on evidence, says that deductive reasoning is of limited value in court in deciding the facts. The whole basis of deduction is the acceptance that a true conclusion may be reached from premises which must be accepted as true and there are no means of ascertaining whether or not the premises are, in fact, true. So, while the formation of syllogisms is valuable in the construction of legal arguments, it is less valuable in reaching correct conclusions on the facts. He considers that inductive reasoning is the method used in arriving at a conclusion but that it is a generalization from known facts, reached as a matter of probabilities. Typically, this relates to conclusions based on circumstantial evidence.[4]

The witness's role is to establish, as accurately as possible, a series of facts for the court. The lawyer may use deductive logic in framing questions and arguments so as to establish or disprove these facts. The court, considering those facts that have or have not been established by the advocates, will then base its verdict on an inductive conclusion.

So advocates need to be able to adduce facts which can be used to establish the accuracy of their sides' point of view. Sometimes, they need no complicated expert evidence. If an accused is seen, by several people, to pick up a knife and cut the throat of the deceased who, thereupon, bleeds to death in front of the crowd, the facts regarding the mode of death are not likely to need amplification save, perhaps, in the specialized field of assessing the state of the accused's mind at the time. However, if the deceased is found dead with a single stab-wound of the heart, in a house where only he and the accused were present at the time the court will require expert evidence to assist it in establishing which of the several possibilities can be taken to be the true one. The distinction between homicide and suicide is clearly important to both the defence and the prosecution and the court will need to know how reliable an opinion the witness is likely to give, how certain he is of his opinion in either direction and on what he bases it. Can he give evidence that the court can accept as proof of fact or is he, at best, talking of a matter of probability—and, if so, how highly can he rate the probability?

Qualities in the witness

In part, the court addresses this task by considering the witness himself. At the outset of giving his evidence, the side that has called him will establish his credibility, by asking him to state his qualifications and to name the post that he holds. At its simplest, a consultant physician who holds a doctorate and is a fellow of the Royal College will be presumed to be more knowledgeable and have more experience than a senior house officer possessing qualifying degrees only. But additional information will be sought if more than one consultant physician is to appear in the case. A recent publication[5] refers to this matter of the 'weight' of the evidence and we can scarcely do better than recapitulate the determinants which the authors isolate as those which the court is most likely to consider:

(a) the witness's first-hand knowledge of events;
(b) the extent of his experience in similar work—to which we would add, in the medical context, his publications;
(c) his standing in his profession;
(d) the status of the book, standards, or research material relied on to support the view he has taken;
(e) the judge's view of the thoroughness of the witness's investigations;
(f) the credibility of the witness;
(g) the impression given of the witness's honesty and reliability

This introduction normally takes only a few minutes in a British court, although the process might be quite lengthy in America and involve a great deal of detail. However, there is a distinct difference in that the witness in the USA has to be 'qualified' as an expert by the particular court—'OK, son, you're qualified' can give a surprising boost to one's morale!

The other side may, in its turn, ask questions which seek to diminish the witness's authority in the eyes of the court. This may sometimes backfire on the lawyer concerned. A colleague of ours, a consultant physician, was called to give an opinion in a case of alleged phosgene poisoning. The defence counsel, confident that no one could have had experience of clinical care of such a case since the First World War, asked the physician, disparagingly, what personal experience he had of phosgene poisoning, expecting the answer 'none'. Disconcertingly, however, the physician replied that he had cared for twenty patients with this condition. It emerged that he had treated a number of firemen who had been overcome by phosgene fumes while fighting a fire at a chemical works. The lawyer was suitably deflated.

Expert evidence as to factual observation is unlikely to be challenged unless circumstances have thrust a relatively inexperienced professional into the limelight. An inexperienced pathologist *could* mistake a skull suture line for a fracture but, in general, no competent doctor should be in any doubt about his findings at examination, which should be acceptable to all concerned.

However, as soon as he begins to express opinions or draw conclusions from his findings, he may be required to prove them and to have them tested by the court. The fact of a stab-wound being found should not be in doubt, and will not be questioned, but an opinion that the wound was self-inflicted will be challenged and will need explanation.

The witness may be able to prove some matters by referring to the generally accepted body of medical opinion. In this, he needs to be well read and knowledgeable in the area under discussion. Counsel often have textbooks lying on the table before them. Generally, this is as much a matter of psychological warfare as anything because, in our experience, they rarely use them. However, they may ask the witness if he is familiar with the views expressed in So-and-So's textbook, and read out a sentence that apparently refutes the witness's views. If it is a well known and recognized textbook, the doctor may know that the sentence referred to precedes another section which actually supports his views, and which he can quote back at the lawyer. It may not be so easy when, say, giving evidence abroad or, within our multi-racial society, where a lawyer indoctrinated elsewhere may be using a textbook written by an author of similar ethnic origin. In any event, time may be gained by asking to see the passage and it may be useful to point out that the edition is outdated—for this is almost invariable. If the book quoted is one he does not know, he should certainly ask to be allowed to see it for a quick glance at the context of the section that the lawyer is using may show that the sense of the passage is being interpreted incorrectly. If a genuinely contrary view is being expressed, then he must acknowledge that fact. It may be an isolated opinion in an obscure text, and the doctor may be able to discount it and adhere to his opinion, but he would be most unwise to go to court without first making sure that a good body of published opinion supports his views and there is nothing to prevent the witness offering the court another textbook in order to demonstrate its existence. Even if not called upon to use it, it is comforting to have at hand some material which gives information in simple statistical form. The availability of a reference on the incidence of head injury in children falling accidentally can be very reassuring when giving evidence in a case of child abuse.

A classic, and very widely quoted, example of the expert humbled is to be found in the trial of *R* v. *Rouse*. Counsel for the prosecution, Mr Norman Birkett, was commencing the cross-examination of an expert engineer and fire assessor, a Mr Isaacs.

What is the coefficient of the expansion of brass?—I am afraid I cannot answer that question off-hand.

If you do not know, say so. What do I mean by the term?—You want to know what is the expansion of the metal under heat.

I asked you what is the coefficient of the expansion of brass? Do you know what it means?—Put that way, probably I do not.

You are an engineer?—I dare say I am, I am not a doctor, nor a crime investigator, nor an amateur detective, I am an engineer.

What is the coefficient of the expansion of brass? You do not know?—No, not put that way . . .

The whole purpose of the rest of this evidence was rendered ineffective for the purpose of the defence by this admission at the outset of lack of knowledge by the witness.[6] The passage is exemplary, with the benefit of hindsight, on two counts. First it is quite incredible that an 'expert' should not understand the *meaning* of a term which is relatively common knowledge, irrespective of whether or not it is related to the case. Secondly, the answer: 'Of course I do not know the precise figure but we can look it up', followed by the production of a pocket book of physical constants, would have been perfectly acceptable and goes to prove the point we have just made.

Published wisdom will support a point of view to a limited extent only. Soon the doctor is likely to encounter the problems caused because the court is not only seeking to establish a set of proved facts but also needs the evidence by which to establish these facts as precisely as possible. The processes of medical reasoning are rarely able to say that a matter is proved absolutely for medical rules are not absolute like physical laws. Thus the melting point of ice is known precisely. Frozen pure water will melt at the same point; and the effects of altering the pressure, or adding any salt to the water, are also precisely known. But the body temperature of an individual at death cannot be known, unless it is measured at that time. It may vary from one person to another by several degrees. Thus, although the rate of cooling of a dead body is an acceptable method of estimating the time of death, it can never yield more than a very approximate result because the starting point of the particular curve of cooling can never be known.

This frequent inability of the medical witness to state a conclusion with the certainty that the court needs is a source of great irritation to the lawyers who expect a high degree of certainty from a scientific process, and of frustration for the doctor who finds it difficult to explain why he cannot be more precise. Hounded by a feeling of inadequacy, the witness may seize on any opportunity to be apparently more dogmatic and this may have disastrous results.

The following experience of one of the authors is an example. The case concerned a possible manslaughter resulting from a death due to complication of an injury. The patient developed a fatal pulmonary embolus following a period of immobility due to the injury. Our opinion was that the injury, the embolus, and the death were related but this could not be held to be absolutely certain. There was the chance that the thrombosis could have occurred spontaneously and, to add an apparently scientific gloss, a reference was quoted to the effect that 75 per cent of such thromboses were due to trauma and 25 per cent were spontaneous.[7] But, asked the lawyers, did this mean that a *history* of trauma put this case definitely into the group *resulting* from injury? And were there other factors that could affect the onset of thrombosis? Yes, said we, obesity, varicose veins, and the like. 'What was the victim's weight?' asked the lawyers, 'and how much did that alter the odds in this particular case?' and 'how many percentages should one allow for the presence of varicose veins?' At that point we realized that we had no valid statistics, no idea of what to allow for these additional factors, and a positive wish that we had never strayed beyond the well-tried, but not very helpful, formula of: 'more probable than not, but impossible to give an exact figure'.

Statistical considerations

Yet, as more knowledge and better tests become available, it becomes increasingly important to try to refine medical opinions and to give the courts as much help as possible in reaching their conclusions. In some areas, one can do this with reasonable mathematical certainty. For instance, in blood group analysis, the establishment of gene frequencies, and the discovery of ever more testable systems, has enabled a mathematical calculation as to the likelihood of exclusion from paternity of a given man to rise from 18 per cent using the ABO system alone to over 98 per cent using all the systems available to a high class laboratory. Now, of course, DNA profiling has dramatically improved that kind of identification; using the average DNA profile of 11 bands, the chance of exclusion is 1 in 2.7 million.

However, evidence as precise as this is uncommon in medical practice and the use of the known incidence of a condition in the population is unlikely to assist the witness very greatly in criminal trials, where what might happen in 99 other incidences out of 100 has no relevance to this one case, and where the witness needs to state with certainty what this episode was due to. Empirical evidence may, however, be helpful in establishing probabilities in civil cases. Thus, reverting to the pathology of deep vein thrombosis and pulmonary embolism, the fact that 75 occurrences out of every 100 will be due to injury and 25 will be spontaneous may be helpful to the court in assessing the balance of probabilities; but things are seldom that simple even in civil matters. If an otherwise healthy person suffers an injury and, after precisely seven days immobilization, develops signs of a deep vein thrombosis followed shortly afterwards by embolism, then the witness can be reasonably certain that the embolus is a result of the injury, especially if it arises in a leg which has been injured. How certain can the witness be if a longer period, say a month, separates the original injury and the onset of thrombosis? The connection will be even less certain if the interval is two months. But by how much? If one can be 100 per cent certain of a causal connection when a thrombosis occurs seven days after an injury, is an interval of one month a 50 per cent possibility—or is that proportion reached after two months? And what if another event intervenes which may also contribute? In one of our cases, a patient sustained an injury to the leg, which was plastered. The plaster was removed after remaining *in situ* for three months; a fatal embolism occurred the next day. Could one say that the injury was the cause of a fairly fresh thrombosis even up to three months later or had the embolus occurred spontaneously during that time? Was the removal of the plaster the cause of dislodgement and embolism? And if the plaster was there because of the injury, and its removal caused embolism, was that an uninterrupted relationship?

It is partly for such reasons that the courts, themselves, take an ambivalent attitude to percentages and, on the whole, tend to regard statistics as an incremental route to usurping their function. Thus, in the important, albeit obscurely reported, Australian case of *F* v. *R*, it was said:

In my judgement the learned judge in [this] case appears to have allowed a medical statistic to extend the scope of the proper standard of care . . . that must be given to a patient. In doing so the scope of the duty . . . has been handed over to expert medical evidence.[8]

This case was based on negligence due to giving a patient inadequate information—a field in which the courts are, in fact, by no means disinclined to depend upon statistics but, at the same time, to scatter their odds fairly widely. Thus, a 10 per cent chance of a risk of damage resulting from an operation was considered to be significant.[9] Something less than a 1 per cent risk would not necessarily be disclosed.[10] Quite where the cut-off point is set has not been decided and the near impossibility of so doing serves as a reminder of the dangers of straying into mathematical assessments of matters which depend upon biological variations (see also Chapter 11).

An example of the court getting into some difficulty in this way is given in the case of *Hotson*.[11] Here, a child developed avascular necrosis of the femoral head following injury and there was an admittedly negligent delay in making the diagnosis. It was agreed that the condition would follow inevitably in 75 per cent of such injuries and it was alleged that the negligent diagnosis had converted the 75 per cent chance into one of 100 per cent; the Court of Appeal therefore upheld an award of 25 per cent of the agreed quantum on the basis of a loss of a 25 per cent chance of recovery. Clearly, however, an individual either recovers or he does not and, in this particular case, intervening negligence either did or did not materially contribute to the development of avascular necrosis—the liability is that of 100 per cent or nil depending upon the balance of probability; chance, in this context, means no more than that, if 100 people suffered the same injury, 75 would develop avascular necrosis and 25 would not. [12] The decision of the Court of Appeal was, accordingly, reversed on the grounds that the damage was done at the time of injury and that the delay in treatment did not affect the issue.

The practice of law and medicine differ in that, in the latter, there is generally opportunity for reflection and for a change of tactic. However, the problems facing the law are of a different quality. Everything has already happened and, as in an examination question, the participants are faced with a set of facts and told to solve the problem from these. There is no chance to study a progression of events. Moreover, the law is interested only in one particular case at any one time. All other cases of murder, or indecent assault, or disputed paternity are irrelevant except in so far as there are precedents which can be applied to this case. But as we have seen in Chapter 5, the circumstances in which the court can consider 'similar cases' are extremely limited—the conditions must be uniquely or strikingly similar to the evidence in the case at trial. [13]

Thus, the medical witness has to adapt his usual process of thought to the needs of the court and this is not easy—nor always possible. When asked whether a certain action produced a certain result, he will instinctively react by saying 'probably' or 'so far as I can tell', because that would be his usual stance when dealing with a problem in his practice. But the court needs more precision than this if it is to do its job and the lawyer calling him will try to get him to say that he is sure that such-and-such is the case and very often, the doctor may find it impossible to be dogmatic. But if the situation is such that he does feel that he can say that he is sure, then the opposing lawyer, or even the judge, may press him to show his reasons so as to test whether the fact can be established sufficiently firmly for the court's purposes; and the opposing lawyer will try to show that he cannot support his definite opinion.

So how can he be sure—and how far can he go to prove the matter for the criminal courts or establish the balance of probabilities for the civil courts? The latter is obviously the easier case, because it is much nearer to what the doctor normally does and how he thinks. None the less, he will need to use more than just his clinical judgement and intuition and will be required to show either his own, or other scientists', empirical feelings as to the condition in question. The problem then resolves usually into two parts. First, there is the diagnosis of the condition—how sure is he that the patient has, say, contracted a particular industrial lung disease; and, secondly, there is causation—what is known, and can be shown reliably, as to how the disease becomes established, what is its incidence in a particular occupation as compared with the general population and so on.

For instance, the doctor can, perhaps, show that a patient has the clinical history, examination findings, X-ray appearances, and biopsy results which show, certainly, that the patient suffers from asbestosis. Then, it may be shown that the occurrence of asbestosis in this particular occupation is x per cent as compared to y per cent in the general population. It may, further, be demonstrated in a series of cases that exposure for more than z years is necessary before the disease develops and that the patient has worked for $z+10$ years in that occupation. Thus, a convincing argument may be developed to show that there is a strong probability that the patient's condition is due to his employment. It may even be possible to determine mathematical expressions for the degree of probability. Much work has been published in recent years on the use of statistical and logical theorems in the determination of the accuracy of diagnosis. Many of these are based on Bayes' theorem, which deals with the effect of further experience on modifying previously held assumptions of probability. Macartney gives an intriguing example of its use in the process of diagnosing a congential heart lesion in a child through the different stages of a clinical examination, each stage giving numerical values for the various alternatives in the differential diagnosis. [14] Work of this type may provide the court with mathematical expressions of increasing accuracy of diagnosis in the future. Even so, it is debatable whether the purposes of the court will be much better served by such 'scientific' methods than by a simple expression of opinion by an experienced doctor and of his confidence in it. As Eggleston says:

In deciding which version [of the facts] it will accept, the tribunal may well have regard to the probability of either version being true, but it is more likely that the tribunal will decide which set of witnesses to believe by considering their demeanour, the internal consistency of their evidence, and other indications of veracity or mendacity. [15]

Or, put in another way:

. . . probability is a quality of belief about human affairs rather than a mathematical statement. It is an expectation that something has happened, so far as criminal trials are concerned. It can be stated in terms of degree, but it cannot be quantified. [16]

We have to reiterate that, to a large extent, the value of an expert doctor's evidence depends on his own qualifications and experience, not on mathematical expressions. Quoting Eggleston again:

A medical man who is asked to diagnose a disease may not be able to recall in detail all the experiences that have told him that certain observed facts make it probable that the patient has a particular disease. Moreover, the experience on which he can draw is not limited to his own. Textbooks, journals and discussion with colleagues will have built up a store of knowledge which he may well be unable to recall in detail, but which he may have generalised into rules which give him a high percentage of successes in diagnosis; that is to say, there will be a high degree of probability that his opinion is correct. To say that an expert can give an opinion in such circumstances, therefore, is to say that he can express an estimate of probability without being required to provide a precise statistical basis for the estimate. [17]

In practice, mathematical calculations as to probability are unlikely to have much of a useful place in medical evidence, because of the lack of reliable statistics. There are obvious exceptions. They include the field of blood grouping, and serology generally, where one is discussing a precise factor which is inherited once and for all, fixed, and is unaffected by any other factors. Thus, a mathematical formula can be applied. Statistics are available from general published medical experience which may be of help to the civil court. Thus a person's weight is related to his height; averages and percentiles are available from which to determine a normal weight for that height, what the probability would be of anyone being close to this figure, or some way from it or how close to it a hypothetical person might be. But when it came to the point, a glance at the person might give a better answer.

But, attempting a mathematical expression of probabilities will be a very precarious exercise when it comes to a specific case demonstrating a series of related events and circumstances that are unique in that an exactly similar set of events is most unlikely to have happened before. 'Statistics' are then more likely to mislead the court than is a more general opinion, expressed on expert knowledge.

Consider the case of the death of a man with chronic bronchitis and cor pulmonale who died from bronchopneumonia following head injury. Clearly, bronchopneumonia is a likely consequence if the head injury has rendered him unconscious and immobile. It may be possible to find statistics that show the occurrence of pneumonia as a complication of head injury. If six cases out of every ten in a published series did so, then one could say that the probability of developing the complication was high—60 per cent or better than even. But what is the probability of the man contracting pneumonia as a consequence of his chronic bronchitis? There are unlikely to be any statistics to give a probability to set against the other for the sequence may depend on the extent of the disease, the time of year and the ambient temperature, whether he has contacted a source of infection recently, and so on.

And to what extent will the cor pulmonale have played a part in the death? Clearly it must have some effect; a healthy heart might have carried the man on long enough for a battery of antibiotics to have defeated the infection. But is it accelerating death from pneumonia that is due to the chronic bronchitis or that is due to the head injury? Or a bit of both? If all the statistics were available, and the probability of a known case of chronic bronchitis getting bronchopneumonia were known to be for example, 20 per cent, then one could say that the probability of a man with head injury and chronic bronchitis contracting bronchopneumonia due to his head injury alone was $60 - 20 = 40$ per cent—less than even and, therefore, not probable. And, again, by how much does the contribution of the cor pulmonale alter the statistics? If eight of a series of ten other men with heart disease died from bronchopneumonia more rapidly than ten other men without heart disease but with pneumonia, one could say there was an 80 per cent probability of the heart disease accelerating infection resulting from injury. But this factor could not be allowed meaningfully against the 40 per cent that has already been established for the effects of the head injury. Before doing so, one would need to study a series—matched for age, weight, and all other factors—of men with identical head injuries, with and without chronic bronchitis and cor pulmonale who had received identical treatment. It is clear that any attempt to introduce mathematical precision into such situations is almost certain to mislead the court with a spurious impression of exactitude which, in fact, is less reliable than an opinion given with the acknowledgement that, while it is based on genuine expertise and existing medical knowledge, it is imprecise.

Such a situation is well understood by judges. As Stone says:

> Moreover, in special situations the mathematical basis of probability may be applicable, for example the overwhelming numerical improbability that any two sets of identical fingerprints could have been made by different persons. While the support which may exist for an inductive conclusion can be thought of as a matter of degree, outside of the special type of situation where mathematical probability is applicable it cannot be quantified. It can only be described qualitatively by using words such as slight or conclusive.
>
> For conviction, the law, in requiring that guilt be proved beyond reasonable doubt, expresses the effect of an overwhelming degree of probability in terms of the state of belief which it produces. [18]

Nevertheless, with the rapid increase of knowledge in diagnostic logic, information technology, and computer science, it is likely that the comments of this chapter will cease to apply in the not too distant future. On the one hand, the application of logic to diagnostic problems is developing strongly. The use of Bayes' theorem has already been alluded to and new developments in logic itself, such as 'fuzzy logic', and 'relevant logic', are likely to have considerable impact on the problems of an imperfect science such as medicine. [19] Equally, considerable effort is already being applied to the use of statistical methods and mathematical expressions of probability in the field of forensic science. That discipline, which in general deals in constant factors, offers more promising material to work with than does medicine. Examples are to be found in the publications of Evett and of Aitken. [20]

Before it is possible to derive meaningful figures for use in the courts, it is first necessary to collect data with this object in mind. Precision of opinion for purposes of medical evidence has not, up till now, been a prime objective in the minds of researchers while time and resources are scarce commodities among those who give the evidence. Very large banks of data, with adequate matching of similar circumstances, would be needed if the results of such an exercise were to be significant. Only then would really useful information be available to expert witnesses in their efforts to assist the courts. But until that time is reached, the doctor would be wise to avoid attempts to impress the court by introducing basically unsound mathematical expressions other than when addressing one of the very few clear cut issues in medicine. In short:

It will be an extremely rare case where mathematical techniques will make a decisive contribution to the resolution of forensic uncertainty.[21]

Forensic experts, experienced in the requirements and expectations of a particular judicial system, accept that standards of proof are measured in degrees of probabilities based on personal knowledge, training and experience. Numerical or statistical evaluations of such standards of proof may be either inappropriate or misleading when applied to expert opinions.[22]

If the doctor is insufficiently sure of his opinion he should say so. The ends of justice will not be served by a doubt cloaked in scientific obscurity.

References

1. Cameron, Lord 'The expert witness' (1989) Paper presented at the British Association in Forensic Medicine, 19 July quoting, in particular, *Hendry* v. *H M Adv* 1987 SCCR 394.
2. *Cross on Evidence* (6th edn, 1985) London: Butterworths, p. 310.
3. Walker, R. J. (ed.) Walker and Walker *The English Legal System* (6th edn, 1985) London: Butterworths, p. 564.
4. Stone, M. *Proof of Fact in Criminal Trials* (1984) Edinburgh: W Green & Sons, pp. 377–379. For discussion, see Kind, S. S. 'Proof of fact in criminal trials' (1987) 27 *J. Forens. Sci. Soc.* 29.
5. Reynolds, M. P. and King, P. S. D. *The Expert Witness and His Evidence* (1988) Oxford: BSP Professional Books, p. 18.
6. Normanton, H. *Trial of Alfred Arthur Rouse* (1952) Notable British Trials Series, London: Hodge, p. 244.

7. Knight, B. 'Fatal pulmonary embolism: factors of forensic interest in 400 cases' (1966) 6 *Med. Sci. Law* 150.

8. *F* v. *R* (1983) 33 SASR 189 per Legoe J. at 200.

9. *Reibl* v. *Hughes* (1980) 114 DLR (3d) 464 quoted with approval by Lord Bridge in *Sidaway* at 663.

10. *Sidaway* v. *Bethlem Royal Hospital Governors and others* [1985] 1 All ER 643.

11. *Hotson* v. *East Berkshire Area Health Authority* [1987] 2 All ER 909.

12. As emphasized by Lord Mackay at 914.

13. *R* v. *Beggs* (1989) Times, 4 July.

14. Macartney, F. J. 'Diagnostic logic' in Phillips, C. I. (ed.) *Logic in Medicine* (1988) London: British Medical Association, p. 43.

15. Eggleston, R. *Evidence, Proof and Probability* (1978) London: Weidenfeld & Nicolson, p. 137.

16. Stone, ref. 4 above, p. 368.

17. Eggleston, ref. 15 above, p. 125.

18. Stone, ref. 4 above, p. 380.

19. Slaney, J. K. 'Formal logic and its applications in medicine' in Phillips, ref. 14 above, p. 31.

20. Evett, I. W. 'A quantitative theory for interpreting transfer evidence in criminal cases' (1984) 33 *Appl. Statistics* 25; Aitken, C. G. G. 'The use of statistics in forensic science' (1987) 27 *J. Forens. Sci. Soc.* 113.

21. Cross, ref. 2 above, p. 151.

22. Ferris, J. A. J. 'Forensic science and the justice system in the late twentieth century' (1987) 27 *J. Forens. Sci. Soc.* 147.

Appendix A

Deaths reportable to the coroner

The doctor who examines or is aware of there being a body in any of the following circumstances is advised to inform the coroner as soon as possible:[1]

- Unattended deaths in which there is no doctor able to certify medical responsibility for care during the terminal illness or when the doctor has neither seen the patient in the last 14 days of life nor after death.[2]
- Sudden deaths either unattended as above or unexpected.
- Deaths suspected of not being due to natural causes including those that may be due to accident, suicide, or homicide.[3]
- Deaths associated with induced abortion, therapeutic or criminal.
- Deaths due to poisoning of whatever nature including those associated with alcohol.
- Drug associated deaths—both therapeutic and addictive.
- When death was apparently associated with surgical or medical treatment, prophylaxis or investigation.[4] Any death in which the standard of health care may be questioned.
- Deaths due to industrial disease, poisoning, or accident.[5]
- Deaths occurring while in prison or under police custody.[5]
- Deaths associated with want, exposure, or neglect.
- Obscure infant deaths including those believed to be instances of the sudden infant death syndrome.
- Deaths of children in foster care.
- Deaths of persons in receipt of a disability pension due to war service.
- Any deaths which the doctor considers should be properly investigated for any other reason.

Notes

1. Strictly speaking, the doctor is not thus bound as it is the statutory duty of the Registrar to do so acting on the details given in the

certificate of death. But it clearly saves much time if the doctor undertakes the task; this is the usual practice.

2. This provision does not necessarily hold in respect of the Procurator Fiscal in Scotland unless the deceased's residence is unknown.

3. Although such deaths are likely to provide suitable organ donors, no donation can be performed using a cadaver reported to the coroner or Procurator Fiscal without their specific authority (Human Tissue Act 1961, s. 1(5)). Even then, authority for the *operation* remains with the person in lawful possession of the body.

4. The fact that a 'brain-stem dead' patient is to be removed from ventilator support is no reason *per se* for reporting to the coroner or Procurator Fiscal; the relevant factor is the reason for *admission* to intensive care.

5. Such deaths result in a mandatory fatal accident inquiry in Scotland.

6. The list of cases to be reported to the Procurator Fiscal is slightly more detailed but is essentially similar except where noted above. There are also occasional archaic references to public health which are of no present day concern.

Appendix B

Medico-legal fees agreed between the Crown Prosecution Service, the Lord Chancellor's Department, and the British Medical Association

(as at 15 May 1989)

Attendance at court—criminal cases

Expert witness

	£
Preparation per hour	40–58
Attendance at court (full day)	200–290

Professional witness

	Maximum £
Less than 2 hours' absence	40.60
Less than 4 hours'	61.00
Less than 6 hours'	91.40
Over 6 hours'	120.00

Witness to fact

Up to 4 hours' absence	14.85
Over 4 hours'	29.70

Recommended fees for reports and qualifying work—civil cases

Doctors regularly employed as experts

	£
Per case	151.50

Plus additional fees for conferences, etc. on the basis of occasional appearances below.

Doctors called in occasionally

Per half day	average	146.00
Per hour	minimum	28.00
Consultants	minimum	40.00

Attendance at court—recommended rates—civil cases

Expert witness

	£
Half day (average)	265.00
Minimum per half day	146.00

Professional witness

Half day (average)	126.00
Minimum per half day	88.00

Coroners' inquests

	£
Post-mortem exam and report	46.50
Special post-mortem	130.10
Attending to give evidence,	
each day	27.60
each additional day	37.10

Notes

Fees for attendance at court may be paid by the Crown Prosecution Service or the Lord Chancellor's Department. Those for professional witnesses or witnesses to fact are fixed but the expert's fee is flexible; in general, the range relates to the expertise needed in the particular case. Witnesses for the defence are paid by the solicitors; since legal aid is tied to the LCD's rates, most solicitors will expect to limit fees accordingly.

Fees in civil cases are based on a contract between the doctor and the solicitor but, when costs are awarded, the rate will be assessed by a Taxing Officer who may use the criminal rates as a guide.

A fee which is agreed 'subject to taxation' means that it will be limited to the decision of the Taxing Officer. The solicitor can appeal against what is thought to be unreasonable taxation but the doctor cannot.

(All adapted by kind permission from *British Medical Association, Fees for Part-time Medical Services*, supps. 31 and 33, revised August 1988 and May 1989.)

Appendix C

Medico-legal fees payable in Scotland

Paid by the Crown Office in criminal cases

Professional witnesses

	£
Engaged not more than 1 hour	33.90
1–4 hours	56.40
4–6 hours	84.70
more than 6 hours	112.80

Expert witnesses[1]

Engaged not more than 1 hour	44.00
1–4 hours	90.30
4–6 hours	135.50
more than 6 hours	180.60

Post-mortem examinations

Post-mortem fee	46.50
Special post-mortem fee[2]	130.10

Fees payable by the Legal Aid Board in civil cases[3]

		£
Report on examination and opinion	range	50–131
Post-mortem examination	range	66–165.50
Attendance at court	half day maximum	55.00
Perusing reports prior to giving evidence max		55.00

(Adapted from FM 74 and FM 80 (1988) by courtesy of the Crown Office.)

Notes

1. As in England, payment at these rates depends upon the expertise required for the case rather than on the status of the witness.
2. Generally a matter of the importance of the case (e.g. murder) or the difficulty of examination (e.g. severe burning).
3. (1989) 34 *J. Law Soc. Scot.* 191. Rates in criminal cases follow those for the Crown.

Appendix D

Road Traffic Act 1988, s.4

REPORT ON MEDICAL EXAMINATION   F.97
NOTE FOR EXAMINING DOCTOR

The form of Report includes reference to most of the tests, etc., usually carried out by doctors. Its purpose is to inform the Procurator Fiscal of the evidence which the doctor may be expected to give at the trial. There is no compulsion, however, on doctors to carry out all of the tests and, on the other hand, they are not necessarily exhaustive of those which may be made. If a doctor carries out any other tests, particulars should be included either in the form or separately. The form, when completed, and any additional communication should be enclosed in an envelope addressed to the Procurator Fiscal, marked "CONFIDENTIAL" and sealed. If, however, the doctor, obtains any information in answer to the first four questions under the heading 'Examination: History' which indicates that the person is ill, is having medical treatment or has significant disability, he should inform the police officer in charge of the police station where the examination takes place.

NAME (in full) ....

ADDRESS ....

OCCUPATION ....

AGE.....................................

PLACE OF EXAMINATION ....

TIME OF (a) MESSAGE RECEIVED ....

(b) ARRIVAL AT STATION ....

(c) EXAMINATION ....

OFFICER(S) PRESENT AT TAKING AND DIVISION OF URINE SPECIMEN ....

....

EXAMINATION: HISTORY?:

Any evidence of illness or injury? ....

Is the person under medical treatment? ....

Is the person subject to fits or diabetes? ....

Are there any significant deformities or abnormalities? ....

....

When was food last taken? ....

GENERAL:

General Demeanour and Behaviour:...

....

....

STATE OF CLOTHING: ....

....

SPEECH: thick, slurred, or over precise ....

CONDITION OF MOUTH, e.g. presence of dentures or any deformity ....

PULSE: rate and character ....

TEMPERATURE: (if thought necessary)..

STATE OF TONGUE: ....

BREATH: odour, hiccup ....

EARS: deafness or discharge ....

HEART: ....

BLOOD PRESSURE: ....

LUNGS: ....

REFLEXES: ....

EYES: Eyelids, red or swollen? ....

      Conjunctivae ....

      Evidence of squint, etc. ....

      Any gross visual defect: are glasses used? ....

      Pupils and reaction ....

      Nystagmus ....

      Can he converge? ....

MANNER OF (*a*) walking ....

      (*b*) turning sharply ....

      (*c*) sitting down and rising..

      (*d*) picking up coins from the floor ....

      (*e*) standing on right leg ....

      (*f*) standing on left leg...

      (*g*) standing on both feet with eyes shut...

      (*h*) touching point of nose with eyes shut ....

          (1) right hand ....

          (2) left hand..

      (*i*) knees bend..

WRITING: Name and address or copying from a book ....

....

MEMORY OF INCIDENTS within the previous few hours and estimation of their time intervals:

....

....

....

REMARKS BY EXAMINING PHYSICIAN ....

....

....

....

....

I hereby certify that in my opinion at the time of examination the ability of the above named person to drive a motor vehicle properly was not * impaired through drink or drugs.

Signed...

Medical Qualifications ....

Date...

* Strike out when not required

(5630) 398886 20m 4/76 CP(A)Ltd.

Note

This *aide-mémoire* is in use throughout Scotland. We are not aware of a similar officially approved form being available in England. (F.97 kindly supplied by Dr W D S McLay, OBE.)

Index